THE BUILDING SOCIETY STORY

THE
BUILDING SOCIETY
STORY

HERBERT ASHWORTH

©Sir Herbert Ashworth
B.Sc.,(Econ), LL.B., FCBSI

First Published 1980 by
Franey & Co., Ltd.,
Burgon Street,
London, EC4V 5DP

ISBN 0 900382 38 4

Printed in Great Britain
by
Bookmag,
Henderson Road,
Inverness.

FOREWORD

Sir Herbert Ashworth, B.Sc(Econ), LL.B., F.C.B.S.I., Chairman of the Nationwide Building Society, has been involved in the building societies movement for well over half a century. He joined the Burnley Building Society in 1925 and moved in 1936 to the Portman, where he became General Manager in 1948. He joined the Co-operative Permanent – now the Nationwide – as General Manager and Secretary in 1950, subsequently becoming a Director and then Chairman. During his association with the Nationwide, the Society's total assets have grown from £60 million to £4,000 million.

Sir Herbert was Director and General Manager of Hallmark Securities from 1961 to 1966. He was Chairman of the Housing Corporation from 1968 to 1973.

He is therefore in a unique position to tell the story of the growth of the building societies from the days when they were largely self-help institutions, set up by working-class men and women seeking to better their housing conditions after the industrial revolution, to the point at which they have become a major financial institution, dominating the savings market and responsible for the fact that 55 per cent of the United Kingdom's houses are owner-occupied.

Sir Herbert has seen at first hand the steadily growing involvement of Governments in housing and building societies, and the chapters covering the last two decades tell a fascinating story – to some extent a depressing story – of the aims and effects of Government policies.

PREFACE

In this story of the building society movement I have devoted most of my space to the events of the last sixty years, for it is in this period that the real growth has occurred along with the great increase in owner-occupation. Accordingly, I have given only a short account of the years from 1775 to 1914. For those who wish to know more of the earlier history reference may be made to the pioneer work "Building Societies: their origins and history" by Seymour J. Price (Franey & Co. Ltd., 1958) and to "The Building Society Movement" by E.J. Cleary (Elak Books, 1965). The latter book has not received the recognition it deserves.

Having been engaged in building society affairs all my working life, I am by no means an impartial observer. I believe that they are admirable institutions which have made a significant contribution to the welfare of the people of this country by fostering saving and promoting home-ownerships, but despite my bias I hope I have not omitted all the warts.

April 1980   Herbert Ashworth

CONTENTS

Chapter 1

TERMINATING SOCIETIES

In the second half of the eighteenth century the mechanisation of industry led to changed systems of production in Britain. Workers were increasingly employed in factories, mills and workshops. Many market towns and villages (especially in the North) were transformed into ugly factory towns, which expanded by drawing on the surrounding rural population. Moreover, such was the pace of change, they grew rapidly at a time when there were no planning laws, density requirements or sewage regulations. And this movement from country to town was encouraged by the bleak prospects for many agricultural workers following changes in farming methods, the enclosure of common land and the severity of the poor laws, which drove out-of-work labourers from one parish to another.

The workers in the towns were far more vulnerable than those who lived in the less crowded rural areas. Although earning higher wages, when illness or unemployment occurred they were far less likely to find friendly help. In a rural community members of their own family and others were accustomed to give assistance. And whilst all but the skilled and better-off farm workers were poorly housed in what we would regard today as primitive cottages and hovels, on the whole living and working conditions tended to be safer and healthier in the rural areas.

So the new urban work-force needed some protection against misfortune and found it in the Friendly Society. These societies originated in the late seventeenth century and spread rapidly after 1750. They were mutual associations to provide, from the contributions of their members, cash payments in the event of sickness or infirmity or for immediate necessities arising on the death of a member or his wife. It is estimated that at the end of the Eighteenth Century there were about 7,000 of these societies. The first Friendly Societies Act was passed in 1793 to give them encouragement and legal protection.

Other types of mutual association were also formed. Money clubs, into which the members paid weekly sums and balloted for the right to a loan of the week's proceeds, were popular. They enabled families to buy clothes and furniture. There were also small sick and burial clubs and savings groups.

Some of these clubs and societies were formed under the aegis of a Sunday

School or nonconformist chapel. Some sprang up among miners or groups from other occupations who established trade clubs which were the precursors of trade unions. And many centred on a local inn where, encouraged by the landlord, the members met to transact their business. He provided them with a room and provided himself with regular customers.

The idea of forming building clubs or societies to provide houses followed on from these efforts at mutual protection and improvement. That is the reason why many of the early building societies were associated with a local inn. It was not uncommon for the landlord to be made the custodian of the books of the society.

The earliest society is thought to have been established in Birmingham in (or about) 1775. It was known as Ketley's Building Society and met at the Golden Cross Inn of which Ketley was the landlord. We have no more information about this society than can be gleaned from three advertisements which appeared in a local newspaper in 1778 or 1779, each offering for sale three shares in the society. According to the third of these notices some £80 had been advanced on these shares and (although we have no information as to the amount of the subscriptions or terms of loan) it seems reasonable to suppose that the society had been operating for two or three years. On this slender but nevertheless concrete evidence it can be said that the society must have been formed about 1775.

Several other societies were established in the Birmingham area between 1775 and 1781 and thereafter the movement began to increase and spread. Most of the early societies were located in the Midlands and the North of England, the areas to which population was shifting under the influence of industrialisation. Altogether, we know of some seventy societies which were formed between 1775 and 1825. There must have been many others of which there is no record.

The earliest societies were essentially building clubs. They aimed to take regular subscriptions from their members (usually, in these early years, about twenty in number) until funds were accumulated sufficient to provide the members each in turn with a house. The society then disbanded. It was thus a terminating society, devoted to a single, limited purpose.

An early society about which we have precise information is one formed in the village of Longridge, near Preston in Lancashire. This Society was established in 1793 under the guidance of Robert Parkinson, the perpetual curate of the chapelry of Longridge. There were twenty members of whom nine were yeomen (i.e. small farmers or countrymen above the grade of labourer) and among the rest were weavers, spinners, stonemasons, a carpenter, a shopkeeper and a travelling dealer.

These early societies, small though they were, went about their affairs in a

business-like way. Rules were drawn up, officers appointed and fines imposed for non-attendance, late payments and for swearing and drunkenness at meetings. The Longridge Society's rules provided for a committee of three members, an entrance fee of one guinea and a subscription of 10/6 per month plus 3d. for the expenses of the monthly meeting. Non-payment of the subscription for three months or upwards rendered the member liable to expulsion, in which case his share was to be sold for the benefit of the Society.

Each house was to be balloted for at the time work was about to commence. When the house was ready for occupation, the member to whom it was allocated was then at liberty to occupy it himself or to put in a tenant. A rent was deter-mined, which was payable to the Society in either case. This charge was payable by those who received houses so as to equate their position with that of those who were not so fortunate in the ballot. Payment of rent (and, of course, sub-scriptions) ceased on termination of the society.

The Longridge Society agreed to purchase a site suitable for the erection of 20 houses. The price of the land was £200. Here arose the first problem. The money was to be paid within one year, but a year's subscriptions would only produce £126. And then there was the building work to be started. The dif-ficulty was overcome by Robert Parkinson, who arranged for loans to be made to the Society, he himself being one of the lenders.

Once the land was acquired, the Society embarked on the building of the houses in blocks of four. Further loans were arranged in the early years, and all the houses were built within about five years. By 1804 the payments had been completed and the loans repaid, enabling the Society to terminate its existence. The cost of each house was just under £100. The total subscription by each member was £75.3.0., the remainder coming from the rents charged in respect of the earlier houses.

The Longridge Society was a model of its kind, although it was greatly assisted by the loans which the Rev. Parkinson arranged. The early terminating societies had many methods in common. But they also varied in some ways. Some organised the building of their houses by direct labour, including sometimes the services of one or more of their own members. Others contracted to buy a group of houses from a builder; some bought the land and put the building work out to tender.

But gradually societies gave up building houses. It was found that making an advance of money to enable the member to build or to buy an existing house was a simpler and more satisfactory way of proceeding. It avoided the problems many of the early societies experienced from defaulting contractors, bad workmanship or delays in construction. There was another disadvantage in the

society undertaking the building: not all the houses could be built at the same time. A start would be made with say two or four and then there would be a pause until further funds had been subscribed. When houses were thus built at intervals of a year or two there was the problem of ensuring that they were identical. Members were entitled to expect the same treatment, no better, no worse; but this was difficult to achieve and led to grievances. The problem occurred in the case of the Longridge Society after the first four houses had been built. It was proposed to make some slight improvements to the second set of four, which aroused the wrath of those in possession of the first four and led to a solicitor's letter protesting that the proposals were "contrary to the true principle and spirit, as well as to the words of Rule 9 of the Club, to make this difference and inequality amongst the members". It proved more satisfactory to let each member make his own purchase or contract, a like sum being appropriated to each. The houses (or the cash advances, when societies ceased to build) were allotted by rotation, or by some form of ballot or, in later years, by bidding for advances.

It would be wrong to leave the reader with the impression that these early societies were wholly working class in origin. The usual subscription of ten shillings per month was, in relation to the current wage rates, a heavy sum to pay. In the 1820s the wages of a London artisan were about 30/- per week, those in the provinces getting 24/-. For town labourers the corresponding rates were 16/- and 12/-. From such information as exists it is clear that in the early Societies members of the lower middle class were much in evidence. Men who were independent, earning a comfortable living and able to save; those in highly skilled and highly paid occupations; these were the men to whom a building society was likely to appeal and for whom house purchase was financially practicable. It is not surprising that Birmingham with its multiplicity of small, prosperous metal firms should have been the birth place of building societies.

Nor were societies confined to those who wanted a house for their own occupation. The presence in the membership lists of shopkeepers and innkeepers who normally lived above their own premises indicates an interest in investment. And because the interest in property investment was fairly widespread, a number of societies permitted a member to have more than one share. When a second Longridge Society was formed in 1798 some of its 26 members belonged to the first Society. The Hall Union Club which was the first Society to be formed in Burnley (about 1799) had among its members:— lawyers, a curate, a schoolmaster, textile manufacturers, innkeepers and tailors. The 31 houses which were built in one street had 19 owners; in another street there were likewise 31 houses, owned by 27 members of whom only four were owner-occupiers. It

seems likely that in a number of these early societies saving and investment was the main purpose of the members.

In the first quarter of the nineteenth century a few building societies registered as Friendly Societies under the Act of 1793, thus emphasising the kindred spirit of self-help but also establishing for them a clear legal position and exemption from stamp duties. The remainder came under no Act of Parliament and therefore had no clearly defined legal standing. Indeed, in 1812 the question of whether building societies were illegal associations was raised in a law suit involving the Greenwich Union Building Society where the defendant (a guarantor to a member of the Society) pleaded that the Society was not established either by Act of Parliament or Charter or other legal authority; and that the defendant's obligation was void by virtue of a Statute of 1720. The Court found in favour of the Society, which meant that while building societies had no recognition from the State, nevertheless their activities were not illegal in themselves. Had the judgment gone the other way, it would have created a serious position. It would have meant that all existing societies (save those registered as friendly societies) were illegal, that their rules were not enforceable against their members and that they could not validly enter into contracts.

Two decades later (in 1836) the first Act of Parliament intended to protect and encourage building societies was passed. By this time they had taken firm root. There were societies in many parts of the country and some towns could boast several societies. This made possible local co-operation in defence of their mutual interests. One such matter became an issue in 1835 when the prospect arose of a change in the law relating to stamp duties which would render the transfer of shares liable to such duty. This was a serious matter to terminating societies because of the importance to members of being able to transfer shares freely. Penalties for default in paying subscriptions were heavy and the only way in which a member (unable for one reason or another to keep up his payment) could escape them was by selling and transferring his shares to someone else wanting to become a member of the society. The imposition of stamp duties on this way out of trouble would have been a discouragement to joining a society.

Petitions pleading against the imposition of the stamp duty were sent to Parliament by a number of societies (some of them acting together) and eventually the Chancellor of the Exchequer* agreed to receive a deputation from societies in Manchester and Liverpool. The delegates not only made their protests on the subject of stamp duty but took the opportunity to explain to the Chancellor how societies operated and the objects they were trying to achieve. He was agreeably

*The Chancellor was Thomas Spring Rice, afterwards Lord Monteagle.

impressed by what he was told and decided that building societies ought to have the benefit and protection of a special Act of Parliament.

There was another reason why the Chancellor wanted to encourage building societies. Savings banks had been established under an Act of 1817 and the rate of interest they were permitted to pay had to be subsidised by the Exchequer. By encouraging building societies it was hoped that people would save with them rather than with the Savings Banks, thus reducing the burden on the Exchequer.

The Chancellor was as good as his word. A Bill was introduced and quickly became the Building Societies Act, 1836. Too quickly! For it was a badly drafted Act and the Courts were to spend much time interpreting its obscure clauses. In an endeavour to make short cuts the Act expressly applied to building societies the provisions of the Friendly Societies Acts of 1829 and 1830 "so far as they were applicable". But there was no guidance as to the circumstances in which those Acts would be regarded as being applicable to building societies.

Nevertheless, the 1836 Act did provide a legal standing for building societies and conferred on them a number of benefits. They were exempted from the Usury Laws; their mortgages could be discharged by a receipt of the trustees without the need for a deed of reconveyance (a considerable economy); transfers of shares were exempted from stamp duty; and all building societies established prior to the Act could obtain the benefit of it if their current rules were deposited and certified. The certifying barrister for this purpose (as for the Friendly Societies) became the Chief Registrar under the Friendly Societies Act of 1846. Under the 1836 Act the certification of rules was the only matter on which societies were subject to control. The protection given them by the Act was therefore obtained in exchange for little loss of freedom. What they did suffer from was the uncertainty arising from the obscure wording of the Act and from the further doubts as to whether later amendments to the Friendly Societies Acts applied to building societies.

The 1836 Act was designed to encourage building societies. In that it was successful and the number of societies increased fairly rapidly. They spread over a wide area and the 1840s saw a number of societies formed in and about London. We cannot say with certainty just how many societies were created or were in existence at any one time, since no returns were required to be filed. It is possible that by 1850 there were about 1500 active societies. Having regard to those which had terminated successfully and those which had come to an untimely end, a figure of 1500 would mean that many more than this had been started.

As societies increased in number in the first half of the nineteenth century, changes took place in their structure and their working methods. The earliest societies were small and their membership was restricted to those who wished to

own a house either for their own occupation or as an investment. But under the influence of the friendly societies and of the saving banks which sprang up from the beginning of the century many people were acquiring the habit of regular saving. Building societies took the opportunity to adjust their operations in order to enrol members who wanted to save without wanting to borrow money for house-purchase. So, even at this early stage, many terminating societies had two distinct classes of subscribers, borrowers and investors. But those who were savers only, were regular subscribers – not paid-up shareholders.

There was also a tendency for societies to have a larger membership – instead of 20 or so members the number was often as high as 100 in the 1830s and there were terminating societies with as many as 250 members in the 1850s.

Of the three methods by which advances were allocated the two simpler ways – by ballot and by rotation – were the least popular. The practice of bidding for advances became the most favoured. At a duly convened meeting the chairman would offer an advance of, say, £120 for sale and the members would bid against each other as to how much discount on the loan they would agree should be deducted. Some societies had a printed scale of discount, the discount diminishing year by year according to the length of time the society had been in existence.

A fair discount in the first year of a fourteen year term would be £60 on a share of £120 – i.e. the member would obtain a loan of £60 interest free. After five years the discount would be £45, the member thus receiving a loan of £75. The member would continue to pay his monthly subscription until the termination of the society. Where the right to an advance was determined by ballot or rotation and no discount was exacted, the member paid interest on the loan, usually at about 6 or 7 per cent (which took the place of the rent payable in the earlier societies, as we saw in the case of the Longridge Society).

The system of bidding for advances was open to abuse. Members who had no intention of borrowing might force up the bidding against someone who was keen to obtain the advance. Or a member would speculate by outbidding the genuine borrower and then sell him the right to the advance, making a profit for himself. Members who were thus driven into accepting a loan at too high a discount were in essence paying a high rate of interest for the amount of cash they did get.

There were other disadvantages in the working of a terminating society. One of these was that as all members had to contribute equally it was difficult to attract new members after a year or two because they had to make back payments to put them on equality with the original subscribers. To save ten shillings each month was one thing; to find a lump sum of £10 or £15 was quite

another. Back payments were thus a serious obstacle to joining an existing society.

Again, if members relied on their own subscriptions to raise funds from which advances were made, progress was slow. It meant that some members had to wait a long time for a loan. This difficulty could be overcome by borrowing money. It was also overcome by including members who only wanted to save. But if either of these ways was adopted then a few years of activity would be followed by years in which funds were flowing in for which there was no demand.

One way of overcoming these problems was to run a series of societies. By starting a second society when the first was well under way, those who had missed the first society could join the second, without having to make back payments. Moreover, the second society could borrow the surplus funds of the first society. And so on to the third and subsequent societies. The series of societies would be managed by the same officers and the process of interlocking by lending and borrowing could continue indefinitely. There were nearly forty societies in one group in Sunderland and fifty-two in another in Liverpool. In the hands of competent managers a series of societies could be, and often was, highly successful. In less skillful hands it could be disastrous.

Other difficulties were encountered by terminating societies. One was a matter of arithmetic. Many societies operated on tables which were hopelessly unsound, the managers of many small societies having little knowledge of accountancy or actuarial science. From these tables, calculations were made of the amount due to a member who wished to withdraw from the society and for making advances by ballot or rotation. Where advances were made by bidding, the tables were no longer properly applicable, which would not have been of any consequence if interest had not been paid out to withdrawing members. Some societies went further and treated discounts on advances as profits already realised. Withdrawing members obtained the benefit of this practice to the loss of members who remained. Societies also made promises which were completely unrealistic. One advertised that "from the peculiar advantages offered by this society, the investing members will reap about 20 per cent interest for the use of their subscriptions". Another held out that "borrowers will scarcely pay at the rate of 2 per cent interest for their loans". Those who promoted societies on such optimistic statements caused widespread disappointment and dissatisfaction. The society either wound up or was under the necessity of extending its lifetime and the payment of subscriptions by several years. Some of the men concerned in launching societies on extravagant promises undoubtedly ran them to make as much money out of them as they could. There was danger to the movement from their activities.

Chapter 2

PERMANENT SOCIETIES

The continuity sought by the expedient of running a series of societies under the same management was achieved in a much more satisfactory way by the establishment of permanent societies. It was also a simpler way. Investors and borrowers were recognised as two different classes. This did not prevent someone saving in a building society for the purpose of becoming a borrower at a later stage; just that he was at first one type of member and, later, the other. The society itself was open-ended; it could enrol new savers at any time and in any number; it could make advances to borrowers (either existing or new members) subject only to the availability of funds; and it could make arrangements with each borrower as to the terms and repayment period of his loan. Thus the permanent society had a range and flexibility which could not be achieved by the terminating society. To the men who were running a series of terminating societies, the permanent society offered a great simplification of their operations, although by no means all of them took advantage of the new system.

The credit for devising the permanent society has generally been given to Arthur Scratchley, an actuary by profession who acted as adviser on Tables of Repayment to many societies and who wrote the mid-century standard work on building society methods and principles of operation. In the later editions of his Treatise he himself asserted that he had first put forward the conception. But Cleary* claims it was another actuary, J H James, who first advocated permanent societies, in a pamphlet published in 1845. The evidence would appear to support that view. Nevertheless, it was Scratchley who had the greater role in influencing the movement in the direction of the permanent principle.

The first few permanent societies were founded in 1845 and 1846 – two in London (Metropolitan Equitable and National Equitable) and four in the provinces (including the Ramsbury, which is still in existence and can claim to be the oldest society which started life as a permanent society). Scratchley himself started a permanent society, the London & Metropolitan Counties, in 1848.

Scratchley published his Treatise in 1849, explaining the new principle much more clearly than James had done and at the same time demonstrating wit'n

*E.J. Cleary, *The Building Society Movement* p 49 (Elek Books, London 1965)

numerous examples, the shortcomings of the terminating society. Notwith-standing these shortcomings, the terminating society did not immediately suc-cumb to its competitor. The permanent society was slower in winning acceptance in the North and the Midlands than in London and the South. Terminating societies continued to be formed in considerable numbers in cities such as Manchester and Liverpool and in towns such as Oldham and Rochdale. This may have been in part due to the strong tradition already established and to the conservative outlook of those who were engaged in managing them, whereas in London and the South the growth of societies was far more recent. Another reason was that Northern societies had remained more steadfast to the idea that each member should become a house-owner, the member who joined simply to save was not so frequently found in these areas.

There was one other development which gave an impetus to permanent societies. This was their use in connection with freehold land societies, for the purpose of which the permanent society was more suitable. Land societies were formed in order to assist people to acquire a vote in parliamentary elections. To be qualified to vote a man must be the owner of a house of an annual value (in the boroughs) of £10; or, in the counties, a freehold of an annual value of £2; or (after the Reform Act of 1832) a leasehold or copyhold of an annual value of £10. Land societies proved popular; some of them were highly successful and many of them attracted to their boards men prominent in parliamentary and business circles. The publicity they received helped to spread the idea of home-ownership.

These societies had thus a political motive. Their promoters (who were, in some cases, Liberals and, in others, Tories), aimed to extend the franchise, trusting that the persons they helped to acquire a house or a plot of land would be grateful enough to use their votes in favour of the party to which they, the promoters, belonged. Land was bought (not by the society but by some of those connected with it) and was then sold off in plots with an annual value of not less than £2, the society lending money to the purchasers.

The idea of using building societies in this way was first thought of and put into practice by James Taylor, who was the secretary and founder of the Bir-mingham Land Society. He told the story of how he registered the Society with the certifying barrister:— "Its rules are similar to those of an ordinary building society: in fact its first rule declares that it shall be a benefit building society. This is essential to its legality. We are enrolled under the Benefit Building Societies Act, and have received the signature of the Government agent, legalis-ing our Society. I remember two-and-a-half years ago being in London with John Tidd Pratt, Esq. the barrister appointed by the Government to certify the

rules of building and friendly societies, and I remarked to him on the impropriety of calling a land society a building society. His answer was, 'It don't matter, what it is: if you want the benefit of the Act, you must declare it a building society, whether it is one or not! 'Very well', said I, 'you christen the child; we give it another name, and we have an idea our name will become the more popular of the two – it is a right child with a wrong name".

There was for some years an active land society movement and a number of the land societies became firmly established. Over one hundred were formed in the decade from 1847 to 1857, the three largest being the Birmingham (Liberal) the National (Liberal) and the Conservative the latter being formed in 1852 to counter the Liberal societies. These land societies reached the peak of their activity in the 1850s.

There were two reasons why the movement thereafter diminished. One was that, with the passing of the Company Act, 1856, a company was found to be a more suitable vehicle for carrying out the purpose of buying and selling land to create more voters. The other was that as the franchise was gradually extended by legislation their original purpose became less important. Many of these societies being registered as building societies (although calling themselves land societies) then turned their attention to the normal business of building societies, thus adding to the growing number of permanent societies.

Perhaps the most notable of the freehold land societies was the National, established in London in 1849. Richard Cobden, Joseph Hume and John Bright were actively associated with this Society. It was registered under the Building Societies Act, 1836 as the National Permanent Mutual Benefit Building Society but was known as the National Freehold Land Society until 1894 when the name was altered, to comply with the Building Societies Act of that year, to the National Freehold Land and Building Society. In the early years the purchase of land for division and sale to the "forty shilling freeholders" was made by trustees who bought the land as private persons since the society itself was not permitted by law to own land. The trustees borrowed money from the Society to finance the purchases, but were of course, personally responsible for any loss or profit that might ensue. Within four years the National had become the largest of the land societies. Not only did it find that there were ready takers for the plots of land made available by the trustees on the various parcels of land they purchased in and around London, it also found that there were many savers coming forward to place money on deposit.

The method of purchasing land through trustees was discontinued by the National in 1856 when (under the Company Act of that year already noted above) the British Land Company was formed. The capital of this company was

offered to the members of the Freehold Land Society and fully taken up. The directors were drawn from the board of the Society and the two organisations used the same officers and staff. All the estates owned by the trustees were then transferred to the new company, which henceforth assumed responsibility for all land transactions. This change left the National free to become a savings bank and building society.

The emphasis was thus changing. It was all very well for a man to buy a plot of land in order to obtain a vote. But what did he do with the land thereafter? The obvious course for the society, with ever-increasing funds, was to encourage him to build a house on it. So, the society began to turn its attention to normal building society activity, offering to lend two-thirds of the cost of erecting a house, repayable over a period of ten years with interest at 5 per cent.

The British Land Co. continued the land activities and for some years the loans it received from the society were substantial. As time went on the Company's activities declined and the land movement aims of the Society were overshadowed by its building society operations. In 1877 the two parted company and in the following year, British Land repaid its loans to the Society and henceforth pursued its own path. It is still in existence, a well-known public property company, quoted on the London Stock Exchange.

The National continued to prosper as one of the largest of the permanent societies. It changed its name to the National Building Society in 1930 and entered into union with the Abbey Road Society in 1944 to form the Abbey National.

Development of Permanent Societies

The permanent society was devised and operated by men who had been involved in terminating societies. They had made an important break with terminating societies by dividing investors and borrowers into separate classes ..i by the establishment of on-going activity. Nevertheless they were not altogether free of the past and for some years many of the practices to be found in terminating societies lingered on. At first, most permanent societies adopted the practice of bidding or tendering for advances, issued only subscription shares and imposed fines on their officers as well as their members. It must be remembered, too, that they were established under the 1836 Act and governed by the same legal decisions which had caused so much concern to the terminating societies.

The evolution and development of permanent societies took place over the remainder of the century. By 1900 their membership and funds far outweighed those of the remaining terminating societies. They gradually threw off the con-

straints of the terminating societies' methods. They were able to obtain incorporation under the Building Societies Act, 1874; and under the Building Societies Act, 1894 they had to submit to proper audits and a prescribed form of account. They had also been placed firmly under the control of the Chief Registrar. Some of the permanent Societies had begun to see the necessity for reserves and liquidity.

As we shall see all this did not come about without disaster. There were frauds and failures. There was mismanagement. But the lessons were learnt and on the whole public confidence, although at times shaken, was never forfeited.

It is interesting to consider how some of the early permanent societies came to be formed. We have already noted one group, the freehold land societies, the aims of which at the outset were political. And we have also seen how some of those who were running a series of terminating societies on a professional basis decided to simplify their operations by confining their activities to one permanent society. There were also instances where those running a single terminating society decided to replace it with a permanent organisation. This happened in Leeds where those operating the Leeds Building and Investment Society, conscious of the limitations of terminating societies, decided in 1848 to establish a permanent society which became the Leeds Permanent. In 1858 the parent society closed down, by which time its offspring had been so successful that it could then claim to be the largest society in the country.

The Bradford Second Equitable (1851) according to its first Annual Report to members "resulted from an opinion entertained by many members of the Bradford Equitable Building and Investment Company that in order to meet the wants of numerous parties desirous of joining such a society it had become requisite to establish a new one on the 'permanent' principle. It is satisfactory to find that this opinion has been amply verified by a larger number of shares having been taken up than in any previous society in this town during the same period; whilst its permanency has thus early been found advantageous in numerous instances as with the entrance of a new member, the society, so far as he is concerned, begins anew, and he has the same period in which to realise his share, or to repay what he has borrowed, that another would have who joined the society at its commencement."

The Halifax Permanent (1853) owes its origin to a small friendly society (the Loyal Georgian Society) founded in 1779. This friendly society early in its career had adopted the practice of lending money to its members for building houses. The society found that this activity was unprofitable and decided to end it. It was this decision which led to the formation of the Halifax, several members of the friendly society taking part. The first meetings of the founders of

the society took place in the Old Coach Inn, which was also the headquarters of the Loyal Georgian Society.

The Marsden (1860) was founded in Nelson (Lancashire) as the result of a conversation at the house of Mr Thomas Holland which turned upon the scarcity of cottages in the neighbourhood and the pressing demand for suitable dwellings for its rapidly increasing population. It was suggested that a building society would be the best means of meeting the requirements of the district. Those present formed themselves into a preliminary committee and two of them were deputed to wait upon "gentlemen of capital and influence in the locality likely to further the movement and to report the result of their canvass".

The Woolwich Equitable, founded in 1847, was preceded by a terminating society started in 1842. In 1843 there was some dissatisfaction about its conduct and a number of participants withdrew and started another society. Four years later they decided to form a permanent society. The prospectus which the new Equitable Society issued argued the case for permanent societies in some detail, setting out the advantages which would be offered to both investors and borrowers. To the investor it offered the distribution of a certain portion of the profits annually, so that a member withdrawing after one year would receive interest on the money invested; and secondly that there would be no back payments. So far as borrowers were concerned, it is worth quoting:— "To the borrower this society offers advantages above many other societies, first because it does not oblige him to submit to the contingencies of a sale and the discount attendant; it does not lend him nominally £600 when the sum is really £300 or £250, but advances the actual amount of the share, out of which a second advantage arises viz:— that while persons who in other societies borrow nominally £600, but really only £300, or less, he must really pay stamp duty on a mortgage deed for £600. In this society the stamp duty will be paid on such an amount only as is actually received by him. Thirdly — he can look forward with certainty to the release of his property, while in other societies a termination earlier than at first proposed is hardly possible, but a much later termination is exceedingly probable. Fourthly — it provides for a release of the property earlier than the time at first fixed by the person borrowing, should he be in circumstances to discharge the sum at any time remaining due on the mortgage, and less 3% on the amount so due, whereas in other societies a release earlier than the period named in the mortgage would involve the *actual* repayment of the amount *nominally* received, which in some cases would be double the amount actually borrowed." This was certainly hard-hitting against the terminating societies.

These societies which gradually took the place of the local terminating

societies were more often than not run and directed by men who firmly believed in the virtues of thrift, sober habits and self-help. They were more concerned with spreading the gospel of saving and home-ownership than with making a profit or income for themselves. The Cheltenham and Gloucester owed its formation to its first President, James Downing, In the course of his duties as Chairman of the Board of Guardians and other social work, he had seen the housing needs of the working population of Cheltenham. He got together a group of nonconformist friends to start the building society in 1850. The Temperance (1854) was inspired by William Shaen, a solicitor, active in many educational and humanitarian movements of his day, who subsequently explained, "I felt that teetotallers were bound together by a feeling of common devotion to a great moral principle, and if we could only get men of good business habits among us, that then we should have an organisation on the basis of which a great business might be raised, besides being of advantage to the great cause of temperance itself."*

The Planet was begun in John Wesley's own chapel in the City Road, London, by members of the congregation and was regarded as a social rather than a business undertaking. At a later stage, the Abbey Road (1874) came into being at the suggestion of a Kilburn builder whose workmen were members of the Abbey Road Church Benefit Society. He advised them to form, in conjunction with the Benefit Society, a building society through which they could purchase houses for themselves.†

The Southern Co-operative Permanent Society was formed in 1884 by members of the Southern Co-operative Guild with the object of making loans to enable co-operative retail societies to purchase shop premises as well as making advances to co-operators themselves. But this idea was soon abandoned and the society confined itself to normal building society business, treating co-operators and non-co-operators alike.‡

Many societies put out prospectuses and leaflets which proclaimed the virtues of thrift and home-ownership in eloquent and even fervent language. One example will suffice. The Cumberland Co-operative was established in 1850. It was intended to act as a freehold land society and also as a substitute for the terminating societies which had been operating in the town since 1837. The prospectus stated:— "The object of the promoters is to induce the industrious

---

*(The Society did, indeed, stand for the temperance movement for over 120 years until it merged with the Bedfordshire to form the Gateway).

‡(Name changed to Co-operative Permanent 1895 and to Nationwide 1970).

classes in this district to make an endeavour to improve their moral and social conditions by the most available of all methods – individual exertion and self-reliance . . . to those who are stimulated to become members by the desire of one day living in their own cot, of cultivating their own garden, and of passing the eve of a well-spent life free from the galling weight of poverty, this society holds out especial advantages. Many who are said to be too straightened in their means to lay by sixpence a week for the purchase of an allotment spend much more than that sum upon articles of pernicious indulgence. Nearly twenty-six millions of money – one half of all the taxes collected in the United Kingdom – are spent annually by the working classes alone in various kinds of intoxicating liquors. One of the most gratifying aspects of this Association is that it will tend to divert from the channels of waste some portion of this enormous sum, which, if laid out in the purchase of assured physical comforts, would give smiling homes to many thousands of families, and impart a stimulus to every branch of industry."

These were the kind of sentiments that were preached by building society men from platforms and by brochure and pamphlet. Under the leadership of the strong nonconformist element which dominated many of the permanent societies, building societies became a proselytising movement, seldom losing an opportunity to advance the merits of thrift and home-ownership.

Chapter 3

METHODS OF BUSINESS

The early permanent societies were fortunate in starting against a favourable economic background. The period from 1850 to 1875 was a period of steadily rising commodity prices and property values. There were years when business was depressed and there were also one or two banking and financial crises but on the whole conditions were helpful to building societies. The London area did suffer from overbuilding towards the end of the 1860s and as we shall see some societies were badly hit by the large number of vacant properties. But this was only a temporary phase in the growth of the London suburbs.

In this Chapter it is proposed to examine the methods and terms of business which the permanent societies adopted in these formative years. Their first task, of course, was to obtain funds in order to lend. In a terminating society, the members subscribed for a share (which, under the 1836 Act, was not to be more than £150) by·paying a monthly subscription. The permanent societies likewise issued subscription shares. The Halifax Permanent adopted £120 as the amount of an investment share, payable at the rate of ten shillings per lunar month; and the subscriber of modest means could have a fifth of a share (£24) at two shillings, per month. The Woolwich Equitable adopted £50 shares at a subscription rate of ten shillings per calendar month. Both societies charged an entrance fee of two shillings and sixpence.

The alternative form of membership was by way of paid up shares (that is, a lump sum investment) but so much under the influence of the terminating societies' methods were the permanent societies that they did not all provide at the outset for this type of share.

The Halifax for instance, did not accept paid-up shares until 1888 and, at first, only for those who had finished paying for their subscription shares and wanted to leave the money with the society. The Woolwich began to take paid-up shares some four years after its formation. The Temperance on the other hand adopted shares of £30 denomination which from the outset could be subscribed for at four shillings per week or taken up in full. Gradually, societies began to run the two classes of shares side by side, but at times when money was plentiful and mortgages hard to come by, they would suspend the issue of paid-up shares.

The Temperance did so from 1871 to 1878.

Permanent societies also took money on deposit, as the terminating societies had done to enable them to make more advances in their early years. This was not essential to the operation of a permanent society in view of its ability to issue paid-up shares. But deposits were popular. Many investors were apprehensive of the idea of taking shares and felt a deposit account was safer. Deposits took precedence over share capital on withdrawal or in the event of a winding-up. Again, the denomination of paid-up shares was generally high and the sub-scription share called for regular payments. Therefore the deposit account was more convenient for both the small and the spasmodic saver. From the Society's point of view there was an advantage since deposits carried an interest rate $\frac{1}{2}$per cent or 1per cent less than was paid on shares.

Deposits were taken on a large scale by some societies, as much as 80per cent or 90per cent of total liabilities. When this happened, there was not much more safety in putting money on deposit than in shares. In the 1860s and 1870s, the deposit departments of some societies took on the appearance of banks and in-deed competed quite severely with the local banks. As the Royal Commission observed in 1872 "nor is it difficult to see that a building society with all its money loaned on freehold or leasehold property, and a constant incoming of repayments by monthly instalments may fairly be preferred, by a portion at least of the public, as a field of investment".

The permanent societies were as eager as the terminating societies to en-courage home-ownership. And the facilities open to the owner-occupier from a permanent society were undoubtedly more likely to encourage him. His re-payment term was certain and clearly defined, and societies accumulated ample funds for lending so that there was no waiting for a loan. But the vast majority of the population were tenants. Those who embarked on house purchase were comparatively few in number. The permanent societies found that house purchase was a plant of slow growth. The savings habit, on the other hand, was more widespread and in consequence there was far more money than was demanded by owner-occupiers. But there was another and much bigger source of mortgage business for societies. It was the investor in house property. Throughout the nineteenth century with the increase in population and the need for more and more houses, house property was a popular form of investment for those with money to invest. When building societies were able to offer mortgages on rented houses, investors found this was a better way to finance their purchases than by way of a private mortgage, which was liable to be called in and then had to be replaced by another, with attendant legal expenses.

Enid Gauldie says "it is worth looking at the kind of person who put his

money into housing, buying a row of houses from a speculative builder or commissioning another to build to his requirements. Not nearly enough is known about these people, but it is clear, from such studies as have been done, that they were seldom big-time financiers. Widows, spinsters and orphans, for instance, seem frequently to have been provided for by the purchase out of family funds of a row of houses which was then expected to provide a small, steady income and sometimes a home within the property. It was through this kind of investor that lawyers exerted their very considerable influence on the housing market, advising investment in housing as a source of small, steady income in preference to greater, but riskier opportunities elsewhere. Tradesmen and shopkeepers purchased rows of houses, living in one, sometimes a slightly superior corner house, and collecting rents from the others".*

There were thus two classes of borrower (the owner-occupier and the investor) each of which was considered normal and desirable. Some societies probably found it easier than others to get owner-occupier mortgages. Much depended upon house building activity, employment and wages in the society's locality. Much, too, depended on the way funds came in from investors. If the build-up of funds was slow, then it was likely that the owner-occupiers would absorb most of it; if funds grew rapidly the Society would seek to lend money on investment property.

The establishment of permanent societies and the rapid increase of the funds at their disposal brought a new element into building society operations. The terminating society had provided for the member who wanted to buy one or two houses for investment – but this was incidental to the main purpose of the society. Now investment property became of far greater significance. The first mortgage granted by the Halifax Permanent was upon "19 cottages, beer-house, brew-house, haychamber, cart shed and conveniences". The first application made to the Woolwich Equitable was for a loan of £200 on two houses in course of erection. The history of the Bradford Second Equitable (1851) tells us that securities offered and accepted in the early years included chapels, Sunday Schools, workshops, stables, beerhouses, shops, warehouses and mills. The majority of loans made by the Bradford Second, however, were granted on dwelling house property – mainly for investment. A large portion of these loans were in respect of property to be built or in process of building, much of it back-to-back housing which was the popular and acceptable method of housing the rapidly increasing industrial workers.

The London societies also made loans to property investors and some of them

*(Enid Gauldie *Cruel Habitations* p. 181. Allen and Unwin Ltd. 1974).

ran into trouble at the end of the 1860s. Housebuilding had gone ahead rather quickly in the London suburbs, demand fell off and builders, speculators and investors found themselves with empty houses which were difficult to sell or to let. The Temperance suffered and by 1872 the directors were saying in their Annual Report that they had thought it advisable to write off a considerable amount for possible depreciation. The Planet which had expanded rapidly was in more serious trouble. The difficulties were due to the Society having distributed each year as earnings the premiums charged on mortgage advances instead of putting proper amounts to reserve; and, secondly, to the volume of properties in possession arising from defaulting builders and speculators. The society survived. One of the members who joined the board of directors and helped to save the society wrote most forcibly about the dangers of lending to the speculative and to the over-sanguine: "Speculative builders were our most dreaded customers. They generally abandoned their securities after a few months' payments. Next to these in mischief were the borrowers who attempted too much. Instead of buying three, four or six houses, the payments for which they could have kept up, even though a part of the property should be for a time unlet, these 'in haste to be rich' customers would take up a terrace or an entire street with the result that when bad times made tenants scarce, having no resources to fall back on, they would collapse into utter bankruptcy. Whenever we had to foreclose on properties thus abandoned we, of course, found them in bad repair and with ground rent and other charges overdue and a big outlay was necessary before any returns could be obtained".

What this director did not comment on was the Board's responsibility for approving borrowers and examining mortgage securities. It would seem that there had been some lack of discrimination. On the other hand it must be remembered that this was the first time any of the permanent societies had experienced a major set-back and the London societies had not foreseen the slump in property. In the last quarter of the 19th century, societies generally were to experience problems with falling rents and properties in possession.

Interest rates paid and charged by permanent societies remained fairly stable throughout the first twenty-five years of their existence. The Halifax Permanent charged 5 per cent on mortgages, paid 5 per cent on shares and 4 per cent on deposits. It may be asked how a society could pay its management expenses without charging its borrowers more than it paid its share subscribers. There were several additional sources of income. Deposit monies at 4 per cent helped to provide a margin; and in the Halifax Permanent (as with many other societies) deposit balances exceeded the subscriber share capital throughout these early years. At 31st January 1879 Halifax deposits totalled £148,000 compared

with £90,000 share balances. Again, interest on mortgages was calculated annually not monthly which over a repayment term of 12 years 11 months gave a considerably higher true yield than 5 per cent. Then the society drew extra income from entrance fees, fines, redemption fees and from a charge on borrowers of three shillings and four pence per annum per share imposed as a contribution towards management and office expenses.

Not only were these extras sufficient to cover management expenses but they enabled the society to pay a bonus from 1856 onwards. In the spirit of mutuality inherited from the terminating societies this bonus was paid to both investing and borrowing members. The same mutual principle was adopted by the Leeds and other societies in their early years, but as time went on the view was taken that any bonuses should be given only to investing members.

From 1859 the rate paid on shares by northern societies was $4\frac{1}{2}$ per cent and the mortgage rate for new loans was reduced to this figure. Deposit rates varied between 3 per cent and 4 per cent, depending on the need for funds. There was little change thereafter, until rates came down another half per cent in 1885.

Societies in London and the south charged higher rates for mortgages than the northern societies and the principal of mutuality was less common. It was stated in evidence to the Royal Commission that the true rate of interest charged by London societies was of the order of $7\frac{1}{2}$ per cent to 8 per cent. In addition to the nominal rate of interest, borrowers were also called upon to pay premiums for their loans. The Temperance charged interest at 5 per cent and advances were made by tender, the successful allotees being those who offered the highest premiums. If a borrower wished to have an immediate advance he could get it by paying an addition of one shilling in the pound upon the premium of the first accepted tender at the last bidding. The Temperance did very well for its investors. At the end of the first year it paid $7\frac{1}{2}$ per cent to its share members and 5 per cent to its depositors. It continued to pay $7\frac{1}{2}$ per cent on shares until 1871, although the deposit rate was reduced to 4 per cent in 1862. In 1871, due to the difficulty of finding suitable mortgage securities in the then depressed London property market, the share rate was reduced to 5 per cent. It was raised to $5\frac{1}{2}$ per cent the following year, when the market was recovering, and remained at that figure for the next forty years.

The normal advance was 75 per cent to 80 per cent of value but there was apparently no hard-and-fast rule especially where the owner-occupier was concerned. Societies operating on a purely local basis knew many of their members and could judge who should be encouraged. Accordingly, the advance might be as high as 90 per cent to someone with a reputation as a sober, industrious workman.

Repayment terms were usually for not more than 15 years. The terminating societies had aimed at a life between 10 and 15 years and the permanent societies proceeded from this basis. The Temperance set a maximum of 12 years and later extended this to 15 years for freeholds. The Woolwich in its original prospectus gave alternatives of 7, 10, 12 and 15 years. But there were societies in Liverpool and Newcastle willing to lend over terms of 20 and 25 years.

Some permanent societies got away to a fairly rapid start and were soon able to employ full-time staff and open a daily office. Others grew more slowly and had to make do with a part-time secretary and a meeting room hired weekly or monthly where the directors and secretary attended for the purpose of collecting subscriptions and other business. The directors also inspected properties offered as security. Sometimes, but not always, they had the assistance of a professional surveyor. Where lending was not confined to one town, societies tended to make more use of professional surveyors. Even at this early stage societies arranged for the valuations to be carried out at fees below those normally charged for this kind of advice. The legal work in connection with mortgages was usually entrusted to one firm of solicitors and here again arrangements were made for a lower than normal scale of charges.

Agencies were opened by some of the more enterprising societies and demonstrated how they could help in accelerating growth. The northern societies were quicker to seize on this method of expansion than the London societies, perhaps because the capital was large enough to offer ample scope for business. The Halifax Permanent opened three agencies in its first year of operation. The Leeds Permanent had eighteen agencies in 1871. The Bradford societies and two in Manchester likewise appointed agents. In London, the Temperance was an exception and appointed numerous agents, some as far away as Lancashire and Somerset.

Chapter 4

THE ROYAL COMMISSION

As we have seen, the vexed question of Stamp Duties induced the early building societies to take a measure of concerted action which led to the passing of the Building Societies Act, 1836. There was subsequent occasions when societies got together to defend their interests or to protest against proposed measures which they considered would adversely affect their operation. One result of the growth of the permanent societies was the emergency of full-time professional managers who were concerned with the wider problems bearing on the movement as a whole and who looked to the future in a way those connected with single terminating societies could hardly be expected to do.

These full-time managers consulted with each other and when necessary collaborated in making representations to the Chief Registrar or to the Government. In 1855 yet another attempt was made by the Treasury to impose Stamp Duty on building society mortgages. This proposal was opposed and eventually rejected by the House of Lords. But the efforts of the Treasury created an awareness of the need for some kind of organisation to follow Parliamentary proceedings and to take appropriate action where building societies were affected. Accordingly, in May 1855, the Liverpool societies formed the Liverpool Protection Association. This was closely followed by the formation of a London association, known as the Land and Building Societies Protection Association; but this Association lapsed in 1860. There was no permanent organisation until the Building Societies Protection Association was formed in 1869.

Other issues besides that of Stamp Duties were giving concern to building societies. One was uncertainty under the law regarding the borrowing powers of societies. The practice followed by many terminating societies of obtaining loans to speed up lending in their early years has already been noted. And we have seen that permanent societies, too, found it useful to borrow money. The power of societies to borrow was questioned in a number of legal cases as was the extent of that power. For a time in the 1850's the Registrar would only certify a rule which required a society's trustees to give their personal security for any loans taken. Later he went further and for a time refused to certify any proposed

borrowing rules. An unsatisfactory position was thus created. Some societies with borrowing rules certified earlier had taken large sums on deposit. Some societies without borrowing powers had also accepted deposits. If borrowing (whether under rules or not) was illegal, what redress did the depositors have? It was not until a test case was brought in 1868 that the Courts decided that the power to borrow (under a rule of the Society concerned which limited the power to an amount not exceeding two-thirds of the amount secured by the mortgages of the society) was valid. Thereafter the Registrar decided that he would register borrowing rules subject to the two-thirds limit. Even so, some doubts remained.

Rulings of the Registrar and the Courts on other matters such as the manner in which societies might be wound-up (of importance to terminating societies) and the redemption of mortgages also indicated that the time had arrived when amendment or replacement of the 1836 Act was desirable. Changes in methods and practice as well as the shortcomings of the Act itself had created a need for more comprehensive and more specific legislation.

This became the objective of the London group now transformed into the Building Societies Protection Association. Despite its title, at the outset it was not representative of the whole country. Its officers were drawn entirely from London societies. It did, however, offer membership to provincial societies, but enrolment was slow.

A Bill to consolidate and amend the law was prepared and approved at the Association's first annual meeting in 1870. This Bill was introduced in Parliament in May, being sponsored by four members, one of whom was W. T. McCullagh Torrens* who had become President of the Association. In June another meeting was held in London at which the London members were joined by delegates from societies in the North-East, Lancashire and the Midlands. They considered the draft Bill which was slightly amended in the light of the discussion. But no further progress was made because in July the Government decided to set up a Royal Commission on Friendly Societies and to include building societies in its field of enquiry.

The Commission's Report on building societies was published in March 1872. The general verdict of the Commissioners was favourable and they were in no doubt that the law relating to building societies was in a very unsatisfactory state. They called attention to the "singular spectacle of a multitude of bodies many of them with numerous members, and wielding considerable money

---

*W.T. McCullagh Torrens (1813-1894) was a barrister, politician and author. In 1868, he introduced the Artisans Dwellings Bill enabling local authorities to clear away overcrowded slums and erect decent dwellings for the working classes. (See Pt 1, Ch 11).

powers, which have wholly outgrown the law by which they are nominally governed."

The Report recognised that the two remarkable features of the period since 1836 were the growth of permanent societies and the development of the loan or deposit system. Of permanent societies it was observed "It is admitted by even an adverse witness that on the whole permanent societies have as yet been judiciously managed; that failures of building societies which used to be very frequent in the epoch of terminating societies alone, are now rare. It is, however, alleged that the growth of them has altogether changed the character and altered the sphere of the building society movement; that it tends to throw this more and more under the direction and into the hands of the middle classes, and to secure to them its benefits. It is, indeed, startling to hear of single advances, not only of thousands, but of twenty and thirty thousand pounds, being made by building societies, sometimes on the security of mills and factories; and it is roundly alleged by some witnesses that when this is the case there is no money to spare for small borrowers, and that the working classes, by whom and for whose benefit the system was primarily devised, are discountenanced and kept away. It is maintained as positively to the contrary, that the smaller advances are always preferred to the larger ones, as being much more secure, by dividing the chances of loss over a wider field, and that the larger ones do themselves benefit the working classes by serving as means of investment for the capital which these classes deposit with the societies, and which might otherwise remain idle."

Two observations may be made on the above quotation. The Protection Association furnished statistics from 250 societies showing that the vast majority of their loans were for amounts not exceeding £300; where large loans were made by societies on other than house property it was because of a lack of small borrowers and some societies were undoubtedly tempted for this reason to take greater risks than was wise.

The other point is that there was some conflict in the evidence given to the Commission on the question whether building societies catered for the working or middle class. Undoubtedly, so far as the permanent societies were concerned, the direction and management had been taken over by the middle classes. And no doubt more and more money was invested by the middle classes. But there is nothing in the record of societies to show that the working classes were discouraged in any way from borrowing; indeed, they were all the more welcome because of the ample funds the middle classes were providing. Yet it is worth noting that the Commission were told (in a complete reversal of the general experience) that in Liverpool working men seldom borrowed but supplied the ma-

jor part of the local societies' capital.

A good deal of the evidence given to the Commission was provided by building society officers, mainly from the permanent societies. Members of the Protection Association were prominent and the Bill which the Association had proposed to Parliament was thoroughly examined by the Commission. There were also critics among the witnesses who complained that building societies encouraged building speculation; that their accounts were often deceptive; that the rates of interest charged to borrowers were exorbitant; that their fines were oppressive and that they did not abide by their rules especially in repayments to members or depositors. No doubt these complaints could have been laid at the doors of some societies. We have seen, for instance, how come societies took deposits without even having a rule authorising them to do so.

It was also argued before the Commission that the privileges they enjoyed allowed societies to compete unfairly with banks and other forms of private enterprise. But the Commission felt that they had "enormously encouraged the building of houses for the working and lower-middle class. Originating with the working class, they must have had great influence in training that class to business habits. There is thus no prior ground why the law should look upon them with disfavour".

There were, nevertheless, those who were of the opinion that building societies ought not to have the privilege of a special Act but should be brought under the legislation governing joint stock companies. The Commission studied this question with care and concluded that whilst the form of the joint stock company was "well suited for all undertakings which require certain definite amounts of capital at starting, it is not so well adapted for those which are capable of growing gradually from the smallest beginnings . . . The two forms of undertaking, we venture, therefore, to think, have an equal right to subsist, the one for the use of those who seek to make capital, the other for those who seek, having made it, to use it." And on this question the Commission concluded "all the various classes of societies which are subject to the jurisdiction of the Registrar of Friendly Societies, the Friendly Society itself, the Benefit Building Society, the loan society, the scientific and literary society, the charitable institution, the industrial and provident society, the trades union, all offer this common element of the predominance of membership and of the gradual growth and diminution of capital. But confining ourselves to the building society, we have come to the conclusion that the institution, however modified since it was first authorised by law, deserves to be maintained as one which within certain limits, usefully supplements, and does not unfairly compete with, the joint stock company."

We shall see in the following chapter that this question of bringing building societies under company legislation was by no means settled by the Commission's verdict and that proposals by the Government were to arouse intense feeling among building society men.

The Commission was of the opinion that exemption from Stamp Duties was neither of vital importance to building societies nor justifiable from the public point of view. They recommended that mortgages up to £200 only should be exempt. They also recommended that societies should continue to be registered with the Registrar of Friendly Societies and that the Registrar should have a limited discretion in certifying rules to enable him to disallow provisions of an inequitable or impracticable nature. On suggestions that building societies' lending activities should be restricted, the Commission saw no reason to limit the size of advances, the geographical area of operations or types of advances.

On the much debated question of borrowing powers, the Commission recommended that the limit should be two-thirds of the total value of the amounts for the time being secured on mortgage; or as an alternative for terminating societies six months' subscriptions.

Chapter 5

THE 1874 ACT

In the light of the observations and recommendations of the Royal Commission the Bill drawn up by the Protection Association was amended and reintroduced. The Home Secretary (H.A. Bruce)*, on behalf of the Government objected to the revised Bill and indicated the kind of Bill it would favour. Notwithstanding the Commission's views, the Government wanted legislation which, in essence, would have put building societies under the Companies Act of 1862. The Protection Association strongly resisted this proposal and relations between the Home Secretary and the Association deteriorated. When the Association's Bill was again before the House of Commons, Bruce attacked it strongly. The Bill was withdrawn and introduced again in March 1873. Thereupon the Government published its own Bill which, in conformity with the Home Secretary's views, provided that all building societies should become joint stock companies and be subject to provisions in the Companies Act.

Building societies were solidly united in opposition to this measure. There was a great outcry from all parts of the country. The protests were so quickly and so effectively made, that within eight days of its introduction the Government Bill was withdrawn for reconsideration. When the new Bill appeared it was no better from the building societies' point of view. More elaborate, its clauses were still based on the Companies Acts. It was described as the societies' "Annihilation" Bill. *The Building Societies' Gazette* observed "We feel that the severest reprobation is due to the insidious mode in which provision is made for the quiet extinction of societies of the class which now exist, and which have, on the whole, worked so well and the substitution of anomalous creations which, it would appear, are to be neither societies as now understood, nor joint stock companies of any intelligible type." And the President of the Protection Association went so far as to say that if it became law many societies would fail and "when a sufficient number had failed the Chancellor of the Exchequer would bring in a Bill for the establishment of Government building societies to be managed by a

*H.A. Bruce (1815-1895) afterwards Lord Aberdare. Gladstone congratulated himself upon having a "Heaven-born Home Secretary". The building society leaders were far from sharing this view.

new tribe of Treasury officials; and the additional millions of savings would go to swell the balances with which the Finance Minister is enabled to deal in Consols".

What the Government appeared to have in mind was that in their own Bills the building society representatives were seeking to protect their position without conceding the degree of supervision to which friendly societies, co-operative societies and provident societies were subjected. But the Home Secretary, instead of pursuing his wish to apply the Companies Acts, would have done better to insist on strengthening the provisions of the societies' Bill along the lines recommended by the Commission: namely, stronger powers to the Registrar regarding rules, accounts and audit on all of which the Commission had made practical recommendations which in drafting their own Bills the societies had chosen to ignore.

The second Government Bill was opposed as vehemently as the first and by agreement it was withdrawn along with the Association's Bill. The Government wanted to think again, but showed no signs of giving way. At this point, however, opinion among the societies was far from unanimous about what should be done. Some of the northern societies, especially in Liverpool and other Lancashire towns were for dropping the idea of new legislation and continuing under the 1836 Act with all its imperfections. They were not only alarmed by the Government's attitude but doubtful of some of the amendments proposed to the Association's Bill. There were also those who criticised the Association as not being a truly representative body. At this juncture the Association had some 188 members of which 76 were in London and the South East, 80 in the North of England and the Midlands with the remainder in other parts of the Country including two in Scotland and two in Ireland. There were some 2,000 societies altogether, so that a plausible case could be made that the Association was not representative. But it was true to say that it was far more representative of the permanent societies than of societies as a whole.

The Protection Association was not disposed to give up the fight and in November 1873 decided to reintroduce its Bill as soon as possible.

Then suddenly events took a turn decidedly to the advantage of the building societies. Unexpectedly in January 1874 Gladstone sought a dissolution of Parliament, suffered defeat at the ensuing General Election and Disraeli became Prime Minister. Assheton Cross, a firm supporter of building societies, was the new Home Secretary. Sir Stafford Northcote, another sympathiser, became Chancellor of the Exchequer. The threat of being brought under the Companies Act had disappeared. The way was open for the passage of a Bill along the lines of that desired by the Association. No time was lost. The Bill received the Royal

Assent in July 1874. It went through with few alterations but the Chancellor was adamant on the question of Stamp Duty on mortgages and the exemption clause had to go.

Events had proved the value of joint action. Building societies had fought hard to get new legislation. They had enlisted the help of influential members of both Houses of Parliament. They had had the assistance of the Assistant Registrar, E W Brabrook (who was later to be a distinguished holder of the office of Chief Registrar). Above all, they had had the leadership of James Higham who had first seen the need for an Association, was its first Chairman and who inspired his colleagues to persist in their quest for a new Act.

James Higham (born in 1821) was one of the first professional building society managers. He promoted the Metropolitan Equitable Society in 1845. A year later he was appointed Secretary of a larger society, St Brides and City of London and by 1848 he was also Secretary of the Eclipse. Higham established the new City Mutual in 1852, the Second City Mutual in 1856 and the Third City Mutual in 1860. These were all terminating societies which were soundly based and ended at their anticipated dates. In 1862 he established a permanent society, the Fourth City Mutual, which is still prospering. Its name was changed to the City of London Building Society in 1956.

Higham was greatly assisted in the formation and work of the Association by the founding of *The Building Societies' Gazette* in 1869. There had been previous attempts to promote a journal dealing with building society affairs but they had not survived for very long. The *Gazette* was not a paying proposition in its early years but through the devotion and interest of Thomas R. Reed it continued to serve, as it still does, the interests of building societies.

The Building Societies Act, 1874 provided that no more societies could be established under the provisions of the 1836 Act but to those societies already existing it gave the option of continuing under the 1836 Act or becoming incorporated under its own provisions. All newly formed societies had to be incorporated. Thus from 1874 there were two kinds of society, incorporated and unincorporated, operating under different Acts. Many societies remained under the old Act. These were mostly terminating societies which if they were in their early years had more freedom (e.g. to borrow) or, if they were in their closing years, did not think it worth while to make the change. To those that did apply, incorporation gave the advantage that they no longer had to have trustees to hold mortgaged property on behalf of the society. This was an appreciable simplification of procedure.

The Royal Commission had suggested that the Chief Registrar should have discretion to strike out or require alteration of rules which he considered in-

equitable or impractical. The Act gave him no such power. What it did, was to stipulate fourteen items which must be dealt with in the rules of a society. Among these matters were the investment of surplus funds, the alteration of rules, custody of deeds, fines, arbitration and dissolution procedures and powers of directors. Provided the fourteen points were properly dealt with and the rules were otherwise in conformity with the Act, the Registrar had no power to do other than certify them. It was left to the members of the society to determine the fairness and good sense of the provisions.

On the much discussed subject of borrowing powers, societies were authorised to borrow up to two-thirds of the sum secured by mortgages. Terminating societies were given the option of the same limit or a sum not exceeding twelve (not six, as recommended by the Commission) months' subscriptions. This was a valuable concession to a terminating society at the beginning of its life.

Other provisions of the Act which may be noted were:

(a)   the liability of an investing member was limited to the amount he had actually paid (plus any arrears), whilst a borrower's was limited to the amount payable in respect of his advance.

(b)   no incorporated society was allowed to own land and buildings except for offices for conducting the business of the society. Mortgaged property coming into possession must be disposed of as soon afterwards as was conveniently practicable.

(c)   societies were compelled to prepare annual statements of receipts and expenditure. A copy of the annual statement had to be sent to the Chief Registrar and another displayed in the society's offices.

The Act gave societies a far more satisfactory framework than the 1836 Act. Having been more carefully drafted and more closely scrutinised, it was free of the ambiguities of the earlier Act. It remained the principal Act for nearly a hundred years. But it did not give the Registrar adequate control over societies which mismanaged their affairs. Nor did it provide adequate penalties for breaches of its provisions. Cleary's verdict* is worth quoting "The 1874 Act, while it provided a reasonable framework for a well conducted society, gave little protection if a society was conducted otherwise. The passing of the Act gave great satisfaction to its promoters and James Higham was justifiably

*E.J. Cleary. Op. Cit. p.100.

rewarded for his able leadership in the struggle.* This satisfaction would have been smaller had it been realised that already the public were looking at each building society, to some extent, as part of an interdependent movement. Thus what happened to one society was certain to affect public confidence in others. In such circumstances something more was needed than a suitable legal framework for well conducted societies. The movement as a whole had to conduct its affairs well. The obvious person to ensure this was the Registrar, but he had to wait until the Building Societies Act of 1894 before he began to receive powers sufficient to fulfil that function".

From the 1836 Act to that of 1874 many hundreds of societies had been formed. But as, under the 1836 Act, no returns had to be made to the Chief Registrar or any other body, no one knew how many societies were in existence at any time and there were no reliable statistics of any kind. The Royal Commission had to be content with guesswork. It was estimated that in England and Wales there were about 2,000 societies in existence at the time of their enquiry. The Protection Association submitted figures which they had gathered from 129 societies. These showed mortgages amounting to £8.2 million and assets of £8.7 million. It was considered that these societies undertook half the total business which meant that the movement had assets of about £17 million. There were some 90 societies in Scotland with assets of about £1.5 million and 17 societies in Ireland whose total assets were negligible.

The fact that by 1871 129 societies were thought to hold half the assets of the movement indicates that permanent societies had forged ahead since the first of them had been formed twenty-five years before. From the middle of the century building societies divided broadly into three main streams:

(a)   the permanent societies some of which (but by no means all) grew steadily and even rapidly. There was a preponderance of larger societies

(*He was presented with a marble timepiece, a gold chronometer and a cheque for one hundred guineas by members of the Association and subscribers to the parliamentary fund.)

in the North as is shown by the following table of the twelve largest incorporated societies according to the Chief Registrar's return for 1880:—

Name	Assets
Bradford Third Equitable	£1,691,621
National Permanent, London	1,601,675
Liberator Permanent, London	1,309,580
Queen's Manchester	1,264,106
Leeds Permanent	1,231,760
Halifax Permanent	973,021
Temperance Permanent, London	734,681
Lombardian Permanent, Manchester	658,141
Manchester & Salford Permanent	599,447
Leeds Provincial	561,292
Newcastle-on-Tyne Permanent	529,188
Burnley	521,953

(b) terminating societies following more or less the pattern of the earlier societies but with a larger membership. Often they were run in series and cities like Liverpool and Manchester had a large number running at the same time.

(c) Starr-Bowkett and other "promoter" societies which had a considerable vogue until the 1894 Act put a stop to balloting for advances. These societies are dealt with in Chapter 7.

To get a view of the pattern of societies we have to move forward to the evidence given by the Chief Registrar to the Select Committee on the 1894 Bill. He told the Committee that the number of societies certified between 1836 and 1874 was 5,500. Of these 690 had been incorporated under the 1874 Act but 200 of these had subsequently dissolved. The vast majority of the 4,800 not seeking incorporation had run their course and terminated. Of the new societies established under the 1874 Act some 500 were permanent societies, 800 were ordinary terminating societies and 1,800 were Starr-Bowkett and other promoter societies.

Chapter 6

THE LIBERATOR CRASH AND THE 1894 ACT

If the period from 1850 to 1875 was favourable to the establishment and growth of the permanent societies, the succeeding years up to 1894 were less encouraging. The United Kingdom was experiencing competition from other rapidly industrialising countries, especially from the United States and Germany. Agriculture was suffering too, from imports of cheap food from overseas. It was a period of falling property values, cushioned only by a decline in interest rates. Against this general background building societies found the going more difficult. But the weaknesses of the 1874 Act produced more immediate problems.

One of these was the number of frauds which were perpetrated. They came from within, through dishonest officials, and from without, through dishonest borrowers and solicitors. There were many cases where the society did not take action for fear of adverse publicity. Others were too large to hide. *The Building Societies' Gazette* reported some thirty cases between 1874 and 1891. A Darlington society lost £45,000; a Swansea society, £35,000; the Sun, London, £30,000; and a Belfast Society, the same amount. These were heavy losses to bear. They demonstrated the need for officers to give adequate security as provided by the 1874 Act. The trouble was that the requirement was often disregarded or the amount covered by a fidelity policy or security was far too small. And there was no means of enforcing the requirement. Over and above this question of giving security, the cases of fraud revealed that lack of supervision by directors and inadequate audits by unqualified and incompetent auditors enabled dishonest officials to make away with societies' funds more easily and over a longer period of time than should have been possible.

The outside frauds came from the forging of mortgage deeds, from landlords stating higher rents than they were receiving and from builders putting forward dummy purchasers. In one case a solicitor pleaded guilty to frauds totalling £300,000, thirty forged leases concerning the same pair of houses. In another, an accountant embezzled nearly £40,000 in the same way, twenty of his forgeries relating to his own house.

As we have seen, societies made loans on commercial and industrial property. After 1880, when societies were flush with money, some were tempted to make

more generous advances on such securities, to be less selective and to accept what were speculative and risky properties. One group of Sheffield societies lost over £60,000 on an iron works built by one of their directors. Another society lent money on a colliery in South Wales which was unprofitable, the loan ultimately standing at £117,000. The society failed, the colliery was eventually sold for £26,000 and one can understand the feelings of a member who at a meeting of the unfortunate society said of the directors "I hope the curse of Heaven will fall on them and I ask you all here to say Amen to that". At which there were loud cries of "Amen, Amen". A Lancashire society made a number of loans on cotton mills, which led to a run on the society when there was a strike of weavers, because it was believed that the mill-owners would be unable to meet their mortgage payments.

When property values were falling (as in these years, they were) rents were also coming down. In consequence, many building societies found (as the London societies had done some years earlier) that some of their borrowers with investment house property were unable to meet their obligations. Societies were then compelled to take the properties into possession and collect the rents. Those with commercial and industrial properties often found themselves in the same position, even if they had not made the kind of rash loans instanced above.

Many societies were inclined to hold on to such possession properties rather than sell at a loss, hoping that times would improve. The 1874 Act did provide that properties in possession should be disposed of as soon as might be conveniently practicable. But no penalty was prescribed nor was any guidance given as to how soon they should be sold after possession was taken. Furthermore, there was no provision for possession properties to be disclosed in the accounts. Hence, there was no inducement to face up to losses and the list of such properties tended to grow as further borrowers failed and the market did not improve.

As time went on the weaknesses of the 1874 Act were becoming more and more apparent. Opinion was forming both within and outside the building society movement that further legislation was needed. After the failures of the Portsea Island and Liberator Societies in 1891 and 1892 respectively, it was clear that action must be taken to strengthen the hand of the Chief Registrar and deal with the shortcomings of the 1874 Act.

The Portsea Island Society suspended payment in December 1891. This was a case of fraud by the Secretary who admitted that he had falsified the accounts of the Society over a considerable number of years. There had been an almost total lack of supervision by the auditors and by the directors. The latter had been in the habit of signing blank cheques at each meeting, leaving the Secretary to fill them up as and when required. The Society was found to have assets of

£435,000 against liabilities of £624,000. And included in the assets were properties in possession on which the total amount due was £168,000.

This was a sad failure but although large the society was still relatively local. Not so the Liberator, which at the time of its crash in 1892 was the largest society in the country, with investors in all parts. To an account of that society and its failure we must now turn.

The Liberator Society was established by Jabez Balfour in 1868. There is little doubt that he was influenced by the success of the Temperance Building Society of which his father was a director. He himself was a clerk in the offices of parliamentary agents and gained some reputation as a Congregational lay preacher. His mother was a writer and speaker, well known for her support of evangelical and temperance movements. He was able, through his family connections, to enlist the co-operations (as directors, vice-presidents and arbitrators) of men who were likely to command support for the society from the rank and file of the nonconformist churches and from the Temperance, Band of Hope and other movements.

By the year 1868 the Temperance Society had, in the short space of fourteen years, built up a thriving and expanding business. Assets totalled £700,000 and it had reserves amounting to £6000. Behind this success lay solid support from the nonconformist and temperance communities throughout the country made possible by the network of agencies which the Society had organised. Balfour aimed at the same groups and employed the same methods. But he did it on a grander scale, setting out to create the largest agency organisation of any society. It was not long before the number of ministers and laymen on the agency roll was over 500. They were paid commissions for the introduction of members and were provided with propaganda material for distribution. In this way the Liberator penetrated rural areas where the population had not hitherto been approached by societies on a widespread scale. The Society was highly successful in attracting funds and other societies (particularly the Temperance) felt the effects of its competitive activities.

For some years it carried on the normal business of a building society and was as successful in attracting borrowers as it was in obtaining funds. But Balfour eventually began to use the Society's funds to finance two building development companies which he also controlled. At first, these companies were mainly concerned with house building but later turned to more ambitious ventures, erecting hotels and blocks of luxury flats. By 1880 (when the assets of the Liberator totalled £1.3 million) some 20 per cent of its funds were represented by advances to these two companies.

In 1880 Balfour went into Parliament as member for Tamworth. In 1883 he

became the first Mayor of the newly created borough of Croydon. He had now become a national figure with a following in the City which enabled him to obtain finance for the many companies he formed. His plans became more grandiose. He formed the London & General Bank in 1882. This and other companies in the Balfour group had dealings with the Liberator, the funds of which were more and more channelled into his speculative ventures. As time went on, some of the ventures went awry and Balfour resorted to doubtful practices, grossly misleading statements and fraud. The directors and officers were little more than puppets. Their confidence in Balfour blinded them to what was going on, although normal building society advances shrank year by year. The Liberator's funds were needed to finance the ever-increasing tempo of Balfour's speculations. When more money was needed than the Liberator could supply, loans were raised elsewhere and the Society relegated to the position of a second or third mortgagee. And if it was not possible to pay the interest due, it was added to the capital outstanding. Land was bought by Balfour (or his two associates, Hobbs and Newman), sold to one of the Balfour companies at an inflated price, the full purchase price being provided by the Liberator.

Eventually, the whole network of companies collapsed in 1892 with the London & General Bank suspending payments. That meant that the Liberator could not meet withdrawals and a compulsory winding-up order was made with liabilities to shareholders and depositors amounting to £3.3 million. Over £3 million was owing to the Society by three of the Balfour companies, most of the securities being second or third charges. There was little for the depositors and nothing at all for the shareholders. The total loss suffered by investors in the Liberator and the various Balfour companies was over £8 million. Balfour fled to the Argentine, was extradited and sentenced to 14 years imprisonment. Five of his associates were also sent to prison.

The dismay occasioned by the Liberator failure was widespread. It was the largest society. Its investing members were to be found in all parts of the country. Its agents were respected members of the community who (in all good faith) had induced simple folk to invest their money. The losses caused hardship and distress to many families. They brought anxiety to the building society movement. For although the Liberator had not carried on a normal building society business yet it was regarded as a building society – and a leading one. There was inevitably a loss of confidence in the movement. Investments fell off and withdrawals mounted. Many societies were seriously affected, and some went to the wall.

The weaknesses of the 1874 Act had now been demonstrated in dramatic fashion. Demands for amending legislation came from the public, from the Press,

from the Chief Registrar and from the Building Societies Association. There were differences of view as to what should be done but in the end the Government decided that its own views should prevail and that its own Bill (rather more drastic than one put forward on behalf of the Association) should be adopted. The Bill became law in August 1894.

The main provisions were as follows:—

1. One of the auditors was required to be a person who publicly carried on the business of an accountant. And the certificate required from the auditors was strengthened. (This did ensure that at least one of the auditors should be a professional. Too often, societies had been content to leave the audit to two completely unqualified local men or lay members of the society).

2. The amounts due on mortgages were required to be shown in the annual accounts in five groups:—
    (a) The amount owing on mortgages not exceeding £500.
    (b) The amount owing on mortgages between £500 and £1,000.
    (c) The amount owing on mortgages between £1,000 and £3,000.
    (d) The amount owing on mortgages between £3,000 and £5,000.
    (e) The amount owing on mortgages over £5,000. Furthermore, particulars of each mortgage over £5,000 were to be shown in a schedule annexed to the accounts. This provision enabled a member of a society to discover whether his society was making an unduly high proportion of its loans on large commercial or industrial properties.

3. The Registrar was given power to appoint (on the application of ten members of a society) an accountant or actuary to inspect the books of the society and report thereon; and on the application of one-tenth of the members (or of 100 members in the case of a society consisting of more than 1,000 members) to appoint an inspector to examine and report on the affairs of the society or to call a special meeting of the society. (These extensive powers given to the Registrar were designed to bring into the open any suspicions or anxieties members might have regarding the conduct or management of a society. It was these provisions to which many societies objected).

4. Balloting for advances was prohibited in all new societies. (This effectively put an end to the Starr-Bowkett and other forms of promoter societies.)*

5. Advances on second mortgage were prohibited except where the same society held the first mortgage. An exception was made for existing societies

*See Chapter 7.

in Scotland and Ireland.

6.　Borrowing powers of societies were limited by excluding from the total mortgage assets (for the purpose of calculating the two-thirds borrowing power under the 1874 Act) all mortgages upwards of twelve months in arrear and the amount due on properties which had been more than twelve months in possession. More salutary still, the Registrar required all such mortgages more than twelve months in arrear or more than twelve months in possession to be listed (with particulars) in schedules to the accounts. (The requirement to print these two schedules led to a gradual decrease in the number of such cases. Societies disposed of possession properties instead of holding them for long periods in the hope that their values would rise. And they became more circumspect about letting borrowers get too far behind with their payments).

7.　No deposit monies were in future to be received except on condition that the society could require one month's notice of withdrawal. (In view of the important part deposits played in most societies' business in those days this was a helpful provision in times of stress).

8.　Directors and other officers were prohibited from receiving gifts, bonuses and commissions in connection with any loan.

9.　The Chief Registrar was given powers, in certain circumstances, to suspend or cancel a society's registration or to dissolve the society. For example, where a society had violated the provisions of the Building Societies Act or where investigation showed that a society could not meet the claims of its members.

10.　All societies still unincorporated, if established after 1856, were to become incorporated. There were some sixty unincorporated societies which had been established between 1836 and 1856 and these were left to carry on under the 1836 Act. These exceptions were allowed principally for the benefit of the Birkbeck Society of which more will be said in Chapter 8.

The 1894 Act thus strengthened the building society law by ensuring that the annual accounts of a society would reveal to the members the extent to which it was granting large mortgages and holding assets in the form of properties in possession. And secondly, it gave the Registrar increased powers to intervene in the affairs of a society if there was evidence or suspicion that it was being improperly conducted.

Chapter 7

THE STARR-BOWKETT AND OTHER PROMOTER SOCIETIES

The Starr-Bowkett societies and their imitators are a curiosity of building society history although they are of little significance in the development of the movement. This story would however be incomplete without some account of their origins and subsequent exploitation.

Dr Bowkett was a medical man, a radical and something of a philanthropist whose concern was to devise a building society which, by having a low subscription, would not be beyond the reach of the poorer classes. He suggested a membership of 100 and a subscription of 9¼d. per week. This would produce £205.16.8d. at the end of a year. A member would be selected by drawing lots, to whom an advance of £200 would be made, free of interest. The advance would be made on the security of a house purchased by the winning member who would then, in addition to his subscription of 9¼d, repay the advance over ten years at the rate of 8/-d per week. Whatever he saved on rent by living in his own house would go to offset this repayment. Further draws would take place as the subscriptions and repayments accumulated. If all went according to plan, the last member would get his advance at the end of thirty-one years and ten years after that the last repayment would be made. Then all the subscriptions would be repaid (together with any surplus arising from fines and defaults) less, of course, any expenses. Thus, in addition to acquiring a house, each member would look forward to a cash return of £60 and possibly more.

In theory, there was nothing wrong with this scheme. In practice, it was difficult to adhere to. Some members found even a payment of 9¼d a week impossible to maintain. Those who were disappointed in the draws for advances became discouraged. After the initial hopes had dwindled, the prospect of perhaps not obtaining an advance for ten, twenty or thirty years brought about withdrawals.

A number of societies was formed in the 1840s on the lines advocated by Dr Bowkett. It was not, however, until the 1860s that this type of society was commercially exploited at the hand of R.B. Starr, who was something of an adventurer and who had dabbled in a number of enterprises. He made some changes in the typical Bowkett society aimed at shortening its life and (by

raising the subscription of a man who had received an advance) making conditions more equal between those who drew their advance early and those who drew late. He obtained a copyright for his amended rules and for the various printed forms to be used by a society. He then began the promotion of societies by organising meetings which he addressed, requiring the newly formed society to pay him a fee of £5 for doing so and for the use of his rules. Before the meeting he made arrangements with a local solicitor and a surveyor to accept appointment with the society and collected from them fees of £25 and £3 upwards respectively. In addition, he charged the society £30 to £40 for providing (from his own printing company, founded for the purpose) copies of rules, prospectuses and other literature. Starr had found a way to make a comfortable living. He promoted one thousand societies between 1861 and his death in 1892. The attraction which drew members to these societies was the gain which could be obtained from winning a ballot. The right to the loan could be sold for cash. The Starr-Bowkett societies thus became increasingly a form of lottery, members joining for the chance of getting, in effect, a cash prize rather than a loan for house purchase.

Starr had his critics, including (in an action against a surveyor for his fee) the Lord Chief Justice, and his activities caused disquiet among the leaders of the permanent societies. He also had his competitors, who imitated his promotion methods and established the 'Model', 'Self-Help', 'Richmond', 'Perfect Thrift' and other series. As many as 1,580 of these various promoter societies (including the Starr-Bowketts) were registered between 1874 and 1891.

When balloting was made illegal in all future societies the game was up and this type of society rapidly disappeared. It was just as well. They did enable some of the lower-paid workers to become home-owners but on the whole they probably did the genuine building society harm by their methods, their terms of business and the commercial attitude of their promoters. Let Chief Registrar Ludlow have the final say, "The establishment of such societies had become a mere trade, while their operations when established had also to a great extent ceased to represent any real additions to the dwellings of the labouring or lower-middle classes and tend more and more to supply a mere outlet for gambling". The rules of these societies "are of the most oppressive description and as such one is astonished to see accepted by persons of ordinary intellect".

Chapter 8

PROGRESS TO 1914

This chapter deals with the progress of societies and some of the events which took place in the twenty years from 1894. The tax problems leading to the inauguration of the special building society arrangement under which interest is paid to investors tax-free (or, more correctly, income tax paid) is dealt with in Chapter 10. And the history of the Building Societies Association to 1914 is related in Chapter 11.

The recovery of confidence in building societies after the Liberator crash was slow. The prosecution of Balfour and some of his colleagues served to remind the public of the failure. The losses and hardships of the Liberator members and depositors were also not allowed to be forgotten for a relief fund was established and appeals on its behalf were made for many years. The total membership of societies diminished by some 50,000 and assets by £10 million within a year or so of the crash. The worst effects of the crisis were then over but it took time for the figures to improve. From 1895 there was a slow improvement to 1911 when there was, as will be seen below, another failure.

In the meantime, the 1894 Act came into force on 1st January 1895 and the new forms of annual account and statement were prepared by the Chief Registrar and became operative from 1st October 1895. One of the most salutary effects which the new form had was on the number of properties in possession. Societies could no longer allow these to accumulate in secrecy. They had to show details of all properties in possession which had been so held for more than one year and all mortgages where payments were more than one year in arrears. Faced with the necessity for revealing to members and the public generally the state and extent of their lame ducks, boards of directors set about the task of disposal with a new-found resolution and urgency. The result was that schedules of both possession and arrears cases (in some cases, horrifyingly large) began to decline and went on declining throughout the years to 1914.

These schedules apart, the new form of account gave a much clearer view of a society's affairs to its members and as all societies had to conform to the standard, it was now possible to make meaningful comparisons between one society and another. The provisions for proper audit and the powers given to the Chief

Registrar were also conducive to improved conduct on the part of officers and boards whose members were now in a much better position to judge their performance and take action, if necessary.

One of the consequences of the run on building societies' funds which followed the Liberator crash was to make societies aware of the need for a certain amount of liquidity. It was not easy to achieve for there were no short-dated gilt-edged securities in those days. The courses open to societies were to put money on deposit at the bank and invest in Consols. The return on both was not encouraging and when interest rates were rising the capital value of Consols trended downwards. The Woolwich Equitable invested £33,000 in Consols and four years later had a capital depreciation of £3,000, while the interest had produced a yield of only 2½ per cent. The Woolwich then decided to find an alternative and succeeded in making an arrangement with a life assurance company guaranteeing a loan of £100,000 if and when it should be required. The premium was 10/6d per cent and it was more profitable to secure liquidity when needed in this way than to put money in Consols at 2½ per cent when it could be lent on mortgages at 6 per cent.

Interest rates paid and charged by societies in this period of twenty years were fairly stable. Changes were few and where they occurred it was usually to discourage the inflow of funds which could not be utilised because of the shortage of borrowers. The Temperance reduced its mortgage rate for new borrowers to 4½ per cent in 1901, and to 4 per cent in 1903. Money was accumulating at the bank and the issue of shares was suspended in 1902 for twelve months. It was suspended again in 1905. The Halifax Permanent found good borrowers difficult to come by and reduced the share rate by one-half per cent in 1896. The Bradford Second found competition for mortgages was severe and reduced its rate in 1895. One reason why there was difficulty in finding outlets for money was that societies had become more discriminating in their lending policies. The 1879's and 1880's had been years of liberal lending on a variety of securities. There followed a period of fluctuating property values and, until the 1894 Act, large portfolios of properties in possession. Societies became more cautious not only because they had to make public their possession properties but also because they had accumulated experience in lending and because they were not as confident of property values as they had been in earlier decades. The emphasis was on the good borrower whose covenant was worth having in bad times.

Societies' progress differed but as a whole building societies had by 1911 recovered from the shock to confidence which the Liberator failure had produced. Unfortunately, there then occurred another disaster which was to disrupt confidence once more. This was the failure of the Birkbeck Society.

Whereas the Liberator Society failed because it was exploited and its funds used wrongly, the Birkbeck came to grief for very different reasons.

The Society was founded in 1851, remained unincorporated after 1874 and, as we have already noted, was one of the sixty societies which were allowed to remain unincorporated after 1894. The reason why it was important for the Society to remain unincorporated was the limitation on borrowing powers imposed on incorporated societies. For although the Society was registered as a building society it was in fact a bank and was popularly and widely known as the Birkbeck Bank. From the outset this Society had aimed to provide a service to people of small means to whom the ordinary joint stock banks made little appeal. It had therefore placed much emphasis on the deposit side of its business. Deposit accounts could be opened with sums of £1 upwards on which interest at the rate of 2½ per cent per annum was allowed. Current accounts were available for sums of £25 upwards. All these monies were payable on demand. The major portion of the Society's funds was held in Consols, Indian, Colonial and Corporation Stocks, in freehold ground rents and in cash. With such large call liabilities it would have been imprudent to have large amounts in mortgages.

But the times were not running in favour of the Birkbeck. Interest rates were tending to rise over the early years of the twentieth century which meant that the values of Consols and other fixed interest investments were moving downwards. The Birkbeck had withstood adverse changes of this kind in earlier years. It had suffered from a high rate of withdrawals at the time of the Liberator crash, paying out £500,000 in one day. It was helped out by a loan of a similar amount from the Bank of England and public confidence was restored.

The Bank of England was called upon to intervene again in 1910 following the widespread circulation of an anonymous letter suggesting that the Birkbeck may have been seriously affected by the failure of the Charing Cross Bank. This started another, more serious, run on the Birkbeck. Although the suggestions in the anonymous letter were denied and announcements made that the Bank of England was again offering substantial help, nevertheless depositors were alarmed and before the excitement died away some £3 million had been withdrawn. This meant realising securities. Consols, for example, which had been bought at an average price of over 100 had to be sold at 80. This was a severe loss. And the Birkbeck was further weakened by the fact that the market value of the remaining securities was well below the book value.

A further run on the Bank took place in May 1911, this time for no apparent reason. But the directors decided that in view of the weakened financial position they could no longer carry on and in the interests of the shareholders and depositors presented a petition for the winding-up of the Bank. There was a

deficiency of nearly £1 million and in the end shareholders and depositors received 16/9d in the £.

In the case of the Birkbeck there was no suggestion of dishonesty or fraud. The decline in gilt-edged securities was the main reason for the failure, coupled with the fact that the directors and officers were not sufficiently experienced in banking business, which required a much more flexible approach to the disposition of assets than they had displayed.

Regarded as a bank, the Birkbeck was reckoned to be the sixth largest in the country in the year 1891. Regarded as a building society, it was by far the largest society, having assets of over £12 million, before the catastrophic run in 1910: yet no more than 10 per cent of its assets were devoted to mortgages. It was far more of a bank than a building society and it was a pity that in 1894 it was not compelled to either become incorporated or change its registration to the companies register. Although universally known as a bank, once it had decided to wind up it had to use its registered title as a building society. This did not help other societies and they suffered from the failure. As with the Liberator crash, the total assets of the movement declined sharply, from £76 million to £58 million.

The Birkbeck was the extreme case of a building society being used as a bank. Other societies, as we have seen in an earlier chapter, expanded their deposit departments and competed with local banks, but utilised their funds in mortgages. There seems little doubt that there was some conflict of views in the early formative years as to the role a building society could or should play. And that there were those who, like the Birkbeck directors, felt that their function could well be that of a popular financial institution, mid-way between a bank and a building society in the narrower sense. The Acts of 1874 and 1894 put an end to that concept for incorporated societies.

Nevertheless, the banking function continued to have its attractions and it is interesting that the two Halifax societies (the Permanent and the Equitable) established separate banking companies. In 1900 the Equitable established the Halifax Equitable Bank and ten years later the Permanent followed by forming the Halifax and District Permanent Banking Company. In each case it was closely associated with the building society and the two banks profited from the confidence and trust in which the societies were held. The banks' branches were housed in the same buildings as the branches of the society. Both banks established themselves upon a sound footing, but after the failure of the Birkbeck there was some feeling that banking business was a field best left alone by building societies. The example of the Halifax societies was not followed by other societies, and in 1917 the Permanent Bank was taken over by the Union Bank

of Manchester and in 1927 the Equitable Bank was merged with the Bank of Liverpool and Martins.

The period under review is notable for the rapid fall in the number of societies. As the old terminating societies disappeared the total fell from 3,642 in 1895 to 2,286 in 1900 and 1,506 in 1914. Between 1883 and 1891, 1,745 societies were incorporated; between 1898 and 1914 only 370 societies came on to the register. By 1914, total assets of all societies amounted to £66 million.

Chapter 9

THE INCOME TAX ARRANGEMENT

The success of building societies in attracting funds has undoubtedly owed much to the arrangement with the Inland Revenue under which interest on shares and deposits is paid free of tax. That is not strictly a correct way of putting it, for the tax on the interest is paid by the society at a composite rate based on the average income tax liability of investors as a whole, computed on the basis of sample returns. The composite rate is agreed each year by the Inland Revenue. However, to the building society investor the amount he receives is free of tax in his hands if he is liable to tax at the basic rate or less. If he pays at a higher rate then the interest (grossed up) is brought into calculation.

The arrangement under which the building societies have been able to pay interest to shareholders and depositors on this basis was inaugurated in 1895. It has been amended on a number of occasions since. In view of its importance to societies over the years an account of its origins must be recorded.

Until the arrangement was proposed by the Inland Revenue in 1894 the tax position had been a source of uncertainty. There were three questions which cropped up from time to time. The first related to investors. Could building societies be compelled to deduct tax from dividends and interest paid to investors, leaving the investor who was not liable to tax to reclaim from the Inland Revenue the amount deducted? The second concerned borrowers. Should those borrowers who were taxpayers be allowed to deduct tax from the interest content of their mortgage payments?

The third was a question for the society. Was it liable to pay income tax on its earnings? This third question was bound up with the other two, for if a society was held liable on its earnings it would be obliged to deduct tax from amounts paid out by way of interest to its investors. And the situation would be complicated if borrowers were allowed to deduct tax from the interest which they paid to the society.

For a time building societies argued that they were analogous to Friendly Societies, which had been expressly given exemption from income tax in 1842 and again in 1853. The Revenue did not agree with this contention, but building societies continued to maintain the position that liability to, or relief

from, tax was a matter, not for societies, but for individual investors and borrowers. And that it was up to the tax authorities to deal with each individual on the basis of his own tax return. The Surveyors of Taxes (as Inspectors of Taxes were then known) were by no means as subject to centralised direction as today. Hence, a ruling by the Inland Revenue in 1866 given to a Sunderland society that a building society had no annual profits chargeable under the tax laws, and was not therefore liable to taxation or required to deduct income tax from interest paid to investors, was ignored by a number of Surveyors. Spasmodic demands were made on societies in different parts of the country. Several members of the Protection Association reported that they had protested against demands on their own societies and that non-liability had eventually been conceded.

But the Inland Revenue were aware that, with the growth of building societies and the increased range of investors, they were losing revenue because many recipients of building society interest were not declaring it in their tax returns. Building societies were asked to make returns of members receiving interest. This was strongly resisted on the grounds that it would be a disclosure of confidential information and that it was anyway an obligation which the Inland Revenue had no power to impose on societies.

The position regarding borrowers was equally unsatisfactory. Societies firmly refused to allow borrowers to deduct income tax from interest paid. The Inland Revenue likewise refused to grant relief of tax to borrowers on their personal assessments. So borrowers felt hard done by, especially as they were entitled to deduct tax from interest paid to a private mortgagee.

The whole question of tax relating to investors and borrowers remained in a thoroughly unsatisfactory and indeterminate state for several years. Then, in 1887, the Inland Revenue attempted to resolve it by publishing a Memorandum of Arrangement. This provided that interest from borrowers with incomes below £150 p.a. was to be exempt from tax and borrowers who were not so exempt were to be entitled to deduct tax from interest payments. It also provided that societies should make a return to the Inland Revenue of the interest paid or credited to depositors and shareholders whose incomes amounted to £150 a year and upwards, from whom the society would have a right to deduct tax, whether the society exercised the right or not.

The Association condemned these proposals on the ground that societies would not be justified in disclosing the individual accounts of investors. It was then made clear that the Memorandum provisions were optional and would be applied to a society only at its own request. Notwithstanding this statement by the Treasury several Surveyors of Taxes endeavoured to make societies in their

areas comply with it. The Memorandum of 1887 had certainly not cleared the air. Finally, the Inland Revenue in 1894 issued a further Memorandum containing alternative arrangements, known as 'A' and 'B'. Arrangement A was virtually a repetition of the terms of the Memorandum of 1887. Arrangement B was the new and significant document. Under this scheme (which was to initiate the tax-paid arrangement so valuable to building societies) the society adopting it was to pay the tax on half the sum distributed to shareholders and depositors in the previous year. In return, the investors would not be taxed on the interest they received. Borrowers were to have no claim on the society for a rebate of tax on mortgage interest, but if the borrower's income was below £160 p.a. he would not be charged property tax and if above £160 the authorities would allow against his property tax an amount equal to the mortgage interest paid by him to his society.

This was a solution which established clearly the position tax-wise of the building society, the borrower and the investor. It was one which operated simply, saving much administrative work in tax offices, avoided repayment claims and probably resulted in more tax being collected. An increasing number of societies opted for Arrangement B. It continued virtually unchanged until 1916 when substantially increased tax rates led to modifications. As will be seen, substantial amendments to the scheme took place in later years.

Chapter 10

THE BUILDING SOCIETIES ASSOCIATION

In the moves for new legislation which eventually led to the passing of the 1874 Act, the Building Societies Protection Association established itself as the main body speaking for building societies. Evolving from the London Association, its membership was still dominated by the London societies and its officers were drawn from those societies. In drafting proposed Bills and in its negotiations with the Government, it sought the co-operation of provincial societies. The conference it convened in June 1870 was attended by building society leaders from Liverpool, Manchester, Newcastle, Sunderland and elsewhere. And the Association sought at all times to carry these leaders along with it in the several draft Bills it submitted and the negotiations it conducted. It offered membership at a nominal fee to provincial societies.

But when the 1874 Act was passed most of those who joined failed to keep up their membership. From a total of nearly 200, the number dropped to about 70 by 1877. An attempt was made to regenerate interest by appointing three provincial members to the executive committee but those appointed failed to attend meetings and were eventually dropped.

The Association (the word "Protection" was deleted from the name in 1886) continued to keep a watchful eye on legislation likely to affect building societies. In fact, parliamentary affairs absorbed most of the time of the executive committee. They supported for a time efforts to obtain leasehold enfranchisement and the registration of titles. They succeeded in obtaining for leaseholders the right to apply to the Courts for relief against action taken by landlords for forfeiture of leases. And on the subject of arbitration, they obtained an Act of Parliament (the Building Societies Act 1884) to rectify a situation created by a decision of the House of Lords. A society had taken action against a borrower who was in arrears. That borrower argued that proceedings should be stayed, as one of the society's rules required all disputes with members to be settled by arbitration. His contention was upheld in the High Court and, on appeal, by both the Appeal Court and the House of Lords.

Now this was a serious matter for building societies. The dilemma was obvious: if there was no 'dispute' that a borrower was in arrears, there was nothing

on which to arbitrate; on the other hand, the society was unable to recover the money by Court action. It was also realised that under this judgment there were wider implications, for other matters involving the interpretation of mortgage deeds and legal decisions might have to be referred to lay arbitrators.

By the time the case had been finally decided by the House of Lords, the Association was ready to take action. A private Bill was promoted and quickly passed which declared that the word 'disputes' in the Building Societies Acts should be deemed to refer only to disputes between the society and the member in his capacity as a member. It was not to apply to any mortgage deed or any contract contained in any document and was not to prevent any society or any member from obtaining legal redress in respect of such mortgage or contract. The building society movement heaved a sigh of relief. The Association had achieved a notable success and, as a reward, saw its membership increase to over a hundred.

As may be imagined, the Liberator crash in 1892 and the passing of the 1894 Act was a period of intense activity for the Association. The immediate reaction of the executive in the days following the suspension of payments by the Liberator was to maintain a low profile. The minutes recorded that although the gravity of the crisis was fully realised by the Committee, they had decided that it would be unwise to issue a statement to the Press with a view to reassuring depositors and members. After a careful survey of the facts before them they decided that the issue of such a statement would tend to arouse fresh discussion and thus increase rather than allay the apprehensions and fears of the investing public. Perhaps it was not only for this reason that they preferred not to issue a reassurance. They may well have had evidence or, at least, indications that other societies were going to find themselves in trouble, which would have made any general statement worse than useless. In fact, some societies were under great pressure from members and depositors wanting to withdraw and a few did fail to withstand the demands made on them and were forced into liquidation.

But if the Association maintained a low profile in the wake of the Liberator crash, it was soon in the forefront of the discussions and negotiations leading to the 1894 Act. There was much work involved and it was at this juncture that a new leader emerged. He was Edward Wood, the Secretary of the Temperance Society. He was strongly in favour of the main changes which the proposed legislation was designed to create and opposed those both within and without the Association who wanted to preserve the *status quo*. He was supported by a substantial number of leading societies and was the most influential voice in support of the new legislation.

The membership of the Association increased to 134 in 1895. Of these, 48

were Metropolitan societies and 86 came from the provinces. The number was still disappointingly small. One suggestion made by the secretary of a provincial society was that to induce societies to join the Association the Annual Meeting should be held in different parts of the country. Accordingly in 1898 the meeting was held in Bradford and was followed by the reading of four papers and a dinner attended by some 200 delegates and guests. A suggestion was made at the Annual Meeting that the executive committee should be enlarged. Edward Wood took up this suggestion and a Committee was formed of the executive and nine provincial representatives. As a result of its deliberations the number of London members of the executive was reduced from twelve to nine and an equal number of provincial members added. As a result of this change the strength and influence of the executive was greatly enchanced, for most of the new members came from societies far larger than those of the London members.

Another Bill came before Parliament in 1899 which caused much concern to the Association. This was the Small Dwellings Acquisition Bill, the purpose of which was to empower local authorities to advance money to home buyers. Joseph Chamberlain (then Colonial Secretary) introduced the Bill, his object being to encourage owner-occupation and relieve the shortage of houses. The building societies, with ample funds at their disposal and not enough owner-occupiers coming forward, saw this as unnecessary and possibly harmful competition. The Association was so concerned that a conference was convened in London at which it was agreed that considering the facilities afforded by Building, Friendly, Co-operative and kindred societies for the purchase of small freehold and leasehold properties, the Bill was unnecessary. The effect would be to deprive building societies of a great part of what they regarded as the most legitimate, safe and satisfactory portion of their business.

It was also agreed that Mr Chamberlain should be asked to receive a deputation. He agreed to do so, but it soon became obvious to the building society men present that he had been badly briefed by his officials about the activities of building societies and their ability to meet the mortgage needs of home-buyers. Although he stood firm on the principle of the Bill he agreed to modify its terms to meet some of the objections raised on behalf of building societies.

On this occasion the man who impressed not only Chamberlain but also his own colleagues was Edward Wood who made a forceful speech. R.H. Marsh, the Secretary of the Association wrote "Towards the end of the interview Mr Wood rose and it was intensely interesting to note the impression his speech created. It was short, clear, admirably phrased and delivered, and when he sat down one felt he had placed building societies and their work in a position in the

estimation of the Government circles which they had never occupied before".

The chief provisions of the Act as passed were:— maximum advance not to exceed 80 per cent nor £240; no loan to be made on a house valued at more than £300; interest ½ per cent above local authority borrowing rate for Public Works Loan Board; repayment term, not exceeding 30 years; property to be freehold, or a leasehold of not more than 60 years unexpired. The Act was permissive, not mandatory, on local authorities. Few availed themselves of the powers. The number of loans made before 1914 was negligible. The fears of the building societies were soon set at rest. But the Act is important for the use made of it in later years.

In 1903, Edward Wood was elected Chairman of the Executive, a position he was to occupy for ten years. In those ten years the Association was to find itself closely engaged in political affairs, as the Liberal Government of 1906 introduced a number of controversial Bills, some of which dealt with housing, land, conveyancing, public health, rates and other subjects in which building societies were directly interested. There was also Lloyd George's famous Budget of 1909 with its proposed land taxes.

The deep divisions which this reforming legislation created were reflected in the Executive Committee and among building society men generally. Some were supporters of the Government and others were bitter opponents. Edward Wood sought to maintain the unity of the Association and the annual report for 1910 stated the position which has been maintained ever since "The Association, throughout its history, has carefully refrained from identifying itself with any political party or organisation, and men of very decisive views on political questions have worked, and do work, together harmoniously on its committee".

Edward Wood, on grounds of health and age, retired from the chair of the executive in 1913. By this time new men were making their voices felt, including Enoch Hill of the Halifax. There was a growing feeling that the Association had perhaps concentrated too much of its activities on pending legislation and not enough on building society development and publicity. There were also proposals for the establishment of area organisations and committees, the implementation of which came a decade later.

But these indications of demand for change were a recognition of the essential part the Association had to play in the building society movement. It was now firmly established and the criticism came from those who wanted to make it a more useful organisation.

Chapter 11

HEALTH AND HOUSING IN THE 19th CENTURY*

The great changes which had taken place in agriculture and industry in the latter half of the 18th century and the early decades of the 19th century had produced a series of complex social problems in a comparatively short space of time. Health and housing were not the least of these. There were others. One was labour conditions: the long hours of harshly disciplined factory working; the employment of children in cotton mills; and of women and children in the coal mines; and the exposure of workers to industrial diseases, as in the pottery industry. Another was the relief of the poor, which was granted under a system which was inefficient, demoralising to the poor and costly to the ratepayer. There was the need for more widespread education, as industrial changes took place and more skilled workers were needed. At the beginning of the 19th century the majority of children grew up unable to read or write.

Until 1832, Parliament made no real attempt to deal with these social problems. It was the age of *laissez-faire* and it was widely believed that government should not intervene in economic affairs. Moreover, the property-owning classes were still influenced by the events of the French Revolution. They believed that reform was an encouragement to revolution. But by 1832, the extension of the franchise to the middle class could no longer be denied. The Reform Act of 1832 was a significant landmark of the 19th century. For in the long term, it opened the way to further extensions of the franchise. It was also the herald of other reforms over the following twenty years.

The initial legislation on each social problem was not of a comprehensive, far-reaching character. Reform was a process of moving from experimental and tentative steps to bolder, more decisive legislation as public opinion moved forward and as the inadequacies of the first Acts were demonstrated. And this was especially true of health and housing.

Another difficulty in the path of effective action in the towns and cities was

*This chapter has no direct bearing on the history of building societies in the nineteenth century. But because housing legislation in the twentieth century has had an intimate connection with building society activities, it is felt that a review of the nineteenth century legislation may not be without interest to the reader.

the lack of efficient local government. The older towns were chartered boroughs but the powers of the corporation were limited and the members were often corrupt. The newer industrial towns had no ruling body of their own and were often dependent upon the decisions of a nearby landowner possessed of the ancient rights of Lord of the Manor. In the countryside, the Justices of the Peace dispensed such local government as there was, not only sitting on the Bench, but dealing with administrative matters such as the relief of the poor and the repair of roads and bridges.

It was recognised at the beginning of the period of reform that something more effective was required if the measures passed by Parliament were to be acted upon at local level. Accordingly, the Municipal Reform Act of 1835 provided that the chartered boroughs should have town councils elected by all ratepaying householders. Unchartered towns could adopt the same system. The Act set a new pattern for local government in England. But it did not produce active and efficient town councils overnight capable of putting into operation the legislative reforms of Parliament.

Even in those progressive towns where municipal reforms were quickly effected, there was strong opposition to housing reforms by property investors and other vested interests. And town councils were often reluctant to take action which involved additional levies on their ratepayers. This was a vital factor. For although, over the second half of the century a comprehensive code of housing legislation was built up, it was not mandatory but permissive legislation which local authorities could please themselves about adopting. Parliament was prepared to give extensive powers to the local authorities; it never reached the point at which it was prepared to accept that it was the responsibility of the State to provide housing for the poor. Therefore, it is not surprising that the local authorities having to foot the bill for housing improvements or for rehousing, were so often inclined to do nothing.

Nevertheless, much was achieved in the second half of the century by successive Health Acts. If the practical results of the Housing Acts were less satisfying, at least a body of housing law was built up on which much of the action to improve housing in the twentieth century was based. It is worthwhile, therefore, to give here some account of the steps that were taken to improve the conditions of the towns and ameliorate the lot of those who lived in the overcrowded, insanitary and poverty-stricken central urban areas.

Housing conditions in both rural and urban areas were far worse in 1850 than at the beginning of the century. In rural areas it was a case of decay as families moved into the towns and little was done to provide the poorest of those who stayed with decent accommodation. There were big landowners who

took a pride in their villages and built houses for those whom they employed. The skilled workers of the countryside – the shepherds, gamekeepers, blacksmiths, horsemen, dairymen, wheelwrights and thatchers – were valued and looked after by their employers or earned enough to enable them to enjoy adequate housing. The unskilled workers had to put up with miserable hovels, unplastered stone walls, mud floors, decaying thatched roofs, with a pile of straw to serve as bedding – these were the conditions of the poorest in many parts of the rural areas.

But it was in the towns that the conditions deteriorated so rapidly in the first half of the century. Between 1800 and 1850 the population of England and Wales doubled to 18 million. The population of the major cities and the manufacturing towns far more than doubled. Cities such as Birmingham, Liverpool and Leeds trebled or quadrupled their numbers in this period. To provide for this growth a vast increase in housebuilding took place.

Some of it was undertaken by the manufacturers themselves. Employers found it worth while to provide housing during the rapid expansion of trade simply because of the need to attract labour to the new factory sites. Except in one or two cases, the employer was not concerned to see that these houses were carefully planned or built. He was under no obligation to provide water, drainage or other amenities. Houses were also provided by speculators and investors determined to obtain the greatest return on their capital.

Although there was much housebuilding the pressure of demand was maintained by the growth of population and the migration to the towns. Inevitably, the result was overcrowding in the poorer parts of the towns. Families crowded into the tenement houses, cellar dwellings and back-to-back houses which were grouped together to form dismal streets and narrow courts. The streets were unpaved and undrained and refuse accumulated. So far as water was concerned, many depended upon rain water cisterns or shallow wells. It was the practice of owners of house property to erect a pump for the use of a given number of houses. This pump would be rented to one tenant who would charge the others for drawing water. There were other places where a stand pipe was put up and water came on at certain times. Those who wanted water had to rush to get it before the supply ceased.

Until the 1830s only a few middle-class people were aware of the extent of the deterioration which had occurred in the town centres. In many, the inner areas had been forsaken by people with the means to leave and these areas were rarely entered except by those who lived in them. In the 1830s and 1840s, the pitiful state of the towns became much more widely known. This was due to the publication of census and mortality figures: the Reports of the Poor Law Com-

missioners: the founding of a number of societies concerned with social studies and statistics: and the cholera epidemics of 1833 and 1848. The mortality rates were startling. They demonstrated how much lower was life-expectancy in the towns; and how much lower in the worst parts of the towns than in the best. The mortality statistics were supplemented by the reports of the Poor Law Commissioners revealing an appalling state of poverty and squalor. Edwin Chadwick was the secretary to the Commissioners and he was instructed to organise a sanitary enquiry which would give a true picture of the condition of the people. The Report, published in 1842, was a thorough survey of all types and sizes of towns and villages. It condemned the existing legislation as inadequate and the local executive authorities as inefficient. A Royal Commission on the Health of Towns followed and its Reports, like Chadwick's, showed the failure of legislation to bring drainage and water supply to the poorer districts and emphasised the need for building regulations.

Public enlightenment as to the wretched conditions in which the poor struggled to survive was enhanced by the work of the new societies undertaking statistical studies which sprang up about this time. The Statistical Society of London and the Manchester Statistical Society (the latter's purpose being "the collection of facts illustrative of the condition of society") and similar bodies in half a dozen large cities all helped to make known the hard facts. Moreover, approaching their studies in a scientific manner, these societies' reports commanded respect both at local and national level.

Then there were the cholera epidemics of 1832 and 1848. Cholera, unlike many other diseases, did not kill only the sickly, the under-nourished and the poor. It was no respecter of classes and there seemed no way of escaping its attack. Nevertheless, it was believed by many to originate in dirt and filth so prevalent in the slum areas. It was not until 1848 that it was proved by Snow to spread by infection from mouth to intestine, usually through the water supply. Either way, there was need for action on public health improvements.

So the campaign for public health was started in the 1830s and the 1840s. It was a campaign for sanitary laws to deal with existing evils. As yet there was little effort to deal with housing as a subject in itself. That was to come in the second half of the century. It must be admitted, too, that as housing conditions had been allowed to deteriorate so much, remedial measures in the fields of sanitation, drainage and water supply were the priority. Insofar as they also applied to new housing they can be regarded as the first steps in housing improvements.

The first general Public Health Act was passed in 1848. It set up a Public Health Board with Chadwick as a member. It aroused great opposition from

property owners and others whose interests were affected by reform or the cost of reform. The Act was permissive, rather than compulsory. The Board's powers were inadequate to compel local authorities to act themselves. Yet the Act was at least a recognition that public health had become a subject of government responsibility.

Because of continued opposition the Public Health Board was dissolved in 1858 and its functions were divided between the Home Office and the Privy Council. Efforts for the improvement of conditions continued in spasmodic and piecemeal fashion. Acts were passed to meet various aspects of health such as nuisance removal, sanitation, prevention of disease and sewage utilisation. These separate Acts caused administrative confusion and complexity, each group designating a new authority for the purpose.

The confusion was such that another Royal Commission was appointed in 1869 to sort out the mess. The Commission reported that in its opinion just about everything was wrong with the public health system. It recommended that the piecemeal legislation should be consolidated and that the administration of public health should be made uniform and compulsory throughout the country. The Report resulted in two Acts. The first was the Local Government Act of 1871, which dealt with administration, establishing sanitary districts and authorities and making it obligatory on each authority to appoint a medical officer of health and an inspector of nuisances. The second was the Public Health Act of 1875 which codified the law on the subject and placed on local authorities the duty to attain the standards laid down.

Improvement was not instantaneous. The Local Government Board was not the most dynamic of bodies and local authorities needed prodding into action. The provision of sewage schemes and other improvements was costly; and the worse the problem, the greater was the cost to the ratepayers. However, the powers and the duties were now settled and the next quarter of a century saw great improvements.

Housing legislation followed in the wake of the Health Acts. The studies and reports on health, poor law and mortality statistics also revealed the need to do something about overcrowding, the improvement of dwellings and the provision of housing for the poor.

The earliest model dwellings associations endeavoured to give a lead. They were the Metropolitan Association for Improving Dwellings of the Industrial Classes (1841) and the Society for Improving the Conditions of the Labouring Classes (1844). These Associations hoped to show that model housing for the poor could be built and rented to show an acceptable, if modest, return on capital; and that the private investor could be induced to provide similar

dwellings. The model dwellings which the Associations erected were criticised for their forbidding exterior appearance, but internally their standard was higher than working-class people were used to. They attracted not the poor and neediest but higher paid workers better able to afford the rents. The private investor and speculative builder did not follow the example of the two Associations although other charitable groups were formed to do similar work.

One of the members of the Society for Improving the Conditions of the Labouring Classes was the Earl of Shaftesbury. His interest in that Association's endeavour, his membership of the Board of Health and his concern with the conditions of the poor generally led him to take up the cause of housing in Parliament. He was responsible for the Lodging Houses Act of 1851. At this time, there were many families without homes of their own, including families on the move in search of work and those of Irish imigrants who were coming over to this country in large numbers because of the famine in their own land. For these families the only refuge was the lodginghouse. They were numerous both in London and the industrial towns and conditions in many were appalling, as Shaftesbury had seen for himself.

The aim of his Act was to encourage the building of respectable accommodation in which families could find shelter. But lodging houses, properly and decently run, could never be a profitable undertaking and local councils were not prepared to burden their ratepayers with the inevitable loss. Few adopted the Act. Where they did, their experience was not such as to encourage other councils. Huddersfield was one town that did, with the result that people came from other towns to take advantage of the facilities afforded. This was not calculated to encourage other towns to spend ratepayers' money on housing to be occupied by men and women from outside their borough.

So the Act remained for the most part unused. Another Act, the Common Lodging House Act of 1853, was however applied with vigour throughout the country. This Act gave powers for the inspection of existing lodging houses to ensure that they should be reasonably clean and to impose some limits on overcrowding. Action was taken under this Act because it involved local authorities in little expense.

Other legislation followed in the 1850s, which, although producing little in the way of actual results, did indicate that Parliament was beginning to grope its way towards solutions for the many housing problems. In 1855 Acts were passed for both Scotland and England which gave powers for associations of persons "acting in the public interest" to take over dilapidated property. These Acts were passed in the hope that housing associations would be formed to take over and redevelop the sites of these dilapidated properties. Their significance is that they

did foreshadow the future process of compulsory purchase.

The Metropolis Local Management Act of 1855, which established the Metropolitan Board of Works, was accompanied by a Building Act which provided London with a higher standard of building practice than that prevailing in the provinces and also made compulsory the appointment of medical officers throughout London. The Metropolitan Board carried out some 50 improvement schemes between 1855 and 1888 when it was superseded by the Local Government Board. Only in its later scheme of slum clearance and street widening was any provision made for the rehousing of families whose homes were demolished. Another Act of 1855 (The Nuisances Removal Act) is worth noting because it contained the phrase 'unfit for human habitation'. Not that it achieved much in the way of practical results. Vagueness of definition, lack of co-operation by local authorities and the unwillingness of medical officers to force the issue when they well knew that it would only result in the occupants being made homeless, were all against this kind of housing remedy.

Another step forward was made in 1858 when the Public Health Act 1848 was amended to enable local authorities, if they so desired, to ban the building of back-to-back houses.

In 1866 The Labouring Classes Dwelling Houses Act authorised the Public Works Loan Board to make advances to local authorities and other bodies such as railway companies and housing associations for the building of houses. The loans were to be repayable over a period not exceeding 40 years at an interest rate of not less than 4 per cent. Only one local authority (Liverpool) took advantage of the Act, but a number of housing associations were granted loans.

The next step forward in housing legislation comprised what are known as the Torrens and Cross Acts. The Torrens Act of 1868 provided for the improvement or demolition of houses which were unfit for habitation. The Act permitted the inspection of premises. If they were found to be in bad condition, the local authority had then to tell the owner what work was required to make them habitable. In the event of the owner failing to do what was indicated then the local authority had power either to close or demolish the property.

The Torrens Act was not a success. The Cross Act of 1875 was designed to be more comprehensive. Instead of dealing with slum areas in a piecemeal fashion, it provided for the purchase and demolition of areas of slum property. But it did not encourage local authorities to undertake rehousing. Instead, they were to undertake the street planning, paving and sewering of the cleared site and then sell or lease it to builders or other persons who would build on it under conditions imposed by the local authority. If local authorities did build houses they were under obligation to dispose of them to private owners within ten

years. The procedure under the Act was cumbersome, for each scheme of improvement had to be submitted to Parliament. Between 1875 and 1884 only a dozen towns had obtained provisional orders and of the schemes carried out Birmingham's was the only one of any size.

Amending Acts were passed in an endeavour to make the original Torrens and Cross Acts more effective and in 1881 a SelectCommittee was appointed to consider how the expense and delay and difficulty in carrying them out could be reduced and what had prevented the building of dwellings to the full extent contemplated under the Acts. The Committee found that the chief obstacle was cost. Compensation to owners, the expensive procedure and the obligation to sell or lease the land for artisan dwellings; all these were impediments. An amending Act which followed did little to improve the situation.

The next event of importance was the appointment of a Royal Commission on Housing in 1884 instigated by the hardening of public opinion on the subject of housing reform. The Reports of the Commission demonstrated that in all parts of the United Kingdom the large cities and towns were still alarmingly overcrowded. The prime cause was the poverty of those at the bottom of the wage scale. So many families had to be content with a room or half a room in a dilapidated old tenement. And the pressure on these families had been increased by the sanitary policy pursued over the years of demolishing the worst slums and driving the inhabitants into the adjoining districts to make more overcrowding. When dwellings were demolished the Commission found that being centrally situated the cleared sites were sold off for commercial development. Even if they had been sold to housing associations or private builders at nominal prices it would still have been impossible to build to let at rents equal to what families were paying before demolition or alternatively, at rents these families could afford. Where housing was built for those who were displaced by slum clearance, the new houses were too dear for them. They were rented by others earning higher wages and having more secure employment. The local authorities thus found themselves with a different and superior class of tenant than that for which the rehousing projects were intended. This was similar to the experience of the model dwellings associations.

The Commission's exposition of the housing situation was valuable, but it did not contain much in the way of constructive suggestions for the future. And this is scarcely to be wondered at for there was one step which no one was yet prepared to take. That step was the provision of housing for the poorest families on a subsidised basis. If this was to be found necessary in the 20th century how much more so was it indispensable to a remedial housing policy in the second half of the 19th century. Housing conditions were then far worse; the poorest

families were then far poorer. Dr Marion Bowley has written "The official housing policy, as far as one existed, was limited to making it legally possible for the local sanitary authorities to deal with the slums at their own expense, if they liked. Broadly speaking, the fundamental idea remained negative. The object was primarily to prevent or destroy insanitary housing conditions rather than to create good conditions. The actual provision of houses by local authorities remained a step taken only in the last resort."[*]

The Housing of the Working Classes Act 1885 followed the Commission's Report. It eased the terms on which loans for improvement schemes could be obtained, limited compensation to owners and also provided that local authorities need not purchase property against which demolition orders had been made. It also enjoined the local authorities to act under the housing powers they had been given. But nothing much was done. The Housing of the Working Classes Act, 1890, was of greater importance. This was a comprehensive measure consolidating previous housing legislation, amending it where it was thought desirable and making new provisions for more effective action by progressive local authorities. That the Act was more effective than the Cross Acts was due not so much to its new provisions but to the changing attitude to social reform and to the improved local government machinery for implementing the Acts following upon the establishment of the county councils in 1888.

Two more measures may be noted. In 1900, the Housing of the Working Classes Act gave to the boroughs the power to build houses for the poor, not merely to build for rehousing those displaced by clearance orders. And, in the Housing and Town Planning Act 1909, the building of further back-to-back houses was prohibited.

Thus, although not a great deal had been achieved and that only by the most progressive authorities, nevertheless, the ground work had been laid and a substantial code of legislation built up which was to be of practical guidance for the efforts made to improve housing conditions in the years following World War I.

---

[*]*Housing and the State.* Marian Bowley p.3. (Geo. Allen & Unwin Ltd. 1945).

Chapter 12

WORLD WAR I

By 1914 building societies had gone a long way towards restoring confidence on the part of their members after the Birkbeck failure. Both membership and assets were showing recovery. The advent of war was a further blow but societies came through the war years in reasonably good shape. They did not make much progress. It was a marking-time period. Their total assets only rose from £66 million to £68 million and the membership remained steady at around 625,000.

War-time Anxieties

Nevertheless, the war years were not free from anxieties. There were problems of liquidity, of interest rates, of war damage and of war-time legislation. And, as time went on, considerable discussion about what was to happen when the war was over.

At the outset financial tension was increased by the raising of the Bank Rate to 10 per cent, the closure for three days of the Stock Exchange and all the banks, and a Government declaration of a moratorium on liabilities. It was only to be expected that there would be a run on cash because of the fears which a crisis generates. For some weeks building society withdrawals were above normal. They were met without difficulty and soon subsided.

A more serious threat to societies' funds came in 1915 when the Government began to raise loans to pay the cost of waging the war. The loans were sought from the public at higher rates than building societies were paying. These higher rates, coupled with appeals to subscribe to the loans on patriotic grounds, resulted in a heavier and more sustained drain on building society funds than had occurred in 1914. The Halifax, for instance, paid out over £1 million compared with £500,000 in 1914. The situation thus created was perhaps the most difficult one with which societies had to deal during the whole course of the war. The obvious course was to raise rates to investors. But that was possible only to a limited extent. For no societies had an interest variation clause in their mortgage deeds. A number of societies in the north had a six-months' calling-in

clause, and some of them used it to put up mortgage rates by ½ per cent. The southern societies' rates for both investors and borrowers were higher than those of the northern societies and so they were not as badly affected.

As it turned out the problem was only a temporary one. House building ceased and the demand for mortgages declined from £8.7 million in 1914 to £4.4 million in 1917. From 1916 onwards societies' liquidity increased and they were able to turn the Government's generous borrowing terms (as high as 6 per cent on some loans) to their advantage by profitably investing their surplus funds with the Government. By 1918 the liquid assets of the movement as a whole amounted to some 20 per cent of total assets.

Growing Housing Shortage

Whilst building societies were more or less at a standstill, changes were taking place in the housing situation which were to be of significance for their future operations. House building had been at a low ebb in the years immediately preceding the war. During the war years hardly any houses were built at all. It has been estimated that no more than 240,000 additional dwellings were provided between 1911 and 1918. On the other hand, owing to the increase in population and the abnormally high marriage rate of the war years, the number of families had risen in the same period by some 850,000. Thus by the end of the war there was a shortage of about 600,000 houses without taking into account the need for replacing the worst of the houses built in the nineteenth century.

Early in the war a new factor was introduced into the housing area – that of rent control. It was brought in as a war-time measure, as other controls were, to ensure that the prices of the main necessities of life were kept at reasonable levels. The controls applied to a wide range of dwellings, and the rents were frozen at the levels prevailing at the outset of war. Price controls of this kind, introduced in war-time, are designed to afford temporary protection, with the intention that as soon as supplies are back to normal they can be dismantled. So far as rent controls were concerned, it was going to be a long time before things were back to normal. Few people, however, expected that they would remain for more than three or four years after the war.

During the second half of the war years, although the extent of the housing shortage was not fully appreciated, nevertheless both the Government and the Building Societies Association recognised that special measures would be needed to expand the house building industry and promote the supply of houses. The Association set up a committee to study what was required. The main question this committee set out to answer was not how owner-occupation could be en-

couraged but how private enterprise could be induced to build houses for letting. This was not surprising as renting was for most families the normal tenure and much of societies' money was loaned to private landlords.

It was obvious to the committee that building costs were going to be high, for prices generally had risen and in any case there would be pressure on the building industry as commercial and industrial buildings would also be wanted. Even so, the problem was regarded as short term. The committee was of the opinion that the cost of building would be 50 per cent above the economic value for the first year after the war, 40 per cent for the second, 30 per cent for the third and that thereafter the cost should approach what would then be normal. "Normal" in this context they envisaged as being some 20 per cent above pre-war prices. The committee made recommendations which had as their objects the restoration of public confidence in house property as an investment, effective means of encouraging and helping investors and owner-occupiers to meet the housing shortage, and proposals for the provision of funds. Among the suggestions made were that builders or purchasers should be relieved of charges for making streets and sewers, that houses erected under approved conditions should be exempt from rates for a period of years, and that subsidies should be paid to builders equal to the difference between cost and economic value. It was also suggested that where new houses up to £500 value were bought by owner-occupiers they should be exempt from income-tax.

Government Committees

In the meantime the Government had set up committees to look at various aspects of the housing need. One – the Carmichael Committee – was asked to look at the ways in which the provision of building materials could be accelerated, and how the speedy demobilisation of building trades workers could be organised. A second – the Tudor Walters Committee – was asked to make a practical examination of house design and to consider the requirements of the people for whom they were intended. The Committee recommended that the design of housing should allow for such improvements in living standards over the next half century as could be foreseen. It was of the opinion that families would require more space, more privacy and the provision of individual rooms for separate activities. A minimum area of 900-950 sq.ft. was proposed; three bedrooms and a bathroom. It recommended variety in site planning and a density in urban areas of no more than twelve houses to the acre. The Committees' recommendations and the type-plans which were incorporated in its Report were a major influence in post-war housing design in both private and local authority housing.

The third Committee – the Salisbury Committee – was asked to look at the housing shortage and to determine how many houses would be needed at the end of the war. It reported in August 1917 and suggested that 300,000 houses would be required immediately, an estimate which was far too low. The Committee also recommended that housing must be made the duty of local authorities.

By this time the Government had established a Ministry of Reconstruction with Christopher Addison* in charge. The Building Societies Association put their proposals to him but found him unresponsive. He accepted the proposals of the Salisbury Committee and in February 1918 announced that local authorities were to be made responsible for the immediate post-war housing drive.

*Christopher Addison served as Minister of Reconstruction and later as Minister of Health under Lloyd George. He later joined the Labour Party, serving in the Second Labour Government (1929–31) as Minister of Agriculture; and (as Viscount Addison) Leader of the House of Lords and Dominions Secretary in the 1945 Attlee Government.

Chapter 13

HOUSING 1919–1923

From 1919 onwards housing legislation had far more impact on building society lending operations than in the past. Housing policy varied (as it still continues to do) with changes of government and fluctuations in financial and economic circumstances. And as policy changed, so did the emphasis on local authority or private enterprise building, the attitude towards subsidies, the Rent Acts and the drive for slum-clearance. This being the case, it is necessary to give some account of the various measures that were passed in the attempt to solve the housing shortage.

The 1919 Legislation

As we saw in the last chapter, the Salisbury Committee recommended that local authorities should be made responsible for the initial housing drive. The Government accepted this recommendation. Working-class houses were needed in large numbers and in order to let newly-built houses at reasonable rents they would have to be subsidised. Permissive powers to build houses for local needs had been given to local authorities by the Housing Act 1890. They were now made obligatory by the Housing and Town Planning Act 1919. The local authorities were required to assess the needs of their districts and then make and carry out plans for the provision of the houses required. The broad aim was to build 500,000 houses over a period of three years. The level of controlled rents of working-class houses was to be taken as a guide to the rents to be charged for the new houses. Variations could be made for the better amenities of the new dwellings and for the rent-paying capacities of the tenants. The deficits on the housing accounts were to be borne by the local authorities and the Treasury. But the liability of the local authorities was limited to the product of a 1d rate. The rest was to be found by the Treasury.

This particular form of residual subsidy has been the subject of much controversy. It has been criticised on the ground that it provided no check on the additional losses which arose from inefficiency or extravagance on the part of local authorities. It certainly did not encourage them to keep building costs down, nor to manage their housing estates economically. On the other hand, the

1919 Act was only the first of many experiments in the housing field. Local authorities were mostly new to house building. The Government was anxious for results, and if too large a financial burden had been imposed on local authorities, they might well have dragged their feet.

As it was, it soon became apparent that it would take time to produce the houses. The tasks of assessing needs and formulating plans, of getting Ministry consents and obtaining tenders could not be done in a matter of days. The Government therefore decided that some encouragement should also be given to private builders. This took the form of a lump-sum subsidy on houses conforming to prescribed size limits. This subsidy was made available from the beginning of 1920.

After the initial preparation stage the local authorities set about their housing tasks with enthusiasm. By April 1921 contracts had been placed for the erection of 160,000 houses. Then the axe fell. In July 1921 the Government decided to bring the subsidies (both local authority and private enterprise) to an end save for those houses which had been started or for which contracts had already been placed. What was the reason? The answer is the need for retrenchment on the part of the Government. The immediate post-war years produced a short-lived boom which lasted through 1919 and the first half of 1920. Costs and wages in the building industry rose sharply. The whole industry was under pressure. Demand for buildings of all kinds outstripped the capacity of the industry which was still rebuilding its labour force.

This post-war boom was not confined to this country. Nor was the break. World prices and trade collapsed. From the middle of 1920 the building industry began to suffer a fall in demand. Unemployment rose, wages fell and so did the cost of building materials, With these trends local authorities could look forward to securing lower tender prices. But, unfortunately, the Government had been spending freely in a number of directions, and were under pressure to effect drastic economies. The housing drive was one of the victims. It was brought to a halt and there was to be no new housing policy until 1923.

The result of this first effort to deal with the housing problem was that local authorities built 170,000 houses and a further 39,000 were built by private enterprise with the aid of the lump-sum subsidy. Nearly all these houses were completed by March 1923. In addition some 54,000 houses were built by private enterprise without the aid of subsidy.

So the first post-war experiment in housing came to a sudden end. The 250,000 houses built by 1923 had fallen far short of target. In the meantime the number of families had increased by some 460,000 with the result that the housing shortage was far worse than at the end of the war.

Several factors had emerged. The local authorities had demonstrated that they were capable of getting houses built. The 1919 subsidies were not withdrawn because the scheme had failed but because it was successful and therefore too costly for the Treasury to bear. "The truth is", says Dr. Bowley "that the country was faced with the dilemma of having large numbers of working-class houses built at immense expense or having very few houses of this type built and saving the public purse. Public opinion, local and national, wanted the houses. The Government's promises to provide houses for heroes and the Minister of Health's pressure on the local authorites to carry out the Government's wishes reflected this decision".* Ways and means would have to be devised of producing a subsidy scheme which would encourage administrative efficiency and greater financial responsibility. But, from now onwards, local authorities were to play an important role in housing.

It had been demonstrated, too, that there were families willing to buy houses for owner-occupation (both with and without subsidy) on an encouraging scale. 93,000 houses may not seem a high total spread over some three years; but in the circumstances, having regard to the high costs of building, it was a significant beginning. And in view of the pressures on the building industry, the labour shortage and the preoccupation of the larger firms with local authority contracts, it was probably as large a total as the industry was capable of producing.

A third factor which became more evident as time went on was that rent control was going to be difficult to dismantle. The Rent Acts were prolonged in 1920 and even extended to houses with a higher rateable value than had been covered by the 1915 Act. Some relief was given to landlords by permitting them to increase rents and to charge more for repairs and rates where rents were inclusive of these items. In 1923 the Rent Acts were again renewed.

With the continuation of rent control it also became clear that houses were not going to be built for letting by private investors, notwithstanding that newly erected houses were exempted from control. For one thing, the Rent Acts had shaken the confidence of investors in property. Again, high building costs and high interest rates meant that rents for new property would be well above controlled rents for similar property. If building costs declined, then houses built later could be let more cheaply, which would drive down the rents of the earlier more expensive houses.

How did building societies fare in this immediate post-war period? There was some frustration at being given no direct part to play in the housing drive. And some rancour that the war-time proposals put forward by the Association had

*Bowley Op. Cit. p. 33

been ignored. When the huge cost of building the local authority houses became public knowledge, criticism was voiced by many building society leaders. Typical of their comments was: "It would have been better if Dr. Addison and the paid officials in his Department had left the provision of houses to experienced men of affairs, such as directors and officials of building societies. There is no doubt that hundreds of millions of money could have been saved and better houses provided". And another said "If the Government could have been persuaded to assist house building through the machinery of approved building societies working under Government guarantee, I venture to assert that more houses would have been built at much less cost to the community than under the wasteful methods adopted".

Mortgage Lending Increases

Nevertheless, building societies were not short of mortgage business in the early post-war years. It came in the main from the existing stock of houses. First, there was the demand at enhanced prices from purchasers of vacant-possession houses. Secondly, many property investors, discouraged by the Rent Acts, decided to sell houses as they became vacant, rather than re-let. And many of them also decided to offer their houses to the sitting tenants at a figure somewhere between the rental and vacant possession values. Here was a new source of mortgage business. Something like 90% of the total stock of houses was rented and it required only a small percentage of these houses to turn over to owner-occupation to provide building societies with an appreciable flow of additional business.

A third outlet for funds was provided by newly built houses. How many of these were mortgaged to building societies is not known. Probably not a high proportion. It is likely that many of the unsubsidised houses were built at this point in time for middle-class families who could afford to pay cash or would look to banks, insurance companies or private mortgages for their borrowings. It must also be borne in mind that building societies were by no means exclusively lending to owner-occupiers. There were commercial properties of various kinds on which many societies made loans. And although many property owners were discouraged by the Rent Acts, there were others who were willing to buy rented property and sought mortgages.

Building society advances had averaged about £9 million per annum for several years prior to 1914. From 1918 onwards they rose as follows.

1918	£6,970,000	1921	19,673,000
1919	15,840,000	1922	22,707,000
1920	25,094,000	1923	32,015,000

This progress was not made without some anxiety about house prices, which first escalated sharply and then started to fall back in 1922 and 1923, though not, of course, to pre-war levels. In 1919 and 1920 existing houses with vacant possession were selling at three to four times pre-war prices. New houses were showing a similar increase. The wholesale price index of building materials (based on 100, 1913) rose to 311 in 1920 and then fell to 242 in 1922. A reliable index for new construction was that of the average tender prices (excluding land) for the erection of local authority houses. This was as high as £930 in August 1920 but had fallen to £700 by March 1921 and to £463 by March 1922.

Valuation Problems

Building societies were hard put to it to determine a basis of valuation which would be safe and yet not unduly deter business by reducing the loan offered to the purchaser to an unacceptable figure. One manager (writing in November 1921) stated that his society's policy had been to limit lending on good-class existing houses to twenty times the ascertained pre-war net annual income. On new houses built since the war loans had been restricted to half the gross cost. Another society estimated as far as possible the pre-war selling price and added one-third to that figure to arrive at present value, on which they lent 75 to 80 per cent.

By 1923 J.C. Head (Chairman, North West Building Society and a highly respected chartered surveyor) was of the opinion that there was little likelihood of a return to pre-war prices:— "Some of the war changes have become permanent; the large number of houses required owing to war marriages; the higher standard of accommodation required; the revelation of the comfort provided by labour saving houses, the outcome of the servant trouble; all these keep up demand – – the factor of inflated building cost is also diminishing but in the opinion of many it is already nearly stabilised at a figure of some 70 per cent above pre-war price".

One of the considerations that perplexed valuers and building society officers was that of reconciling rental values with the much higher vacant possession values. In these early post-war years it was widely believed that rent restriction would before long come to an end and with the restoration of a free market, rental value would again become the basis of valuation and what was called the vacant possession "premium" would disappear. But this ignored the inflation which had taken place and the fact that rents were being kept artificially low by rent control. Many building society men, brought up in a world where rented houses and rental values governed the housing market, found it difficult to accept the changed level of house prices. Others found it easier to reconcile themselves

to the enhanced price levels. This difference of approach to valuations was the underlying reason why some societies began to expand more quickly than others. In subsequent years, as we shall see, there were other factors which also enabled some societies, especially those in the south, to grow at an exceptional rate.

Chapter 14

EXPANSION – FIRST PHASE 1924-1930

The years from 1924 to 1930 saw the beginnings of the great expansion of home-ownership and the parallel and rapid growth of building societies. Each year's figures of mortgage lending and asset growth, easily surpassing those of the previous year, surprised even the building society leaders. And they were achieved against a background of by no means expansionary years for the economy as a whole. After the immediate post-war boom the Bank of England gradually regained a firm hold on monetary policy by the adoption of high interest rates, and from the end of 1921 onwards by a rapid reduction in the volume of floating debt. The Bank's restrictive policy was maintained even through the slump of 1921 and 1922 when other considerations would have encouraged the adoption of precisely opposite policies. The purpose of this inflexible attitude was the restoration of the Gold Standard. With the exception of J.M. Keynes hardly anyone of authority or influence doubted the wisdom of this aim; and it was finally achieved in May 1925. As is now generally recognised, that step resulted in deflationary policies being pursued in subsequent years if only to defend the Gold Standard, once it had been re-established.

It was, in consequence, a period of high unemployment with the declining industries such as coal and cotton particularly hard hit. The General Strike of 1926 was in support of the miners, whose employers sought to impose severe wage reductions, the abolition of the minimum wage and the lengthening of the working day. Then in 1929 came the Stock Market crash on Wall Street with serious effects throughout the world. The boom of 1928 on our own Stock Market was followed by a slump in 1929 and the Hatry group crash.

Thus the years of the first expansion were not free from economic and financial difficulties. Why then were builders able to sell houses on the scale they did? And why were building societies able to attract increasing amounts of money with which to make purchase possible? The answer lies partly in the new form of subsidy provided by the Government in 1923; partly in the acute housing shortage which meant that families were prepared to make sacrifices in order to buy homes; partly in the easier mortgage terms which building societies made available; and, so far as funds were concerned, in the attractions of the tax-paid

investment-rate coupled with the efforts which building societies themselves made to enlist new investing members by increased publicity and advertising.

Aid for Private Enterprise

First, the Government measures. Following the abrupt termination of the 1919 Act subsidies, a vacuum was created in housing policy. Nothing was done to fill it until 1923. The immediate post-war coalition Government under Lloyd George was succeeded in 1922 by a Conservative administration. Neville Chamberlain was appointed Minister of Health (in those days the Ministry responsible for Housing). His Housing Act of 1923 was designed to encourage private enterprise to build small houses for sale or for letting. It offered a subsidy of £6 per annum for 20 years or its equivalent as a lump sum, namely £75.* Although this subsidy was also available to local authorities, the Act made it a condition that they should be allowed to build houses only if they were able to convince the Ministry that it would be better if they did so, rather than leave it to private enterprise.

The Chamberlain Act was a return to financial orthodoxy. From the Government's point of view it had three advantages over the 1919 Act. It provided a subsidy which was simple; it limited the liability of the Treasury; and it avoided any inflationary impact on building costs. The Act was also a direct encouragement to private enterprise, to which the builders readily responded. But the Government was still thinking of the housing shortage as a short-term problem. That was evident from the limited period for which the subsidy was to be available. It was to be paid only on houses built by 1st October 1925.

Another point worth noting is that this was the first (but by no means the last) reversal of the roles of private enterprise and local authorities in the field of housing. And that reversal was not to stand for long. For when the first Labour Government took office in 1924, the new Minister of Health (John Wheatley) brought in another Housing Act under which the powers of local authorities to build houses were restored. No longer were they first required to prove that houses could not be adequately supplied by private enterprise. Moreover, although future changes of Government would result in changes of emphasis as to the respective contributions to be made by local authorities and private enterprise, this Act did in fact establish local authorities as a permanent agency in the provision of houses which in the course of time was to make them the biggest landlords in the country. Subsequent Governments may have restrained their

---

*In the event, few, if any, houses were built for letting; and the lump sum payment was almost universally taken by house builders rather than the annual payment of £6.

housebuilding, reduced their subsidies or confined their activities to slum clearance and replacement. But, since 1924, no Government has ever suggested that local authorities should leave the housing field entirely to private enterprise.

Wheatley's Housing Act was undoubtedly one of the most important measures of the first Labour Government. It is notable because it took a long-term view of the housing problem. The Chamberlain subsidies were now to be made available as far ahead as 1939. On houses built by local authorities and by public utility societies (or housing associations as they are now known) the subsidy was increased to £9 per house in urban areas and £12.50 per house in rural areas, payable over 40 years instead of 20. A further £4.50 per house (again for 40 years) was to be contributed by the local authority from its rate income.

Wheatley thus held out the prospect of a steadily expanding house-building programme and was thereby able to make a "gentleman's agreement" (as it came to be known) with the building trade unions under which they agreed to relax their rules so that the number of skilled men in the various trades could be increased. The shortage of skilled men was the principal bottleneck standing in the way of an increased house-building programme. Now recruits were to be admitted to the industry for training.

The Labour Government was short-lived and was followed by another Conservative Government. Again, the emphasis shifted slightly. Local authorities were now urged to concentrate on houses for lower-paid workers and so avoid competing with private enterprise. The Government's main concern, however, was with the size of the subsidies. It was argued that subsidies should not be allowed to drive costs up, and further, that if costs fell then subsidies should be reduced. Building costs did begin to fall in 1927 and went on falling for the next six or seven years. Accordingly, both the Chamberlain and Wheatley subsidies were reduced in respect of houses completed after 30th September 1927. In 1928 the Wheatley subsidies were again reduced and the Chamberlain subsidy was abolished except for houses completed before 30th September 1929. But with the return of a Labour Government in 1929 the second reduction in the Wheatley subsidy was cancelled.

Private housebuilders responded well to the Chamberlain subsidy offer and by 1927 had raised the production rate to 150,000 houses per annum of which more than half qualified for the grant. Local authorities were slower in responding to the Wheatley subsidies but maintained a steady increase up to 1928 in which year a grand total of 260,000 houses were built by private enterprise and the local authorities. Altogether, in the seven years, 1924-30 some 1.3 million dwellings were erected, 880,000 by private housebuilders and 440,000 by local authorities.

How far did the toal of 1.3 million houses built in these seven years go towards meeting the shortage? At the beginning of 1924 there was a need for some 800,000 dwellings and the number of families was increasing at a rate of over 100,000 per annum. Allowance must be made for wastage due to demolition and conversion of existing dwellings to other uses. The deficit in houses had probably been reduced to about 400,000 houses by the end of 1930.

Increase In House-Ownership

Of the new houses, two-thirds were erected for sale, which meant that in the course of seven years the number of owner-occupiers had doubled. This was not a sudden conversion on the part of the public to the virtues and advantages of home-ownership. There were two motives at work ensuring the sale of the new houses. One was the desire to obtain a better, more modern house on the part of those who already had a house which they owned or rented. The other was the sheer necessity for those without a house to find a home to live in. And apart from those fortunate to obtain one of the relatively few council houses, the only way in which these two groups of people could satisfy their needs was to buy.

Of the first group Dr. Bowley has written: "The temptation to move was probably greatest for those families living in the small three or four-bedroomed type of house which compared so unfavourably with the small modern villas. The long, dark passages, cold and depressing sculleries, sordid bathrooms and villainous scarlet brick of Victorian lower middle-class villas could, in the post-war era be abandoned for compact new houses with all sorts of modern conveniences and fittings. The new villas may be stigmatised as jerry-built, they may be despised as pseudo-Tudor or ugly by the sophisticated, but there is no denying their attraction for the young couple with a small family. Nor must it be forgotten that the improvements in transport, better trains, electrification, buses and motor coaches made the outskirts and new suburbs cheaply and rapidly accessible."[*] The families who were prosperous and had saved some capital and who were thus able to make this transition to new houses began the process of trading-up which enabled others less prosperous to buy the older houses. And, at this juncture, as so many of them were tenants, they increased the potential for home-ownership, since, in many cases the landlord then sold his house with vacant possession.

This first group had a choice – they could stay where they were or buy a modern house. The second group had no choice. To buy was the only way to achieve a home. Many of them had married during the war years and had been

[*]Bowley, *op. cit.* p.74.

compelled to live with parents or in one or two furnished rooms. Some were earning good wages and could afford the mortgage repayments. Some were prepared to make sacrifices in other directions in order to buy. The main problem for many was the deposit it was necessary to find to bridge the gap between the purchase price and the 75 per cent–80 per cent loan which building societies were accustomed to lend.

Insurance Guarantees

Let us see how this problem was solved. Building societies had been of the opinion, ever since the war ended, that good use could be made of their funds if only Government guarantees were forthcoming to support their loans. And in 1922 the National Federation of House Builders stated that many people would buy if they were required to find no more than £100. The Federation believed that the Government would ultimately be persuaded to give some kind of guarantee. What the Government did in the 1923 Act was to empower local authorities to give a guarantee to building societies. Where the guarantee was forthcoming, the building society could lend up to 90 per cent. But few local authorities were prepared to give such guarantees and the results were disappointing.

However, the guarantee arrangements gave birth to another form of guarantee scheme. Building societies and insurance companies got together and evolved the single-premium insurance guarantee under which the insurance companies gave a guarantee along similar lines. The borrower paid a single premium which could be added to the advance. In return he could obtain a loan up to 90 per cent. And the building society was indemnified against the extra loss which might be involved in making the above normal advance. This was to prove highly popular and was widely used from about 1925 onwards. It was only at the end of the decade, when builders were looking to less-well-off purchasers, that builders' pool schemes came into vogue cutting purchasers' deposits to 5 per cent and even less. But that is a subject for a later chapter.*

By making it possible to borrow a higher proportion of the price of a house, building societies eased the way for many families. Some lengthening of the term of repayment also helped. The ten or fifteen years of pre-war days had gone by the board. Twenty years was now regarded as normal and some societies were prepared to allow 23 or 25 year terms. Some anxiety persisted among the more conservative societies about the future trend of prices. The expansionist societies took the view that they could accept the existing level, relying on their

*See Ch. 17

borrower's covenant and the margin between their normal advance and the price
to safeguard them against a fall in values.

Building Society Funds

In this first phase of building society expansion their total funds more than
doubled at £371 million. In the ten years from 1920 they had more than
quadrupled. The substantial house building output of this period would not have
been possible without this supply of money. There were other lenders. The
banks, insurance companies and family trust funds provided loans for the better-
off families buying houses in the upper price ranges. When it came to houses selling between £500 to £1500 and purchased by clerks, foremen, commercial
travellers and factory workers the building society was the principal source of
finance.

The societies ended the war years, as we have seen, in a highly liquid position
and were able to take advantage of the initial increase in demand for mortgages,
due to enhanced prices. But that liquidity would not have lasted long. To meet
the increasing demands on their funds it was necessary to attract new investing
members on a larger scale than ever before. Times were propitious. It was not
difficult to obtain the money.

There were several reasons for this. For one thing, increased taxation made
the building society tax paid rate attractive to a new class of substantial investor.
In those days the building society tax arrangement was far more advantageous
to the higher rated taxpayer than it is today. Another helpful and significant factor was that the intensive national savings campaign of World War I had induced numerous families to save regularly. That saving habit had outlived the war.
"The small savings institutions (including building societies, post office savings
banks, trustee savings banks, industrial assurance, co-operative societies funds,
etc.) showed a total of £498 million in 1913. By 1925 the total, which by then
included national savings certificates, had reached £1,375 million and by the
mid-1930s was over £2,500 million. All these agencies reaped the reward
(though not in equal proportions) of the wider saving habit".*

A third — and important — source of funds was the money which was
withdrawn from the housing market by property owners or by those who had
been accustomed to lending money by way of private mortgages. As owners sold
out and did not reinvest in property their money often found its way to the
building societies. So did that of the private mortgagee.

*Bricks and Mortals, Sir Harold Bellman p.137

Nevertheless, without efforts on the part of building societies, much of the money they obtained would not necessarily have come their way. By means of publicity and public relations, branches and agencies, societies sought to encourage new investing members and thereby more funds.

Chapter 15

GROWTH AND COMPETITION

We have seen how the housing shortage induced many families to become home-owners and how this development produced a rapid expansion of building society lending. By 1930 the total funds of the movement had grown to £370 million and the number of members to 1.5 million.

Varying Rates of Growth

Some societies had grown rapidly and had more than kept pace with the growth of the movement as a whole. Others had expanded at a slower pace. Partly it was due to the temperament and outlook of the men in charge. Some were in their seventies, for in the 1920s men did not retire at 60 or 65 – there were few pension schemes. These older men had been profoundly influenced by the Liberator and Birkbeck failures. They did not take kindly to rapid expansion or to property values which were well above what they had been accustomed to in pre-war days.

The Temperance was a notable example of those societies whose watchword was caution. In 1908 it was the largest society. But from 1920 to 1935 its assets increased only from £1.6 million to £4.9 million. "Apparently those who were the leaders could not divest themselves of their Victorian outlook. They considered that the ideal society was one which restricted its operation to its own locality, and, therefore, they were unsympathetic to the opening of branch offices".*

At the beginning of the 1920s the nothern societies held the paramount positions in the league table with the Halifax Permanent far and away the largest society. But the London Societies began to expand at an astonishing rate. They were favourably placed to take advantage of the greater prosperity of London and the Home Counties. Much of the new housebuilding was on their doorstep. By 1929 four London societies (the Abbey Road, Woolwich Equitable, National and Co-operative Permanent) had taken their place among

*From *Queen to Queen*, a history of the Temperance Permanent Building Society – Seymour J. Price, p.82. Franey & Co. Ltd. 1954.

the top eight societies. The following table shows how the situation changed:

The 8 largest Societies

1922	(£ mill.)	1929	
Halifax Permanent	13.9	Halifax	59.3
Bradford Third	5.8	Abbey Road	19.1
Halifax Equitable	4.1	Leeds Permanent	12.0
Leeds Permanent	3.7	Woolwich Equitable	11.4
Burnley	3.3	Bradford Third	11.3
Huddersfield	3.2	National	9.9
Leicester Permanent	2.8	Huddersfield	9.8
Bradford Second	2.2	Co-op Permanent	9.6

(Figures for Halifax Permanent are to 31st Jan of following year; for Leeds Permanent and Woolwich Equitable to 30th September; and for Halifax Equitable to 30th June; all others to 31st December. Halifax Societies merged in 1928.

The Halifax Permanent had taken the lead before 1914 under the vigorous leadership of Enoch Hill. He had pursued a policy of opening branches and agencies and after the war continued this policy. Between 1918 and the merger with the Halifax Equitable in 1928 about 100 branches and agencies were opened. Other progressive societies began to follow the Halifax's lead. Hill himself remarked: "The day of branches has arrived and I am very glad to see that many of the important building societies are realising the advantages and benefits of branch offices".

Advertising and public relations were other means of attracting business. The Association established a Public Relations Committee which did sterling work under the chairmanship of Harold Bellman of the Abbey Road Society. The Halifax and the Abbey Road set an example to the rest of the movement in their own public relations, and in their style of advertising and literature.

Competition Resented

But the vigorous promotion of the most expansive societies was not to the liking of many local societies. Particularly, the incursion of the London societies into the provinces was resented and that resentment was freely expressed. The London societies charged more for mortgages and paid more to their investors. Consequently their advertisements for funds in provincial papers were extremely unwelcome. Furthermore, they paid commission for the introduction of mortgage business. By 1929 the competition was becoming acute. Industry and

population were moving south and the northern societies were not finding all the mortgage business they wanted.

At the Annual General Meeting of the Association in 1929 Enoch Hill said that the favourable conditions in the Metropolitan area and adjacent counties was not the complete explanation of the phenomenal progress of the London societies. He said "it may be fairly asked how much of their success is due to their policy of penetrating the provinces for business, which has become such a marked feature of their operations". And he asked "what had been the effect upon country societies of the practice of paying substantial commissions for the introduction of mortgage business, not only in the Metropolitan area but in many parts of the country". One delegate objected to societies advertising in his local papers, huge advertisements which were a direct appeal to his society's own members. One or two societies threatened to resign from the Association.

It was not only advertising and the payment of commission which created animosity. Branch offices were viewed with apprehension and suspicion by the local societies. The Halifax had to take its share of the criticism on this count. Even the opening of the Halifax's London office gave rise to comment on the part of some of the London societies and Hill defended it on the ground that it was designed to serve the 700 or so members of the society then living in the London area.

But these were irritants which were destined to disappear as time went on and as societies became reconciled to the fact that the geographical spread of the larger societies was inevitable. In the next decade competition for mortgages took another form – the development of the builders' pool and low deposits – while interest rates gradually became unified throughout the country.

District Associations

There were other changes which came in this decade. One of them was the establishment of District Associations, which were to play a useful role in the exchange of ideas and the discussion of policy at local level. The idea of forming district associations had been suggested before the war but nothing was done until 1919 when the South Western Counties Association was established. The example was quickly followed in other areas and soon there were half a dozen such bodies. In 1922, provision was made for district associations to affiliate to the Building Societies Association. They were entitled on affiliation to send two representatives to the Annual General Meeting of the parent Association, but it was to be many years before they were entitled to direct representation on the Council. Nevertheless, they were not without influence on the main issues of the

day; and proved useful in disseminating information among member societies and bringing about an improvement in methods of administration and practice. Most Associations held regular meetings including annual dinners with guest speakers both from within and without the movement, which helped to gain publicity.

Staff Training

In the years to 1930 the growth of societies led to substantial recruitment of staff, and from time to time there was discussion on the need to provide staff training. In April 1920 the Building Societies Officers Guild was started in London by members of various societies' staffs. It received encouragement from a number of London societies and from certain London managers, in particular from Arthur Webb of the Co-operative Permanent who was a keen educationist and fully in sympathy with any proposal for staff training. The Building Societies Association, however, withheld its support arguing that educational and professional qualifications were obtainable by means of the examinations of the Chartered Institute of Secretaries. The Guild also failed to obtain much support in the provinces. Unfortunately, it had stated at the outset that one of its aims was to establish, in consultation with boards of directors, minimum salary scales. The Association and building societies generally were not inclined to look with favour on an incipient trade union and it was probably this unwelcome aspect of the Guild which led to its early demise. Nothing more was heard of it after 1921.

Little more of a practical nature was done except internally by a few progressive societies until the Metropolitan Association held its first week-end school at Hertford College, Oxford. This became a regular annual feature, held alternatively at Oxford and Cambridge. Other associations followed the example of the Metropolitan Association. These week-end schools were a great success and were to lead in the 1930s to the formation of the Building Societies Institute.

The Halifax Merger

By 1930 the number of societies had been reduced to 1026, a decrease of just over 300 from 1918. This was in no way due to amalgamation but to the disappearance of terminating societies and the winding-up of some permanent societies. The desirability of mergers was often canvassed in this period, but the requirements of the Building Societies Acts imposed one daunting obstacle. For two societies to amalgamate it was necessary not only to obtain the consent of both societies at a special general meeting, but also to obtain the written consent

of the holders of not less than two-thirds of the shares of each society. This latter requirement was regarded as practically and physically impossible to fulfil. Yet it was done in the one notable amalgamation of the 1920s. That was the merger of the two largest societies, the Halifax Permanent and the Halifax Equitable.

The intended amalgamation was announced in September 1927 and was said by Enoch Hill to be a natural union of the two Halifax societies and was later described by the Halifax Permanent president as a "marriage". The Halifax Equitable was founded in 1871, eighteen years after the Permanent. It prospered and grew at a quickening pace, especially after J.H. Mitchell was appointed secretary in 1897. By 1914 its assets were £1 million to the Permanent's £3 million. After 1918 Mitchell continued to push the society ahead, determined that even if he could not overtake the Permanent he would ensure that the Equitable expanded just as fast, if not a little faster. This he did and by 1924 he had made his society the second largest in the country. By 1928 the Equitable's assets stood at £14 million compared with the Permanent's £33 million. Still a long way behind, but nearly half the Permanent's size instead of only one-third as in 1914.

Mitchell resigned in June 1927. According to Hobson, David Smith (then secretary and Assistant General Manager of the Permanent) was then approached by the Equitable board with the offer to become their chief executive. "Smith replied that he was quite content with his prospects at the Permanent. He then suggested as a way out that the two societies should merge. Hill, he said, had not at first welcomed the idea, but later adopted it with enthusiasm".* Whatever the reason for his initial hesitation, he quickly realised that the elimination of the local rival and the addition of its assets to those of his own Society would make the Permanent's already large lead over all other societies virtually unassailable.

The amalgamation proved a triumph of organisation. To comply with the law, some 200,000 concurrence forms were obtained from the shareholders of both societies, and the union became effective in the early part of 1928. This success did not, however, pave the way for other amalgamations in the inter-war years.

*A Hundred Years of the Halifax. Sir Oscar Hobson p. 96. B.T. Batsford Ltd. 1953.

Chapter 16

THE FINANCIAL CRISIS OF 1931

The financial (and political) crisis which Great Britain suffered in 1931 was only a part of the world-wide financial storm and economic depression which occurred from 1929 to 1933. A brief account is relevant to our story because it had consequences of significance to building societies and their progress during the 1930s.

The Crisis and Britain

The Stock Market crash on Wall Street in 1929 was the herald of depression and of the collapse of a world inflationary boom. The downturn was much more severe than that of the normal trade cycle. Traditional correctives and reactions were of little avail. The United States collapse had grim results for it affected trade and investment all over the world. Prices of primary products fell heavily, and although this improved the terms of trade for Britain it also meant that the primary producing countries could no longer afford to buy our exports. As a result unemployment mounted. The numbers out of work doubled between June 1929 and June 1930 from one to two million. By the end of 1930 the unemployed numbered 2.6 million. The consequent increase in unemployment pay meant that a heavy budget deficit would face the Chancellor.

But the domestic financial plight was not the only worry. London as an important financial centre held large international balances, mostly short-term holdings which were liable to be withdrawn if lack of confidence produced a run on sterling.

Two reports published in July 1931 served to highlight the difficulties that Britain was facing. The MacMillan Committee on Finance and Industry was set up in 1929 and the May Committee on National Expenditure was appointed in early 1931 as a sequel to a Liberal motion in the House of Commons calling for an independent review of Government expenditure.

The MacMillan Committee pointed to the difficulties of the British trading position and the failure of financial policy to overcome them. It was much influenced by the economic views of John Maynard Keynes who was one of its

members. The Committee's report was a searching and thorough review and suggested that the maintenance of maximum output and employment at home should be one of the purposes of monetary policy.

While the MacMillan Report indicated the weaknesses of the economic and financial position in general, the May Committee's Report dealt with the immediate position. It had a far more dramatic impact. It painted an unduly gloomy picture which immediately undermined international confidence. In order to balance the budget the Committee prescribed rigid economies, including cuts in unemployment pay.

As if this was not enough, there was crisis in Europe, too. It began with the collapse of the Credit Anstaldt Bank in Austria. This was followed by financial trouble in Germany, where the Reichsbank lost millions of marks in gold and foreign exchange. The German economy was on the verge of disaster.

The two crises, domestic and foreign, demanded immediate action, and so far as Britain was concerned, withdrawals of money by foreign creditors, whether because it was needed abroad or because of a lack of confidence in Britain, could only be arrested by the speedy balancing of the budget.

The National Government

The Cabinet Economy Committee proposed increased taxation and economies which included a 10 per cent cut in unemployment benefit, but a majority of Labour Ministers were not prepared to split the party by agreeing to these measures. Ramsay MacDonald and his followers then joined the Conservatives and Liberals in the formation of a National Government.

But the formation of a National Government did not end the financial crisis. Confidence in sterling was not re-established and funds continued to flow out of London. Despite an emergency budget on 10th September 1931, increasing both direct and indirect taxation and proposing cuts in servicemen's, police and teachers' salaries and in unemployment benefits, the situation continued to worsen. On 21st September the Gold Standard was abandoned. The reserves had proved inadequate to save it.

The policy of maintaining the Gold Standard after 1924 had involved a period of severe and continuous deflation. Restricted by this policy, British industry had not shared to the same extent as other countries in the industrial and manufacturing boom which took place between 1925 and 1929. For that reason, when the boom was finished and depression came, Britain was not as badly hit as other countries. Nor did going off the Gold Standard prove the tragic step which the government's financial advisers had so often predicted. It did, in fact, provide the Government with a new flexibility which helped it to

solve its financial problems. The devaluation of the pound relieved the strain on Britain and diverted the crisis to other countries, including the United States and France. Once the crisis was over, Britain's international position was one of relative stability.

But the grave unemployment situation remained. 1932 was a dreadful year in which industrial production, security values and exports all reached their lowest points and the number out of work its highest. Nevertheless, the turning point was reached some time in the latter half of 1932.

The War Loan Conversion

To bring about an improvement in trade and employment, the National Government (which was returned with a massive majority at the General Election in October 1931) decided to promote a cheap money policy. By successive stages the Bank Rate was reduced to 2 per cent by June 1932. This had a two-fold purpose. One was to encourage borrowing by industry and encourage production; the other was to prepare the ground for the unprecedented and bold step of persuading holders of the £2,000 million 5 per cent War Loan to convert to a new stock at a lower rate of interest. It was widely expected that the rate on the new stock would be 4 per cent, but the Chancellor (Neville Chamberlain) decided to make the most of the depressed situation and offer conversion to a $3\frac{1}{2}$ per cent stock.

To do this successfully and avoid a large proportion of holders asking for repayment instead of converting demanded some preparatory measures. In particular, it was necessary to ensure that there was little prospect of obtaining elsewhere a higher rate. Building society shares offering 4 per cent – or even $3\frac{1}{2}$ per cent – with no tax payable were an obvious danger to the conversion plan. But even before the conversion terms were finalised building societies were being flooded with money which they could not use. The successive reductions in Bank Rate had been accompanied by reductions in Bank Deposit Rates. There was a depressed stock market and few opportunities to obtain a safe return equal to that which the building societies afforded. Enoch Hill said "This extraordinary influx of funds is at once a compliment and an embarrassment". And Harold Bellman questioned whether the outstanding lesson to be learned was that one should not allow the movement to be exploited and flooded with funds which by no stretch of the imagination could be described as normal building society money.

From quite early in 1932 many societies had placed restrictions on the sums which could be added to existing accounts or accepted from new investors. When the Chancellor made it clear that the Government would welcome the

disappearance for the time being at least of financial competition liable to prejudice his scheme, building societies were only too ready to oblige by tightening
the restrictions already imposed. The Association was not directly involved, but
Bellman was called into consultation by the Treasury. No doubt it was he who
was the prime mover in a statement issued jointly by the four largest London
societies (Abbey Road, Co-operative Permanent, National and Woolwich
Equitable) on 12th July 1932. In that statement the societies announced that to
avoid being made the depository of substantial funds realised from the sale of
War Loan, invididual investors in the four societies would not be permitted to
increase their present holdings by more than £250 and new accounts would be
limited to £50. The Halifax had also been kept informed and on the same day
announced the closure of its paid-up share department and a limit of £500 on
deposits. Many societies followed these leads but differed in the extent of the
restrictions imposed.

Interest rates were reduced, too. The four London societies mentioned above
reduced their deposit rate to 3½ per cent. And under the lead of the Halifax
societies began to reduce their share rates from 5 per cent to 4½ per cent and
then to 4 per cent.

Demand for Mortgage Rate Reductions

The conversion of War Loan was in the event a highly successful operation. But
once it was done and building societies were seen to be reducing their investment
rates there grew a demand for a reduction in mortgage rates. In September 1932
The Building Societies' Gazette reported: "The Press of the country has allowed
its imagination to run riot on the question of mortgage interest rates during the
past month. Scarcely a day passed, during the earlier portion of the month, on
which the subject was not referred to in glaring headlines; and probably at no
period in their long and honourable career have building societies received so
much concentrated publicity in so short a space of time".

Societies were under pressure to reduce mortgage rates not only on new
mortgages but also on existing loans. This was a situation without precedent. Accustomed to long periods of stable mortgage rates, on the few occasions when
there had been changes they had been restricted to new mortgages. That was the
case in the middle 1880s when mortgage demand was slack; and again in 1920
and 1921 when rates were raised in the boom period. But now there was a completely changed situation: a background of low interest rates; a plethora of
funds; and a substantial body of owner-occupiers demanding along with the
housebuilders that mortgage rates should come down.

The first move came in respect of new mortgages. One or two provincial

societies reduced their rates by 6 per cent to 5½ per cent on new advances in the London area. Then in September 1932 the four large London societies again made a concerted move, reducing their rate for new advances to 5½ per cent, applicable throughout the country, and many other London Societies followed their lead. Many provincial societies reduced their new lending rate to 5 per cent except for the London area.

So far as existing mortgages were concerned, societies were not yet ready to take a decisive step. But with the Bank Rate and other rates holding firm at the lower levels, the early months of 1933 produced a widespread movement in favour of reductions on existing accounts.

By September 1933 the *Economist* was able to report that something approaching uniformity of rates was being secured among the largest societies. The old basic rate of 6 per cent for new mortgages in the Metropolitan area had completely gone. The standard charge for owner-occupiers both in London and the provinces was now 5 per cent. The normal deposit rate had come down to 3 per cent and although there was a greater variation in rates to shareholders it was rare to find a maximum of more than 4 per cent. Even at these rates there was still a need for restrictions on the amount of money accepted, although the restrictions varied from one society to another.

Thus, the consequences of the financial crisis – the conversion operation and the cheap money policy – led to a new level of building society rates and an abundance of funds. The way was opened (as we shall see in the next chapter) for a further phase of expansion and a substantial house-building programme.

In the crisis year of 1931 and the two following years house building and mortgage lending flattened out but despite the discouraging economic conditions remained encouragingly stable. Local authorities averaged 70,000 houses a year and private building accounted for 140,000 a year. Building society advances averaged £90 million a year and in 1933 reached £100 million for the first time.

As the subsidy to private enterprise was phased out in 1929, the number of houses built for sale without subsidy increased. The fall in building costs undoubtedly helped. By 1930 the continued fall in costs had become in total sufficient to stimulate expansion of unsubsidised houses of all sizes. The cost of the cheapest and smallest type of house fell from 12/- per week (or 11/- with the Chamberlain subsidy) to between 8 shillings and 9 shillings per week. There was still an acute housing shortage. And those who were in safe employment were prepared to buy; their real income had increased during the depression.

More worrying for building societies – especially those in the northern regions of high unemployment – were the borrowers who were out of work and

unable to meet their monthly payments. This proved to be much less of a problem than many feared. By recognising the difficulties and allowing payment of, say, interest only, societies eased the situation for many. Some borrowers were able to draw on their savings. Few were prepared to give up their homes.

One burden which societies were called upon to bear in this period was a substantial increase in their tax liability. In search of revenue, the Chancellor decided that a revision of the income tax arrangement must be made and that henceforth societies would not only pay the composite rate on distributions made to their investors, but for the first time they would be charged to tax at standard rate on all undistributed profits.

Chapter 17

EXPANSION – SECOND PHASE 1934-1939

By 1933 it was evident that the worst of the economic depression was over and that better times were ahead. In his 1934 Budget speech Neville Chamberlain said that the country had left Bleak House and might now begin Great Expectations. To encourage that belief he reduced Income Tax from five shillings in the pound to four shillings and sixpence. The cuts in the salaries of teachers, civil servants and other officials which had been made in 1932 were restored.

Housebuilding and Recovery

The economy went on improving in a marked and vigorous fashion. The Government had created the background conditions favourable to a recovery including a balanced budget which helped to restore confidence at home and abroad; tariff protection which reduced manufactured imports; and, of course, cheap money. The improvement was based on the home market rather than on an upswing in exports and it is the opinion of many economists that this recovery was initially set in motion by the increase in housing starts which took place from 1933 onwards.

And it was cheap money in particular which made the housing boom possible. In the first place it encouraged housebuilders to borrow money to resume or expand their programmes. The banks had the money to lend partly because the demands of industry for finance were at a low ebb and partly because the Bank of England was deliberately expanding the credit base. The reduction in interest rates was also one factor (but not the only one) which encouraged housebuying.

Once house building had got under way other sectors of the home market were stimulated. Furniture and house furnishings were wanted and there shortly followed an upsurge in the purchase of electrical appliances and of motor cars. There was a further uplift to the economy from the heavy capital expenditure which the increased production of these goods entailed.

The Builders' Pool System

So far as demand from housebuyers was concerned, low interest rates alone would not have been enough to make it effective. By this time much of the

demand from middle-class families had been satisfied. The main demand would now come from lower paid workers in regular employment, many of whom were anxious to obtain a newly built house, provided the terms of purchase were within their means. This meant building smaller houses and selling them on easy terms. The building societies had been of the opinion throughout the 1920s that 10 per cent was the minimum deposit which an intending housebuyer should find. Accordingly, under the guarantee schemes arranged with local authorities and insurance companies the purchaser was required to find 10 per cent of the purchase price, plus legal costs. Under the builders' pool system adherence to the 10 per cent deposit gradually gave way, making it possible for a house to be bought with a much lower initial deposit.

Builders' pools were evolved in the late 1920s but came into widespread use only in the 1930s. The pool was an arrangement between building society and housebuilder under which the building society agreed to make larger advances than it would normally have done to the builders' purchasers in consideration of the builder depositing with the society a sum of money in respect of each loan. The sums so deposited were "pooled" in the sense that they were treated as one fund which could be drawn upon in the event of a borrower defaulting and the society having to sell his house at a loss. As a further support to the fund the builder was also required to guarantee each mortgage, and if called upon to do so repurchase the property from the society. Thus, if there were default cases, the pool would be drawn on only if the builder failed to honour his guarantee and undertaking to repurchase.

The pool agreement usually called for substantial deposits by the housebuilder in respect of the first loans made under it. An amount equal to the excess advance over 75 per cent would perhaps be required on the first six or ten houses; half that amount on the next six or ten; thereafter, the society would be content with one-third of the excess advance. But there were no standard terms. Each society decided its own policy and would negotiate terms with each builder. Much depended on the standing and reputation of the builder and what the society thought of the quality of his houses. Societies were often played off against each other by builders seeking to get the best terms – competition was sometimes fierce.

When the pools system began advances were usually limited to 90 per cent. Under the pressure of competition and the obvious need to make it easier for lower-paid workers to buy, advances went up to 95 per cent and even higher. Builders began quoting selling prices inclusive of legal fees and advertised their houses for sale on payment of a deposit of no more than £25 or £30. Under pool arrangements the repayment term was frequently extended to 25 years to

make the monthly payment more attractive.

There is no doubt that the pool system made possible the housing boom of the 1930s. The large societies, who were able to provide an assurance of adequate funds, secured a more than proportionate share of pool business. There were many misgivings about the wisdom of forging such a close partnership with the speculative builder. Yet, even those who expressed doubts were willing to go along with the rest. As we shall see in a later chapter, the criticisms of pooling arrangements came to a head with the Border's case and the 1939 Act.

Low deposits, longer repayment terms, low interest rates and falling building costs resulted in brisk sales of houses and accordingly production rose to new heights. From 1934 to 1938 the total number of houses erected averaged about 350,000 per annum. And of these the private housebuilders built around 280,000 each year.

As house production rose, so did the number and amount of building society loans. Lending was at a high level from 1934 to 1938. Additional funds were thus absorbed and total assets of the movement increased from £501 million at the end of 1933 to £773 million at the end of 1939.

Changes in Housing Policy

Local authority housebuilding was left far behind in this boom period. This was because the Government decided that their housing activities should be directed to slum clearance. While the housing shortage remained acute it had seemed pointless in the 1920s to tear down houses even though there were many that were decaying and thoroughly unfit. By 1930 it was considered that a start could be made. The Greenwood Act of that year introduced a new policy and a new subsidy which varied directly with the number of people displaced and rehoused. It discouraged the pre-1914 practice of demolishing slums and leaving the displaced families to find their own alternative accommodation, which so often merely added to the overcrowding of other slums. The new subsidy *per capita* basis also made it easier for local authorities to deal with large poor families. Additional subsidies were also provided for urban areas where rehousing had often to be provided in flats for which construction costs were higher. The Wheatley subsidy was still to be available for houses built for general needs. Local authorites were thus in the position of providing houses for replacing slums and houses (under Wheatley) for meeting additional needs. The results of the Greenwood Act up to 1933 were disappointing, but after that date the larger cities (which contained most of the slums) began to gear up their effort. Another Act in 1935 was directed to the reduction of overcrowding and the

number of houses built for that purpose and for the replacement of slums gathered pace.

With the advent of the National Government yet another change in housing policy took place. It was decided that the local authorities should concentrate on slum clearance and should leave the provision of additional houses to private enterprise. Accordingly, in 1933 the Wheatley subsidy was withdrawn.

Rented Houses Without Subsidies

The reason why the Wheatley subsidy was withdrawn was that the Government had come to the view that cheaper money and falling building costs had made it possible to build houses for letting without subsidy. Private enterprise would be encouraged to produce them. Economic forces operating in a free field would secure a large volume and variety of houses at competitive rents. It was hoped that a number of persons and organisations would play their part; and that private builders, housing companies and associations, finance societies and private investors would all take a share in the ownership of working-class houses. To provide the finance to make this possible, the Housing (Financial Provisions) Act 1933 provided for loans of 90 per cent of value to be made by building societies with guarantees by the Government and local authorities jointly. These loans were to be made at $4\frac{1}{2}$ per cent in London and a defined group of southern and western counties; and at 4 per cent in the rest of the country. That was $\frac{1}{2}$ per cent below the rates prevailing for owner-occupier loans. Repayment was to be over a period of thirty years.

This Act was the culmination of three years endeavour by the Association's executive to achieve a collaboration with the Government which would place building societies in the key role in all housing finance. It was a bold and ambitious bid. How it was made and how the building societies had to be content with a comparatively minor achievement must now be recounted.

It all began with a paper on "Public Money in Housing" presented by Walter Harvey to the Association's 1929 conference. In this paper Harvey criticised public housing on the grounds that subsidies were wasteful because they were not passed on to the consumer and that local authorities had done little or nothing for those who could not afford a rent of more than ten shillings per week.

His main argument was that the most economical and effective kind of help that could be provided was a guarantee to enable buyers to borrow up to 90 per cent. Experience had proved that both local authority and insurance company guarantees carried little risk and that actual losses had proved negligible.

But few local authorities were prepared to operate the guarantee provided by

the Housing Act 1925 and many were themselves lending money to house buyers. Harvey therefore suggested that local authorities should not only cease lending in competition with building societies, but that they should also transfer their existing mortgages *en bloc* to building societies. Local authorities (with, possibly, the Government joining in) should all be prepared to guarantee building society loans. And if the building societies ran short of money through having to transact much more mortgage business, then the difficulty could be met by the setting up of a housing loan, under Government guarantee, to provide the building societies with the necessary additional funds. Harvey also envisaged building societies helping with the slum problem, again provided suitable guarantees were forthcoming.

Suggestions for a National Housing Organisation

The conference referred Harvey's paper to the Executive for consideration and report. Accordingly a sub-committee was appointed (with Harvey as Chairman) and duly reported to the 1930 conference. In between the two conferences it had sent out a questionnaire to member societies to ascertain what degree of support there might be for specific recommendations along the lines of Harvey's proposals. Some 76 replies were received. Some where hostile, some non-committal and a few (less than twenty) were helpful. As the sub-committee said, there was not sufficient support available to warrant the Executive Committee approaching the Government or local authorities with a definite scheme. Having said that, the sub-committee went on to make two very definite proposals. One was for finance to be made available through building societies for the provision of houses for those who could afford to pay only small rents and for those displaced by slum clearance. The other was for the establishment of a national Housing Organisation which would consist of representatives of the Government, of the building societies and of the building industry, with regional boards on which local authorities would be strongly represented. The national body would carry out housing and slum clearance schemes. It would sell houses to those who wanted to buy, otherwise it would let.

The sub-committee, having brushed aside the lukewarm response to its questionnaire, had made proposals of an even more far-reaching character than Harvey's original suggestions. It also proposed that discussions should now be opened with the Minister of Health and the local authorities. The report was accepted at the conference with little comment. It did receive (in August 1930) the commendation of a leader in *The Times* which concluded "Since the War we have spent about £1,000 million on housing, most of it borrowed, and much of

it borrowed at rates of interest which impose a heavy burden on the ratepayers and taxpayers. The building societies have now made a suggestion for an organisation which, as compared with the authorities so far in charge of housing, could certainly operate more cheaply, with greater concentration, with more independence, and with equal regards for the requirements of modern housing. In their present task of exploring further so promising an idea they deserve the hearty co-operation both of the Ministry of Health and of local authorities". Nothing much seems to have happened for some months, but in August 1931 Harvey was able to report that friendly and informal conversations had taken place between officials of the Ministry of Health and building society representatives. And in May 1932 the *Gazette* reported that for a considerable time past the sub-committee had been in touch with the Ministry. There was at last some prospect of building societies being invited seriously to tackle the problem of bringing their resources to bear so that working-class houses could be provided without subsidy. But still it was argued that some guarantee was essential if abnormal advances were to be made.

In April 1932 Hill was saying "If we had the Government behind us to assist in making abnormal loans and being responsible for the safety of those loans, the financial responsibility of the Government would be limited to that infinitely small proportion of borrowers who would be defaulters or who would fail in carrying out their obligations". He added "we could multiply home owners by hundreds and thousands, the Government instead of putting down millions of money and saddling the taxpayer and the ratepayer with this expense for an indefinite period of years, would be only liable for the very small sum represented by the deficits".

The Minister Steps In

The building societies (or some of them) were anxious to form some link with the Government entailing a guarantee which would do away with subsidies. From Harvey's paper in 1929 to Hill's plea for guarantees in support of owner-occupier loans the objectives had varied. The takeover of local authorities' house-lending activities, the setting-up of a National Housing Corporation, the making of loans on houses to let, and involvement in slum clearance had all been canvassed.

At this point the Minister of Health himself gave the housing sub-committee a brief – a much narrower one than they had sketched out themselves. He wanted to end subsidies except for slum clearance. He therefore asked the sub-committee to work out with his officials a practicable scheme to provide houses for less-well-paid workers who would be expected to rent rather than purchase.

And so the scheme was worked out and authorised by the 1933 Act. The building societies had at last obtained what they had long sought, a Government guarantee. But it was not the guarantee which Hill and others had pleaded for, namely to support owner-occupation loans. Nevertheless, it was something of a milestone. The Government was at last recognising that building societies had a part to play in the provision of housing for those who could not afford to purchase.

The 1933 scheme was not however universally welcomed. Some societies said they would not co-operate. Others agreed somewhat reluctantly. Arthur Webb said he "had always regarded it as a fundamental principle of the movement that it should aim at creating owners as against ordinary tenants and he had worked on that theory. In the north, the matter was not regarded in the same way, the view being held that a building society was there to advance money to anyone who wanted it for a particular purpose. That being the case why had they given support to the measure? Building societies were overburdened with capital, and therefore it seemed so far as their surplus funds were concerned they were justified in helping the Government by providing for those who would become tenants but who could not afford to purchase".

Harvey was enthusiastic. "Is it not fair to say", he asked, "that the home buying movement has been overdone, under forced conditions, and that the greater need now is for all classes – houses to let?" Hill announced in May 1933 that the Halifax was prepared to make £10 million available under the Act over the next two years.

The Act By-Passed

There were two drawbacks to the scheme. One was the concessionary rate of interest, which to societies was unattractive so long as they could lend their money to owner-occupiers. The other was that although the Government was sharing the guarantee risk, the local authorities had to work the scheme, approve the plans and agree values with the building societies. This was a discouragement to the builders, for many local authorities were unenthusiastic and some were antagonistic to what they considered a usurpation of their own function of providing houses to let.

In the event, the number of houses built under the 1933 Act was no more than 21,000. The Act has been written off as a failure. Judged by its results that is a fair assessment. It has to be said however that it did not fail because of building society opposition or lack of builders or investors prepared to acquire houses to let. It failed simply because everyone concerned discovered that it was possible and more convenient to build houses to let outside the Act paying nor-

mal building society interest rates and avoiding the necessity of getting local authority approval for guarantee purposes. Between October 1937 and March 1940 no fewer than 163,000 houses were built in England and Wales for letting, approximately one-third of the total number of houses built by private enterprise in that period. Building societies (at least some of them) came to the view that it was safe to lend up to 90 per cent on such houses without guarantee and to accept repayment over 30 years. Some investors built houses solely for letting and some builders gave families the option of buying or renting on the same estate. Building for letting helped to maintain the rate of house production in the later years of the period when the demand from house-buyers was tailing off.

Transfers of Local Authority Mortgages

Another feature of the 1930s was the transfer of existing mortgages by local authorities to building societies. This was not because local authorities wanted to get out of the mortgage market as Harvey had suggested in 1929 they should, but because they were unable (for statutory reasons) to reduce interest rates on house loans. Some of their earlier borrowers were paying 6 per cent and $5\frac{1}{2}$ per cent. By 1935 the building society rate had come down to $4\frac{1}{2}$ per cent, and it was therefore to enable their borrowers to obtain the lower rate that so many authorities entered into arrangements to transfer their mortgages *en bloc* to building societies.

Chapter 18

THE CODE OF ETHICS

The Building Societies Association never had a large membership. In 1921, out of 1300 societies only 250 were members. Nevertheless, it embraced the larger societies and the major part of the assets of the movement. The Association up to this time had had a limited role. Its main activity had been in the field of legislation where it had been diligent in looking after its members' interests, and readily intervening not only when the Bills directed to building societies were before Parliament, but on other occasions when legislation was proposed which might operate to their prejudice. Before 1914 there was some opinion that the Association should do rather more than this. It was felt by some that it should play a more positive role in the field of public relations and should facilitate and encourage the formation of district committees or associations.

The fact is that the Association had neither the organisation nor the finances to contemplate much activity beyond its traditional role. It had a part-time secretary in the person of R.H. Marsh who had occupied the post since 1888. He was highly respected, much loved and efficient within the limits which his practice as a Chartered Accountant and his other interests imposed on him. The Association served the movement well enough in the 1920s when societies were in the first phase of expansion. The newly formed district associations supplemented the work of the Association by providing for the reading of papers on policy and practice and promoting public relations and occasionally passing resolutions designed to prod the parent Council into action.

From time to time changes were made in the constitution of the Association. In 1922, when membership fees were modestly raised, it was agreed that in future they should be based not on membership but on assets. Provincial representation on the executive committee was increased, and in 1926 the name was changed to the National Association of Building Societies. Power was taken to expel a society if its conduct, status or financial position was considered likely to be detrimental to the reputation, welfare or good government of the Association or of the movement.

In 1932 the executive was enlarged: in future it was to consist of 24 elected and up to six co-opted members. It was to be known in future as the Council of

the Association. The power to co-opt, it may be noted, was to enable George Franey, the Editor of *The Building Societies' Gazette,* to join the Council. He was co-opted, not primarily because he was Editor of the *Gazette* but because he had for some time been assisting in an honorary capacity with the secretarial work. The part-time secretary R.H. Marsh was unable to keep pace with the increase in work, especially on the public relations side. Franey had helped with the organisation of the Annual Conferences and in other ways. It was considered desirable that he should participate in Council proceedings.

In the 1920s the Association's activities were mainly concerned with the traditional role of parliamentary watch-dog, housing, guarantees, income tax and public relations. Up to 1931 it had held firmly to the understanding on which the Association was started in 1869, that it should not in any way interfere with the internal working of any member society.

The Association and Competition

By 1931 intense competition for business coupled with the economic depression led to fears that trouble lay ahead. If property values fell (as seemed likely, given the crisis and the rising unemployment figures) what would happen to the borrower who had bought his house with a minimal deposit and a maximum mortgage. He would find that he was unable to sell his house for what was ow-ing to the building society, and would therefore be tempted to abandon his home and default on his mortgage.

In October 1931 the Council cautiously stepped into the minefield of com-petition regulation. The principal bone of contention was the borrowers' per-sonal stake and it was to this that the first communication was directed. A cir-cular was issued which stated "at the executive committee just held it was felt that societies in union would not take it amiss if a word of caution were given in relation to advances on mortgage. This is that it is felt essential that prospective borrowers should have a personal stake in the property to the extent of 10 per cent at least of the purchase price, and that, in the interest of the movement, building societies should protect themselves and it by rigid adherence to this practice for the time being". That was the first step along the road that was to lead to the break up of the Association in 1936 and the formation of two new rival bodies.

Prior to the issue of this first circular a group of societies in London had been considering a wider set of proposals which were designed to check the abuse of building society facilities. These proposals were taken up by the executive com-mittee of the Association. In November 1931 a further circular was issued to member societies, this time dealing not only with borrowers' personal stakes but

with repayment periods, pool deposits, payment of commission and forms of guarantee. The *Gazette* was optimistic that a large measure of co-operation would be secured from societies as the proposals had been received in an extremely cordial manner.

In April 1932 societies were asked to say to what extent the proposals had been adopted and put into operation. There was wide acceptance in principle, but many societies had reservations on one point or another. The main bone of contention was the suggested maximum advance of 90 per cent. This was objected to by societies operating pools on smaller deposits, and often by small societies not operating pools but long accustomed to making large advances to local members whose families had been associated with the society for many years both as borrowers and savers.

In the following months the proposals of November 1931 were modified by a committee of representatives from the six largest metropolitan and the six largest provincial societies and circulated to societies in December 1932. The Council made an earnest appeal for consideration of the proposals in an atmosphere free from prejudice or bias, and with the realisation that the approach to common problems on co-operative lines was usual in movements which had attained the economic significance of building societies. This did not cut much ice with those societies which were competing fiercely for business. At the June 1933 conference T.R. Chandler (the vice-chairman of the Association) who had acted as chairman of the committee of the twelve London and provincial societies said that the apathy of a considerable number of societies, and the definite hostility of a small but important section, had rendered all their efforts vain.

Bellman Becomes Chairman

At this point in time an important event occurred. Enoch Hill retired from the Chairmanship of the Association after a long reign of twelve years, and was succeeded by Harold Bellman. T.R. Chandler stepped down from the position of vice-chairman to allow Hill to occupy that post, but remained chairman of the advisory committee.

From now on the efforts to secure some limitation to competition were to become more intense. Bellman, who had been the moving spirit from the beginning, took up the fight not only for co-operation but for a Code of Ethics and Procedure which would be binding on member societies. He was loyally backed by Chandler, and the two of them went round the country addressing district association meetings and conferences to win support. At the 1934 conference held in Harrogate the Code was put to the delegates, and by an overwhelming

majority and with prolonged applause, the Council was authorised to submit the proposals to all societies on the basis that if a two-thirds majority voted for acceptance, then the Council would be authorised to require all societies to subscribe to the Code of Ethics and Procedure as a condition of continued membership.

When the proposals were later submitted to societies the response was not quite so enthusiastic as the reception given to them at the Harrogate conference. There was a substantial body of dissent. It came from a few large and many small societies. Some were opposed to any measure of control over the running of their own societies. Some were aggressive, competitive societies who wanted to go on competing and did not accept the dangers that Bellman and others feared. But there was also some resentment that those who were the strongest advocates of co-operation were those who had been the fiercest competitors over the last decade. By the end of 1933 the Abbey Road's total assets had reached £41.8 million, the Woolwich Equitable's £23 million. They and the other large London societies had established connections with builders, estate agents and solicitors; they had certainly gained for themselves a large slice of the new house mortgage market. Now these societies were preaching co-operation. Was it to stifle competition and thus preserve their own connections?

By 1934 the number of societies in membership of the Association had increased to 379. 314 of these had less than £1 million assets each (some of them had a good deal less), yet these societies had only three representatives on the Council. To meet their fears that they would receive little consideration it was agreed that they should have five out of ten places on an advisory committee to be set up to administer the co-operation scheme. Some further amendments were made to the recommendations, the most important of which was that, in deference to the small societies, the control of interest rates was left in abeyance.

A Measure of Agreement

The revised scheme was put to societies in October 1934, and they were asked to vote on it. The vote showed a large majority in favour. In an endeavour to obtain unanimity still more amendments were made. Finally a special general meeting was held in January 1935 and endorsed the proposals by an overwhelming majority. It was hoped to make the Code effective from April 1935 but more troubles arose. Societies had been asked not to make changes in interest rates, in the hope that they might shortly be regulated within the Code. But a few provincial societies reduced their lending rate to 4½ per cent and were shortly followed by the large London societies who acted without informing the Council. The London societies argued that their hand had been forced and

Bellman admitted that the request not to make changes had been overlooked. The Halifax Society was intensely annoyed. Bellman tendered his resignation as Chairman of the Association but at the next meeting of the Council a vote of confidence persuaded him to carry on.

And now the Halifax had to be placated. Further delays took place. Further revisions to the Code were made. In February 1936 it was again put to a vote of member societies. Again there was a large majority in favour, a majority which represented over 87 per cent of total assets. But there were forty societies, representing nearly 10 per cent of assets, who voted against the proposals; and a number of small societies – about a hundred – either did not vote at all or expressed doubts without committing themselves either way.

The National Association Wound Up

Events now moved fast. There had been five years of discussion and negotiation. The Council made one final effort to win over the dissidents. It was unsuccessful. So it was decided to go ahead without them. This raised a constitutional question. If acceptance of the Code was to be made a condition of membership, some alteration to the rules of the Association would be required. The Temperance society which had all along opposed a compulsory Code threatened that they would not resign but if kicked out of the Association would take legal action.

The Council therefore took the drastic step – but really the only practicable one in the circumstances – of calling a special General Meeting to pass a resolution for the winding-up of the National Association. This was done in June 1936, and later the same day a new Association (to be known by the old name of the Building Societies Association) was formed with acceptance of the Code as a condition of membership. Over 200 societies joined the new Association. Those opposed to the Code also got together and formed the National Federation of Building Societies; some fifty-five societies with combined assets of £55 million. They included the Northampton Town and County, Leek and Moorlands, Eastbourne, Brighton and Sussex, Cumberland, Lambeth and Norwich Benefit Societies. The Temperance and the Bradford Third were among those who opposed the Code, but these two societies did not join the Federation. Nor did the Leeds Permanent when it resigned from the Association a few weeks after the Code became operative.

With the dissenters gone, the Building Societies Association now had a membership totally bound to observation of the Code. But the difficulties remained. The dissenters were now free to compete openly. And they did. To

protect their business and preserve their builders' connections, societies observing the Code were obliged to seek dispensations in respect of long-standing business arrangements which did not comply with the Code. Apart from dispensations, societies, in the face of competition, found it far from easy to keep their terms of business within the straight-jacket of the Code. It was agreed at the 1937 conference that an attempt at revision and simplification of the terms of the agreement should be made. In the end, the Council came to the conclusion that it was beyond their powers to simplify or to enforce the Code. Bellman said in a final admission of failure "the Code's successful operation demanded qualities which are not always present in our fallible human nature". By 1938 it was virtually dead.

All that remained was for the Association and the Federation to come together. Harvey, who was now Chairman of the Association, and Creighton of the Cumberland society, who was Chairman of the Federation, made the necessary preliminary overtures, and agreement was reached in 1939 for members of the Federation to rejoin the Association with representation on the Council.

Chapter 19

THE BORDERS CASE AND THE 1939 ACT

The 1939 Act came about mainly as a result of the celebrated Borders case. This was a legal action by the Bradford Third Equitable against one of its borrowers in arrear, a Mrs. Elsie Borders. It was started in the High Court in January 1938. It went to the Court of Appeal and ended in the House of Lords in May 1941. The final stages were not of vital importance but the first stages were. It was not only the important legal issues involved which gave concern to the building societies, but also the widespread and unwelcome publicity which the case engendered. This was due in large part to the defendant – the wife of a taxi driver – conducting her own case. She was hailed as a modern Portia fighting single-handed against a large financial institution. The Press had a field day.

The plaintiffs had loaned Mrs. Borders 95 per cent of the purchase price of a house bought for £730 from a firm of speculative builders with whom the society had a pooling arrangement. The action was brought by the society because Mrs. Borders had failed to maintain payments under the terms of the mortgage deed and the society sought to obtain an order for possession of the property.

Two Main Issues

Two main issues arose from the defence put forward by Mrs. Borders. One was the validity of collateral security. Mrs. Borders argued that the builders having provided collateral security under the pooling arrangement, the mortgage was *ultra vires* and illegal under the Building Societies Acts and the Society's own rules. In consequence, she argued, the mortgage deed was unenforceable. On this point the judge decided in favour of the society. He observed "The mortgage in question is not beyond the powers of the Society. It is a mortgage of freehold estate. The security of the freehold estate is not merely nominal. As between the plaintiff and defendant the transaction is one of loan on the security of freehold property. It is not a case in which freehold land has been added to unauthorised security merely to make it appear that the transaction was one of loan upon authorised security when the truth was otherwise."

The other main issue was that of fraudulent misrepresentation. Mrs. Borders in her defence counterclaimed for damages from the Society on the grounds that she had been led by representations made to her both orally and in a brochure issued by the builders to purchase a house in which a number of defects had subsequently appeared. Those representations were that during the course of construction the houses were inspected many times by surveyors from the local authority and from the building society; and that the fact that a leading building society would make more generous advances over a longer period than on any other building estate proved what amazing value the builders were offering.

On this issue the judge found that although Mrs. Borders had satisfied him that it was upon these representations she had been induced to purchase the house, nevertheless she had failed to prove that the Society was in any way responsible for those representations. One fact which may have helped the Society on this point was that just before Mrs. Borders agreed to buy her house the builders had switched to the Bradford Third from another building society with whom they had been running a builders' pool. The brochure had been prepared and published while they were working with the first society. Had that not been the case Mrs. Borders might have been on firmer ground. This question of fraudulent misrepresentation went to the Court of Appeal, where the judge's verdict was reversed. But on appeal to the House of Lords the society won the day.

Collateral security and fraudulent misrepresentation were the main issues which were of moment to building societies generally. So far as the Bradford Third was concerned, they lost their action for possession because the Court held that the society had failed to prove that the mortgage deed produced in Court was one signed by the defendant and her husband (as guarantor). The Court also held the defendants were not estopped from setting up the contention that the actual deed signed by them was signed only conditionally pending the remedying by the builders of some defects to the house which were already apparent at that early stage.

The 1939 Act

The doubts cast upon the validity of collateral security caused much anxiety to building societies, especially as the High Court judgment was delayed for over a year, partly due to the defendant being given leave to amend her defence and counterclaim and partly owing to the services of the judge being required in the Court of Appeal. The issue of fraudulent misrepresentation gave rise to a great deal of criticism of the liaison which builders' pools created between societies and builders. Who was interested in the purchaser? In most transactions, the

house buyer was unaware that he was getting an advance of 90 per cent or 95 per cent only because of the pool arrangements. The Borders' house, it was generally agreed, was badly built. Soon there were purchasers on other estates, alerted by the publicity given to Mrs. Borders, complaining of defects in their houses. Some withheld payments to their societies. Some tenants' and residents' associations were formed among aggrieved owners to make their action more telling.

A fiery Labour Member of Parliament, Ellen Wilkinson, took up the cudgels on behalf of house purchasers. She proposed to introduce a Private Member's Bill which would have placed severe constraints upon building societies. The Building Societies Association, the Chief Registrar and the Government had not been idle, and forestalling Miss Wilkinson the Government announced in February 1939 that they had a Bill of their own in preparation. This was before judgment had been given in the High Court, and while, therefore, the validity of collateral was still in doubt. The Government announcement cleared the air so far as building societies' anxieties were concerned by stating that the Bill would contain a clause validating advances made in the past where collateral security had been taken. The Bill would also define what types of collateral could be taken in future including the terms on which builders' pools could be operated.

The 1939 Act was duly enacted though not without some fierce infighting during its committee stages. The Act did settle the doubts about collateral security, declaring that a society shall be deemed always to have had the power to take into account the value of any additional security for an advance. It further provided that after the coming into force of the Act, a society could take as additional security only those kinds specified in the Act. These included life policies to the extent of their surrender value, guarantees given by assurance companies or local authorities, charges upon money deposited with the society or upon trustee securities. As to builders' pools, termed in the Act "continuing arrangements", financial and guarantee conditions were laid down which were so stringent that after World War II no such arrangements were ever operated.

The Act also provided that notice must be given to a borrower where additional security was taken from a third party, and imposed on societies an obligation to serve the borrower with a notice of non-warranty, failing which the society would be deemed to have given the borrower a warranty that the purchase price of the property was reasonable. It also required of a society that in exercising its power of sale it must take care to ensure that the price at which the property was sold was the best price reasonably obtainable, thus putting on a building society a higher duty than was imposed by law on other mortgagees.

The basic aims of the Code of Ethics were embodied in the 1939 Act. Its

enactment must have given a wry satisfaction to Bellman and all those who had supported him in his efforts to achieve co-operation. For the Bradford Third was one of the societies which had opposed the Code and the dangers that Bellman had foreseen were epitomised in the Borders' case. He must surely have been tempted to say "I told you so". He did later observe "the authorities, in fact, stepped in, as had been forecast, to do what the building societies seemed unable to achieve for themselves. The Act embodied a number of essential protective measures which had formed part of the Code. To that extent there was no cause for regret, but at the same time it would have been much more creditable to the movement had it been able itself to carry out the measures which were subsequently imposed upon it from without. None the less it is satisfactory that this legislation is now binding on all societies, both within and without the Association, and it is unlikely that any misgivings can arise in the mind of the public as to these matters in the future".* The Act did more than protect building societies from the effects of unwise competition. As Cleary points out its aim was also to protect the borrower and make him aware of the conditions upon which he was borrowing.†

*Bricks and Mortals p. 130.
†Cleary, op. cit. p. 223.

Chapter 20

ORGANISATIONAL CHANGES IN THE 1930s

As we have seen, the building boom of the 1930s led to rapid growth, intense competition for mortgage business and strenuous efforts on the part of the Association Council to regulate and curb competition by the Code of Ethics. For much of the decade the Association's efforts were directed to that end and to the attempts to persuade the Government to aid housing by guaranteeing mortgages. But there were other issues which claimed the Council's attention.

Taxation

One was taxation. Building societies had had the good fortune to escape taxation on their surplus. Under the long-standing Arrangement B tax payable had been limited to that payable on dividend and interest distributions. This had been of enormous help to rapidly expanding societies in the 1920s, for it had enabled them to increase their reserve funds at a rate equal to or even faster than the growth of their assets. The Halifax, for instance, increased its assets from £27.2 million to £59.4 million between 1925 and 1930; in the same period its reserves rose from £708,000 to £2.0 million.

This was so favourable an arrangement that it was bound to catch the eye of a Chancellor looking for additional revenue. And so in 1932 it was decided that a revision of the building societies' tax arrangement should be made, and that they should be charged to tax at standard rate on all undistributed profits. The 1932 arrangement, arrived at after much investigation and protracted negotiations between the Inland Revenue and the Association, was finally settled on the basis that it should operate for three years. Accordingly, in 1935 it was again the subject of review. The Inland Revenue had made an exhaustive examination of a large number of building societies' accounts. The total distribution of dividends and interest had risen from £11 million to £17 million, and the average true liability of investors had altered materially. The Association's Income Tax Committee (aided by outside advisers) studied the whole matter very thoroughly, and again there were hard fought negotiations with the Inland Revenue. Finally, it was agreed that the principle of computation should be on the same basis as the 1932 arrangement, that it should operate for a period of four years and

thereafter from year to year. The composite rate was to be in the ratio of 1/8 to 4/6 (the then tax rate). But there was a new feature, namely that composite tax should be paid not only on distributions but also on the tax paid on those distributions on the grounds that the tax paid was also in effect a distribution.

In 1937 the Association was also called upon to do battle on the subject of National Defence Contribution, a new tax designed to help to pay for Britain's rearmament. This levy of 5 per cent on profits was to be applied to building societies' total income less working expenses and interest on loans and deposits. This would have worked unfairly as between one society and another, depending on how much of their liabilities were represented by shares or by deposits. The society with a high proportion of deposit monies would have come off much better than a society which had taken the bulk of its money in shares. And in any case it was considered that the total liability was more than societies should be called upon to bear.

The Association fought hard and successfully. The outcome was that the Chancellor agreed that building societies should pay at the rate of $1\frac{1}{2}$ per cent on total income less only working expenses. This concession reduced the potential liability of the movement as a whole from £1 million to £400,000. This settlement was received with cheers from both Association and Federation members.

The Secretariat

The other major event, so far as the Association was concerned, was the establishment of an adequate secretariat. At the Annual Conference in June 1936, just prior to the dissolution of the National Association, the Chairman (Harold Bellman) said that as a result of the transformation of the movement and the added responsibilities which this entailed, the work falling on the part-time secretary (R.H. Marsh) had been increasingly heavy and exacting. The Council felt the time was ripe to undertake the organisation of special services and facilities for affiliated societies. The existing arrangement not only depended upon the assistance which George Franey (the editor of *The Building Societies Gazette)* provided, but also on the large volume of work undertaken voluntarily by members of the Council. It had therefore been decided to create a secretariat appropriate to the needs of the day. Marsh was to become Honorary Secretary and a full-time Secretary was to be appointed with the necessary clerical assistance. The intention was to have a properly equipped and well-organised secretariat capable of rendering clerical, co-ordinating, advisory and research services demanded of a modern central organisation. It was, said Bellman, an urgent, practical necessity and in no sense a luxury.

The desirability of taking this step had been in the minds of members of the Council for some time. The factor which delayed it was the high regard in which Marsh was held throughout the movement. He had been secretary for nearly fifty years, and there was reluctance to suggest that he should retire. All the same, the need for some change was evident. The possibility of Walter Harvey taking the post of Secretary or Director-General of the Association was mooted. He was keen to take the job and for family reasons would have welcomed a move to London. Nevertheless, he did not wish to sever completely his connection with the Burnley Society of which by now he was a director as well as General Manager. Discussions did not produce an arrangement acceptable to him and the idea was dropped. Harvey was disappointed.

At last, in 1936, Marsh decided or agreed to go. The post of full-time Secretary was advertised, and after the new Association had been established C.G. Garratt-Holden was appointed. He proved an admirable choice, just the kind of able administrator and organiser needed for the setting up of the secretariat envisaged. The only drawback was that the Association had no offices of its own and the new Secretary had to make do with a couple of rented rooms, until in 1938 a lease was taken of 14 Park Street and the Association had at last an eminently suitable home of its own.

The Building Societies Institute

The other major organisational development of the 1930s was the formation of the Building Societies Institute in 1934. At the first Metropolitan Association week-end school in 1929 Arthur Webb had opened a discussion on educational facilities for building society staffs. Both the Chartered Institute of Secretaries and the Incorporated Secretaries Association had by this time arranged for building society law and practice to be included in their Intermediate and Final examinations, but there remained the problem of where students could receive tuition. As a result of the discussions at Oxford courses were established at three centres under the aegis of the L.C.C.; and lectures on building society law were provided by the City of London College. A correspondence course was also made available by the School of Accountancy. And from the beginning of 1930 the *Gazette* began to publish a most useful educational section. Opinion was gradually moving in the direction of a suitable organisation to meet the growing needs of building societies for trained personnel.

What really sparked off the formation of the Building Societies Institute was oddly enough an address given in 1932 by Mr. J.E. Hibbert of the Halifax Society at a week-end school held jointly by the North West, Yorkshire and

Midland District Associations in which he argued against the formation of an Institute. He said that in his opinion too much importance was placed on examinations. He abhorred the intellectual slavery to which the student had to submit. He then concluded by saying somewhat inconsistently, that the examinations of the Chartered Institute of Secretaries were open to all building society employees, and that he would make the passing of these examinations compulsory unless a valid excuse could be put forward which was acceptable to the society's management.*

This address by Mr. Hibbert did not go down at all well and Walter G. Boys (then Assistant Secretary of the Burnley Building Society) spoke strongly and with great effect, saying that some effort should be made by the staffs themselves to improve their status. They could get professional standing only by their own efforts and by setting up some staff organisation for protecting their interests and for giving them the opportunities which they sought. If some of the younger members would start an organisation similar to those of the bankers he would be the first to support them.

This speech aroused enthusiasm among those present, who clearly indicated that they wanted something done. Boys (with Walter Harvey's assistance) responded by enlisting the aid of district associations. The parent Association was not averse to the idea of an Institute, and appointed representatives to a committee convened to discuss and draw up a draft constitution. That constitution was finally approved by the National Executive and recommended for approval by affiliated societies. It was provided that the first Council of the Institute should be appointed by the Association, and of the thirty-five Council members half were to be managers or secretaries and half were to be drawn from members of staffs. Harold Bellman was to be the first President and Walter G. Boys the Honorary Secretary. The objects of the Institute were to be educational, benevolent and social. So its formation was by no means exclusively or even mainly a staff effort. Boys was the man who was really responsible, aid-

*There is little doubt that in making this statement the speaker (as a Halifax man) was following the line followed by Enoch Hill who had been a member of the Council of the Chartered Institute of Secretaries since 1928, and who was at the time looking forward to high office in that body. He did in fact become Treasurer of the C.I.S. in December 1933, senior Vice-President in December 1934 and President in December 1935. He had understandably encouraged members of his own staff to take the C.I.S. examinations, and indeed after the formation of the Institute in 1934 there was no marked enrolment of Halifax members until after Hill had served his presidential year with the C.I.S. It should be added that in 1938 Hill made a substantial donation to the Institute's Benevolent Fund and provided a capital sum to endow the "Enoch Hill Prize" to be awarded annually on the results of the Institute's examination.)

ed by the district associations. On this occasion, unlike the ill-fated Guild, care was taken to exclude specifically from the objects of the Institute the subject of remuneration; no doubt this helped to gain the support of the Association and many societies.

The Institute got off to a good start, quickly preparing syllabuses for Intermediate and Final examinations based on studies relevant to building society law and everyday practice. Walter G. Boys continued as Honorary Secretary until 1938, working in London. But in that year he expressed his wish to resign for personal business reasons, and it was arranged with the Association that Charles Garratt-Holden should combine the office of Secretary with his Secretaryship of the Association, and that the Institute should be housed in 14 Park Street. Boys continued his association with the Institute as Honorary Director of Studies.

The International Union

Another body which came into being during the 1930s was the International Union of Building Societies and Savings and Loan Associations. A Congress of building societies and kindred bodies overseas had been arranged to take place in London on 11th and 12th August 1914. With the outbreak of war most of the American delegation cancelled their sailings, and there were, of course, no European representatives. It did take place, however, with Edward Wood presiding.

Optimistically, it was decided to hold another meeting at San Francisco in 1915. This time there were no foreign delegates, but papers were submitted from England and other countries. At San Francisco it was resolved to postpone any further meeting until 1920. These two gatherings were unfortunate in their timings, and it was not until 1931 that a third Congress was held. The venue was Philadelphia; George Franey acted as Secretary-Treasurer, and Enoch Hill was one of the Vice-Presidents. A strong British delegation crossed the Atlantic, but apart from them and the Americans there were only two German and two South African representatives.*

The fourth Congress, held in London in 1933, under the presidency of Enoch Hill, was the first really international gathering. Delegates from no fewer than seventeen countries were present. The Prince of Wales honoured the proceedings by giving an address on the opening day. The Government gave an official reception and the city of London made the Guildhall available for a Banquet over which the Lord Mayor presided. The Prime Minister [Ramsay

---

*The British party sailed from Liverpool on Friday 1st July, visited New York, Philadelphia, Washington, Niagara, Toronto, Ottowa, Montreal and Quebec, arriving home on 30th August. The total inclusive cost per person was £88.!

MacDonald) was present at a garden party given by Sir Harold and Lady Bellman at their home.

Bellman was the President for the next two Congresses held in Salzburg and Zurich in 1935 and 1938 respectively, both of which were well attended and successful conferences, although the Zurich Congress was held just before Munich amid fears of war. At Zurich a new constitution was adopted and the name changed to the International Union of Building Societies and Savings and Loans Associations. It was agreed that the next Congress should be held in the United States in 1942. In the event it was not until 1957 that the seventh Congress was held in Stuttgart.

Fewer Societies

By 1939 the total number of societies had fallen to 960. There were 854 permanent societies and 106 terminating societies. Of the permanent societies there were 22 societies with assets exceeding £5 million (total £482 million); 75 with assets between £1 million and £5 million (total £185 million); 757 with assets of less than £1 million (total £104 million). The 106 terminating societies had combined assets of only £1.4 million.

Since 1929 there had been some changes among the first eight societies. The Huddersfield had dropped to tenth position, but the other seven were still there. Two of the London Societies had improved their positions, and there were now six dominant societies in point of size, of which four were London based societies.

Assets £million

	1929		1939
Halifax	59.3	Halifax	129.1
Abbey Road	19.1	Abbey Road	51.4
Leeds Permanent	12.0	Leeds Permanent	41.7
Woolwich Equitable	11.4	Woolwich Equitable	40.1
Bradford Third	11.3	National	35.7
National	9.9	Co-op Permanent	31.2
Huddersfield	9.8	Leicester Permanent	16.2
Co-op Permanent	9.6	Bradford Third	15.5

The growth of the large societies brought problems of office accommodation for the ever-increasing staffs, and of adequate strong room space to house the deeds of the mortgaged properties. The Halifax acquired new offices in 1921, enlarged them in 1927, and within eighteen months were finding that more space was needed. Adjoining land and buildings were acquired and a new ex-

tension built and opened in 1931. The Abbey Road erected a new building in Baker Street which was opened in 1927, but it was soon necessary to acquire adjoining properties, and the enlarged Abbey House was opened in March 1932. The National, Leeds, Woolwich and Co-operative Permanent were all obliged to provide new and larger Head Office buildings. Most large societies introduced mechanical posting of accounts in the late 1920s or the early 1930s.

Mergers

After the Halifax union in 1928 there were some, but not many, mergers. Three Birmingham societies amalgamated, the Co-operative Permanent took over the Wellingborough, the Bristol and West absorbed two local small societies, the Steyning and the Littlehampton merged, and the Brighton and Sussex began their long sequence of take-overs (which continued after World War II) by absorbing half-a-dozen societies in the 1930s. It was found that instead of effecting an amalgamation on the Halifax pattern it was simpler for the small society to dissolve and transfer its engagements to the larger society at the same time encouraging its investors to transfer their monies to the latter society. This avoided the necessity of obtaining concurrence forms from shareholders holding two-thirds of the shares of each society.

There was a temptation, however, under this method, for the directors of the dissolving society to secure over-generous compensation for loss of office and distribute an equally over-generous part of the reserve funds to shareholders to persuade them to agree to the dissolution. The Chief Registrar commented in his Annual Reports on this tendency. The opportunity to amend and simplify amalgamation procedure seemed to have been lost when it was omitted from the 1939 Act. But circumstances arising from the war necessitated legislation dealing with friendly societies and other bodies coming within the province of the Chief Registrar. He took the opportunity to amend the Building Societies Acts by inserting in the Societies (Miscellaneous Provisions) Act 1940 clauses which provided that mergers or transfers of engagements could be confirmed without the consent of the holders of two-thirds of the shares. The interests of members and the public were safeguarded by powers conferred upon the Chief Registrar.

The Act also provided that no dissolution would have effect if the intention to transfer engagements was the motive. Instead, it provided that a society might undertake the engagements of another society by special resolution, or, with the consent of the Registrar, by an ordinary resolution of a general meeting or of the board of management.

Chapter 21

THE INTER-WAR LEADERS OF THE MOVEMENT

Of the acknowledged leaders of the building society movement during the inter-war years pride of place must undoubtedly go to Sir Enoch Hill and Sir Harold Bellman. Hill and Bellman were the two men who gave the movement its impetus in the 1920s and 1930s. They both sought personal publicity but each in his different way gained publicity for the building society movement just at the time when it needed to attract more and more funds to finance the growing number of house purchasers. They were ably backed up by others, notably Arthur Webb, T R Chandler, Walter Harvey, and behind the scenes but nevertheless exercising a notable influence on men and events, George Franey. There were other figures who commanded respect and whose contributions to the work of the Association were highly valued by their colleagues. Among them were Alderman C F Saunders of the Principality, G C Cutler of the West London (who served on the executive committee of the Association until his death at the age of 92), and David Lewis of the Cheltenham.

Enoch Hill

Enoch Hill was not only the chief executive of the largest society, but occupied the Chair of the Association from 1921 to 1933. He was therefore the mouthpiece of the movement through the years when home-ownership began to grow and building societies to expand.

Born in humble circumstances at Leek, Staffs, in 1865, he started work at the age of eight as a half-timer earning one shilling per week. In his teens he displayed an enterprising spirit running his own printing business and a bookseller's and stationer's shop. Eventually he became the secretary of the Leek United Building Society, and when the Halifax in 1903 advertised for a secretary he applied for the post. His was one of many applications, he was unknown to anyone connected with the Society and had never set foot in Yorkshire. What brought his name under serious consideration was the manner in which he presented his application for the job. He made use of his printing experience preparing a brochure which included printed copies of his application and testimonials, and providing a copy for each member of the Halifax Board. As a

result two members of the Board were deputed to visit Hill in Leek to see him and the offices of the Leek Society. The Leek was a small society compared with the Halifax, but Hill had doubled its assets and could show evidence of a well-run society. He was offered the Halifax post at the then not inconsiderable salary of £600 per annum. He was thirty-seven years of age.

Hill set about the task of running the Halifax with great vigour. It grew rapidly and by 1913 it could claim to be the largest society in terms of assets, a position it has held ever since. But he also transformed its mortgage business. The Halifax had been content to invest its funds upon a variety of securities and to grant large mortgages. It had at all times welcomed owner-occupiers but had not succeeded in making that class of borrowers its mainstay. In 1904 Hill set out to alter the emphasis of the Society's lending policy. The owner-occupier was to be encouraged. On freehold houses up to £300 loans of 90 per cent instead of 75 per cent were to be available; on houses valued at between £300 and £400 loans of 85 per cent, and on houses valued at between £400 and £600 loans of 80 per cent were offered. On leasehold houses the advance was to be 5 per cent less in each price range. This had a marked effect on the Halifax's business as Hill told the Association Conference in 1911. In eight years the amount outstanding on mortgages under £500 had risen from £207,000 to £947,000, whilst the total amount outstanding on mortgages over £5,000 had fallen from £516,000 to £288,000.

Hill became a member of the Executive Committee of the Association in 1914. Before that he had prodded and criticised the Committee at annual general meetings, suggesting that it might be more active on behalf of the movement. When he became Chairman in 1921 the hope was expressed that he would give effect to some of the ideas which he had advanced in earlier years. It seemed to some, however, that he and the Committee generally were content to carry on in much the same way as they had done in the past. Hill did not seek reform. He was nevertheless a great publicist for the Halifax and for the movement as a whole.

Hobson wrote, "Hill had some of the defects of his qualities. He could hardly be called a modest man. He was not at all averse from self-advertisement and in fact indulged in it quite freely. It was part of a certain flamboyence of character, a revulsion very likely from the severity of his youthful environment and up-bringing".* That flamboyant trait did, however, serve to make him the spokesman for the movement at a time when building societies were beginning to expand. And in his speeches he was a fervent missionary for home-ownership and savings. A typical paragraph from one of his speeches in 1930 runs "We are banded together as co-workers or missionaries in a great and noble cause. We

*op. cit. p.63

are striving to create and foster a spirit of self-help, expressed by home-ownership, by individual endeavour, combined with the will and power to give help to others. We have been trusted with the fruits of great thrift efforts on the part of our members which it is our duty to protect and safeguard".

And he also proclaimed "I think the building society movement to-day con-stitutes one of the greatest domestic romances in the history of our country in recent times. I do not know of anything more thrilling, anything more calculable of creating happiness and joy than for a man and woman to have redeemed a mortgage debt, going proudly home with their title deeds in their pocket feeling that they have a roof over their heads as long as life lasts, independently of anything or any authority".

Hill reigned contentedly over the Halifax and the Association steering the Halifax to new records each year and presiding at the Association's Annual Meetings with a keen sense of the publicity value to be extracted from them for building societies. He had parliamentary ambitions and stood as Conservative candidate at four elections but without success. He was knighted in 1928.

Harold Bellman

Harold Bellman joined the Board of the Abbey Road Society in 1918, became Assistant Secretary in June 1920 and Secretary in 1921. Every bit as ambitious and publicity minded as Enoch Hill, Bellman had the advantage of being based in London, which provided him with opportunities for wide contacts. But first he had to create his own power base. In 1921 the Abbey Road was a £1 million society compared with the Halifax's £12 million. Bellman acted in two ways. He began the rapid expansion of the Abbey Road which raised its assets to £3.6 million in 1925 and then in a most spectacular leap to £19 million in 1929. That advance made it by far the largest London society and second only in the country to the Halifax.

Secondly, he was the moving spirit behind the formation of the Metropolitan Association in 1922, acting as secretary for a year or so before being appointed Chairman. This gave him a useful platform and a loyal following among the London managers and directors. His eyes were soon set on a seat on the Council of the parent Association which like Hill before him he felt could be doing more. At the Annual Meeting in 1922 he said "I think there are some of us, while not unmindful of the records of the past are a little impatient about the future. We feel that the organisation of the Association to-day is not adequate for the status of a great and growing movement". The following year he was elected to the Council and found a congenial and apt outlet for his energies and talents in the Chairmanship of the newly formed Public Relations Committee.

Walter Harvey

Herbert Ashworth

James Higham

Harold Bellman

Enoch Hill

Thomas R. Chandler

George Franey

Arthur Webb

Bellman had a flair for organisation and administration which enabled him to create a well-run society which, although it expanded rapidly, was at all times financially sound and ably staffed. The Abbey Road set new and higher standards in building society advertising, an example which was followed by other societies. In 1930 he was made Managing Director, was knighted in 1932, and became Chairman of the Abbey Road in 1937.

Hill and Bellman were now running the two largest societies and both of them were making the most of the publicity to be derived from their own society's meetings, branch openings and record figures; from the Association's activities; and from international gatherings at home and abroad. Both societies invited each year to their Annual General Meetings some prominent politician or well-known public figure which tended to increase attendances and gain national reportage.

By 1933 the time had come for Hill to retire from the Chair of the Association. He was approaching seventy and his creative years were in the past. It was inevitable that he should be succeeded by Bellman. There were those who thought that Arthur Webb of the Co-operative Permanent had claims to the Chair. But no one could deny that Bellman was the man best fitted for the job, although there were some who admitted it only with reluctance, for the aggressive, expansionist policy of the Abbey Road had not endeared him to all. Some of the resentment against that policy was to colour the reactions to his efforts to impose the Code of Ethics.

It must be acknowledged, however, that it was Hill and Bellman between them who put building societies on the map in the inter-war years. Not only their own societies gained but so did the whole movement.

Arthur Webb

Arthur Webb, son of Thomas E. Webb, the first President of the Co-operative Permanent, was first associated with that Society as an agent when serving as Assistant Secretary of the Battersea and Wandsworth Co-operative Society. He was appointed Secretary of the Co-operative Permanent in 1892, eight years after its formation and at a time when its assets amounted to no more than £25,000. One who knew him well has written "He had at the outset to do everything for the Society, with at times only part of an office and no assistance. He laboured in season and out of season. Few Co-operative Conferences in the South were missed by him. He could be seen and heard anywhere and everywhere among groups of co-operators and other working people, advocating, propagating and planning. Once a week, at the early hour of 6.00 a.m.

he could be seen in Covent Garden placing leaflets in the *Co-operative News* before it was distributed to societies in the South".*

Under his guidance and largely by his personal efforts the Society forged ahead and by 1913 its assets exceeded half a million pounds and it had over 10,000 accounts. This was exceptionally good progress especially bearing in mind that the period from 1892 to 1913 covered the Liberator and Birkbeck crashes. Webb had laid the foundations on which the Co-operative Permanent was to grow rapidly after 1919, and still under his direction take its place as one of the major societies. He was Managing Director from 1928 to 1939, President from 1939 to 1942, and remained a director until he retired in 1951. He died at the age of 84 in 1952.

Webb was elected to the Association Executive in 1903 and served until 1946. Thus he was one of the members of the Executive who when appointed, had a long experience and detailed knowledge of building society practice. He had as it were created a Society. But unlike some of those who had started their careers in the Victorian era, he was ready to take the opportunities which the post-1918 years provided. He was the first building society leader to take up the question of what part building societies could play in housing after World War 1.

As a Wimbledon councillor and a member of the Surrey County Council, Webb took a great part in educational activities. He was always ready to encourage vocational education and training for building society staffs, was a member of the original Council of the Institute and President 1939-41. The Co-operative Permanent was the first society to establish an independent actuarially-based superannuation fund.

Walter Harvey

Walter Harvey worked for the Yorkshire Penny Bank until his appointment as secretary of the Burnley Building Society in 1921. He was then in his late forties. Like Bellman he was one of the new men coming into the movement at the beginning of the expansive years. He had the advantage of his banking experience in the course of which he had been a branch manager and had also served in the head office of the bank. The transition to building society business presented few problems. Moreover there were few sizeable Lancashire societies and soon Harvey was opening branches in Liverpool, Manchester and other neighbouring towns. This first cluster of branches within easy reach was follow-

---

*Dr Albert Mansbridge *"Brick upon Brick"*. A history of the Co-operative Permanent Building Society 1934, p. 55.

ed by London and Birmingham offices, and the growth of the Society was adequate to keep it among the ten leading societies.

Harvey was soon elected to the Executive Committee of the Association and was soon playing a prominent role. Housing and taxation were his principal activities. We have already recounted his part in the Housing (Financial Provisions) Act of 1933. He was also involved in the struggle with the local authorities to obtain a form of guarantee acceptable to building societies. He was for a number of years the Chairman of the Income Tax Committee, and in that capacity was responsible for negotiating the composite rate arrangements. He succeeded Bellman as Chairman of the Association in 1937 when the understanding that a Chairman should serve for not more than two years was adopted.

Harvey's influence was exercised not only through the Association but by his regular monthly column in the *Gazette* which appeared first under the *nom-de-plume* "Observer" and later under his own name. He wrote his column for over twenty years commenting on a wide range of current topics. His views on financial matters were conditioned by his years in banking; he wrote much about housing – the shortcomings of local authorities, builders' excess profits, valuations, housing demand and house prices. Often – perhaps too often – his writings were no more than comments on cuttings from the national and local Press, but they were always of interest to readers of the *Gazette.*

His general attitude was far removed from the flights of rhetoric in which Hill indulged. He summed up his own attitude by saying ". . . one cannot help feeling that the claim to philanthropic service is overdone. I should like to see more stress on building societies as thrift institutions, conducted on efficient business lines, answering mainly as they certainly do, to the ordinary conditions of demand and supply, without any pretence of doing something for nothing".*

Thomas R. Chandler

T.R. Chandler of the Woolwich Equitable was a qualified actuary who in 1906 had taken up appointment as actuary to a large insurance companny in Amsterdam. Neither he nor his wife was particulary enamoured of life in that city, and on being approached on behalf of the Woolwich Board accepted appointment as Assistant Secretary of that Society, becoming Secretary in 1914. He became General Manager in 1929, and a year later a member of the Board. He was appointed Chairman of the Woolwich in October 1957 but died soon afterwards.

Prior to the Abbey Road Society's rapid expansion the Woolwich was the

*The Building Societies Gazette , January 1928, page 3.

largest London Society and Chandler served as a member of the Council. He was Deputy-Chairman from 1926 to 1933, stepping down in that year to enable Sir Enoch Hill to take that post on relinquishing the Chairmanship. He resumed the Deputy-Chairmanship in 1937 and served as Chairman 1939-40, holding that office for one year only at his own request.

Chandler was an able and much loved chief of the Woolwich. In the movement generally he was respected for his calm and dispassionate judgment. He loyally supported Bellman in his efforts to introduce the Code of Ethics. A behind-the-scenes man rather than a publicist, he exercised considerable influence in the deliberations of the Association Council.

George E. Franey

George E. Franey died in October 1974 in his hundredth year. He edited *The Building Societies' Gazette* from 1899 to 1947. But his contribution to the progress of the building society movement went beyond the influence he exerted through the *Gazette* , valuable as that was.

In January 1890 he entered the employment of T.A. Reed & Company and soon became Reed's right-hand man. Reed & Co were shorthand writers, but Reed had also taken on the publication of the *Gazette*. Franey was entrusted by his dying chief with the responsibility of carrying on the *Gazette*. It was only because Reed & Co were official reporters with a large Government and professional connection that Franey able to continue (as Reed had done before him) to subsidise the *Gazette* for some twenty years, after which it began to pay its way.

Franey in his capacity as an official shorthand writer gained a wide experience of men and affairs. Edward Montague, Secretary of State for India, appointed him as his private secretary in 1917-18 when Montague visited India and he was called upon to go back to India in a similar capacity to Lord Kennet, Chairman of the Royal Commission on Indian Finance and Currency in 1924 and 1925. There followed visits to Siam and South America, again with financial commissions of international importance.

He was therefore able to be of great assistance to both Hill and Bellman in the development of the international movement. He co-operated with Hill in reviving the International Congress in 1931 and again with Bellman in subsequent congresses. Testifying to his work on behalf of the International movement Sir Harold Bellman described him as "the producer, working behind the scenes, planning, interpreting, placating, missing the curtain calls, the

limelight and the applause, but earning the hearty good will and admiration of the entire cast".

But it was not only on the International scene that his influence was felt. The men who were at the head of affairs when building societies began their expansion in the 1920s had mainly come from small beginnings, were managing local societies and had a parochial outlook. Franey was able to advise them in their dealings with government, in their public relations, and indeed in their relations with each other. Building Societies owe him much.

Chapter 22

WORLD WAR II

The course of events in the building society movement during World War II
was in some respects reminiscent of that experienced in World War I. In both
there was an initial surge of withdrawals, a fall in mortgage lending and a
growth of liquidity in the culminating years. In both building societies were
marking time; total assets were little changed during the war years. In World
War II they amounted to £773 million in 1939 and had risen to no more than
£825 million by 1945. And in both periods there was a cessation of
housebuilding, a rise in the number of families and in consequence a growing
housing shortage.

But there were differences too. War damage was far more extensive in World
War II and was a more serious threat to building society finances. In contrast to
World War I, World War II was financed at low interest rates; as societies' liquidity ratio increased it became difficult to invest funds at remunerative rates,
and this had the effect of driving investors' rates to low levels.

Withdrawals

The aggressive intentions of Hitler and the Munich crises had given warning of
the possibility of war. Some societies had heeded the signs and increased their liquidity ratios. Others had ignored them. Of the eight largest societies only two
had to resort to bank loans in 1939, the Woolwich and the National, but both
societies had investments far outweighing the amount borrowed. A number of
smaller societies had bank loans of more than the sum invested in securities other
than mortgages. On the whole societies surmounted the initial impact of
withdrawals in the early months of the war. But with the advance of Germany
and the fall of France in 1940 a new wave of withdrawals had to be met. To
help the societies who were short of cash, the Government made a Defence
Regulation permitting societies to require six month's notice of withdrawal. The
Treasury issued a statement to make it clear that the Regulation was permissive
and that it was anticipated that the public would find no difficulty in withdrawing small sums. Some societies availed themselves of this relief but many were
able to pay withdrawals on a normal basis and did not need to invoke the

Regulation. Withdrawals continued to run at fairly high levels until 1942, but thereafter subsided.

War Damage

The threat of war and of damage by enemy aircraft had given rise well before 1939 to concern about the risks to property and how such risks should be covered. The Building Societies Association had made representations to the Government but was told in 1938 that it was not at that time prepared to institute a scheme of compulsory insurance. In January 1939 the Government announced that it planned a scheme which excluded the principle of insurance and placed liability upon the community as a whole. It was envisaged that no compensation would be paid until the total of losses was ascertained and then the Government would make a reasonable contribution. This was cold comfort for building societies since they would have to wait until the end of the war for all losses to be established and to know what compensation would be paid. Eventually the Government decided to introduce legislation embodying a scheme for compensation and compulsory contributions from all property owners. This was effected by the War Damage Act 1941. Compensation was to be of two kinds: a "cost of works" payment where the property was capable of being reinstated and a "value" payment where the property was completely destroyed. The contribution to be paid by property owners was fixed at two shillings in the pound based on the net annual value, payable annually for a period of five years.

Building societies were relieved that the uncertainty was at an end, although not so pleased that mortgagees (although in no sense the owners of their mortaged properties) were required to pay part of the borrower's contributions where the property had a net annual value of less than £150. This meant they had to pay on most of their securities. The amount payable by the mortgagee varied according to the amount of debt owing in relation to the purchase price, and was as high as two-thirds where the debt exceeded three-quarters of the purchase price.

The Association issued circulars and pamphlets outlining procedure under the Act, and gave a great deal of advice which was in turn used by societies to assist their borrowers in making claims. Many societies took it upon themselves to act on behalf of their customers in completing claim forms, inspecting damaged properties, preparing specifications, getting repairs done and resolving claims with the War Damage Commission. The borrower whose house had been completely wrecked was in a less fortunate position than one who was able to obtain a "cost of works" payment and have his house repaired. Compensation based on the 1939 valuation with interest at $2\frac{1}{2}$ per cent would be paid eventually. In the

meantime his mortgage interest would accrue at $4\frac{1}{2}$ per cent or 5 per cent. The War Damage Commission eased the situation somewhat by making interim payments up to a maximum of £800 to enable an owner to pay off or reduce his mortgage so that he could buy another house. The building societies, under the lead of the Halifax, decided in 1944 that they would also help by reducing their interest charges to $2\frac{1}{2}$ per cent in "value payment" cases.

Emergency Legislation

Emergency legislation was necessary, as in the 1914-18 war, to protect the position of those serving in the armed forces. Even before war was declared, reservists and territorial forces had been called up and their position had been protected. If they were borrowers, their mortgage repayments could be suspended. The Courts (Emergency Powers) Act 1939, extended relief to all those whose financial circumstances had been seriously affected by the war. Another Rent Act was passed which brought under control nearly all houses in the country.

Later, in 1940, when France had fallen and the threat of invasion had to be taken seriously, it was decided to evacuate families from certain vulnerable coastal areas. Defence (Evacuation Area) Regulations were made providing for a moratorium in those areas covering rents, rates, hire purchase and mortgage payments.

Thus building societies had perforce to accommodate many borrowers, civilians and serving men, by accepting reduced payments, interest only or no payment at all. Societies exercised tolerance and forbearance. They did not lose by doing so.

Interest Rates

The Government's policy was to maintain low interest rates throughout the war period, and in that it was successful. Bank Rate, initially and as a precautionary measure, was raised to 6 per cent on the outbreak of war, but by October had been reduced once again to 2 per cent. It was kept there. But taxation was severely increased. An interim budget in the Autumn of 1939 raised the standard rate of Income Tax to 7s. It went up to 7/6d and then 8/6d in two budgets in 1940. In 1941 it was raised to 10s. and stayed there. These increases meant that the composite rate paid by building societies on distributions to investors was raised sharply too. When the Standard Rate went up to 10s. the composite rate was raised to 5/9d. Building societies were being squeezed. Lending was minimal and mortgage balances were reducing. Liquidity was in-

creasing and it could not be employed to yield on average more than about $2\frac{1}{2}$ per cent.

Expenses were rising through war damage contributions and the cost of safeguarding records and securities. Narrowing margins meant that rates paid to investors had to be reduced. There were some who argued that borrowers should share in the sacrifice by submitting to an increase in the mortgage interest rate, but this was never seriously contemplated as a practicable course.

Beginning in 1940 there was a general reduction in investors' rates, first to $3\frac{1}{2}$ per cent for shares and $2\frac{1}{2}$ per cent for deposits, followed by a reduction to $2\frac{1}{2}$ per cent and $2\frac{1}{4}$ per cent in 1942. Thereafter as liquidity increased societies were compelled to place severe restrictions on the acceptance of new money and reduce rates still further – down to 2 per cent and even $1\frac{3}{4}$ per cent for new money, although the rate was held at $2\frac{1}{2}$ per cent for existing share accounts until the reduction in mortgage rates to 4 per cent in 1945 brought a reduction to $2\frac{1}{4}$ per cent on shares and $1\frac{3}{4}$ per cent on deposits from the beginning of 1946.

Like other societies the Halifax was severely restricting the inflow of money throughout 1944 and 1945, yet its liquidity was mounting rapidly; at the end of 1945 out of total assets of £135 million, investments and cash at banks accounted for £53 million. This was exceptional, but other societies had also increased their liquidity ratio to more than was comfortable, and the average for the movement as a whole was approximately 29 per cent.

Mortgage Lending

With no housebuilding and little buying and selling going on in the existing house market, mortgage lending fell to low levels. No more than £10 million was advanced in 1941. Thereafter it rose to £16 million in 1942, £28 million in 1943, and £52 million in 1944. With the ending of the war in 1945 and more activity in the house market, the year's lending rose sharply to £97 million. From 1943 onwards when societies were more liquid, competition developed for such mortgage business as was available. Already house prices were moving upwards and the Association issued a warning to societies against accepting what might be only temporary increases in valuations. The Association again became concerned about the terms upon which loans were being made. An attempt was made to frame regulations but it came to nothing.

It was obvious that prices were bound to go on rising in view of the evident shortage of houses and the demand which was showing itself even before the war ended. Was it possible to control them? Could a practicable scheme be devised and operated? The Government thought these questions ought to be examined, and in February 1945 appointed a committee to enquire into the

possibility. W.S. Allison of the Scottish Amicable was a member. The Committee reported in August 1945 that it considered selling prices should be controlled and recommended a scheme which in their view was practicable. The maximum price would be based on the value with vacant possession on 31st March 1939 plus an addition of 50 per cent. The 1939 value would be fixed by a District Valuer. The scheme would operate for a period of five years and the percentage addition would be reviewed after these years.

The vendor of a house would be required to obtain a certificate of value stating the maximum permitted price, and the purchaser would have to produce this certificate when the conveyance was sent for stamping, together with declarations signed by himself and the vendor, stating the price paid and that there had been and would be no other payment or arrangement in respect of the sale resulting in additional payment to the vendor or to anyone else. It would be made an offence to sell or offer to sell or to buy or offer to buy at more than the maximum permitted price.

The Committee recognised that the scheme would throw a heavy burden on the District Valuers and would depend on whether they could be adequately staffed. It was also admitted that at the controlled prices there would be several applicants for any desirable house placed on the market. They examined a number of suggestions as to how a purchaser should be selected, most of which involved the local authority in making a choice based on need. The Committee found themselves unable to make any definite recommendations on this thorny subject.

The Report came in for a good deal of criticism mainly on the grounds that the District Valuers would be overwhelmed by the work entailed, that house sales were going to be held up, that there would be evasion and that the legislation entailed would be very complicated. Nothing more was heard of the proposals.

There was, however, some information in the Report of the extent to which prices had risen between March 1943 and March 1945. The Committee obtained figures from the Valuation Office comparing prices obtained in this period of such houses in England and Wales as had also been sold in the five years ended 31st March 1939. The percentage increase in prices at 31st March 1943 was 33.7, at 31st March 1944, 55, and at 31st March 1945, 83.3. In Scotland the increase was 43.5 per cent in 1943 and had risen to 93.4 per cent by March 1945. By the time the Report was issued prices were almost certainly double 1939 prices and house-owners would hardly have welcomed control at the level suggested by the Committee.

Mortgage Interest Rates

The rate on existing mortgages was maintained at $4\frac{1}{2}$ per cent until 1945 but new loans were made at 5 per cent. In August 1943 the Co-operative Permanant announced that it would make £1 million available at 4 per cent and would agree repayment terms up to thirty years. This £1 million was quickly taken up and the Society reverted to $4\frac{1}{2}$ per cent from the beginning of 1944. This was merely a gesture and had no immediate impact. But in September 1945 the Co-operative Permanent cut its rate to 4 per cent and announced at the same time that existing mortgages would be reduced to 4 per cent from the beginning of 1946. The Huddersfield followed two days later and soon the bulk of the movement had announced similar cuts.

There was strong feeling among societies (expressed at several District Association meetings) that this rather ragged way of making an important change in interest rates was undesirable. This was in fact a turning point in leading eventually to the Association making recommendations and requiring adequate notice from member societies when they proposed to act on their own.

There was some concern, too, that the mortgage rate had fallen to as low a level as 4 per cent. What would happen if interest rates began to rise? It was at this point in time that societies began to think seriously about introducing an interest variation clause in their mortgage deeds. Some societies, especially in the South, were against such a step on traditional grounds. They had always believed that a borrower should have a firm contract and know where he stood on interest rates throughout the term of his mortgage. But times were against them.

Mergers

The war period was eventful so far as mergers were concerned. The number of societies fell from 960 in 1939 to 890 by 1945. This was due in the main to the absorption of a number of small societies by larger societies, or unions between local societies. Not all merger proposals were accepted by members. In 1941 the Dewsbury Society directors agreed terms under which they would be taken over by the Halifax. The Dewsbury was a sound society with assets of less than £2 million. It was obviously going to be swallowed by its much larger neighbour. The members of the Dewsbury did not like the prospect and at the special meeting rejected the proposals and passed a vote of no confidence in the board of directors. At the next Annual Meeting they voted all but two of the directors off the board, replacing them by some of those who had opposed the proposed merger.

In 1942 when the subject of amalgamation was under consideration by the

Reconstruction Committee appointed by the Association and therefore in the words of the *Gazette* might be held to be *sub judice,* the Co-operative Permanent embarked on an intensive and controversial campaign to persuade small and medium societies throughout the country of the virtues of merging with a larger unit. A circular letter was issued and representatives from the Co-operative Permanent were sent to call on societies. The letters and the follow-up calls evoked bitter and heated protests from District Associations. It was felt that the issue was being unfairly prejudged, especially as the suggestion that the question of amalgamations should be considered by the Reconstruction Committee had come from Arthur Webb of the Co-operative Permanent Society. Moreover, it was considered that undue pressure was being put on small societies suffering from a shortage of staff. The Midland was the most militant of the District Associations and the Council endorsed a strongly worded protest which that Association submitted.

The *Gazette* hoped that the Co-operative Permanent would see its way to end an embarrassing and unedifying situation. The Society did decide to send out no more unsolicited letters on the subject of amalgamation, although it felt aggrieved that so much resentment had been aroused. It also maintained that the desirability of the campaign was purely a matter for the discretion of its board of directors. The Co-operative Permanent did not abandon its search for amalgamations, and it did succeed in taking over a number of smaller societies. But it never succeeded in attracting any of the larger societies in its campaign which lasted for seven or eight years.

There were more spectacular events in the merger field. In the Autumn of 1943 the Abbey Road and the National surprised the movement by announcing proposals to unite to form the Abbey National with assets of £80 million. The reason given for this merger was that it would provide greater opportunities of public service for their resources if combined in a single organisation. The proposal was approved by the members of both societies and became effective from the beginning of 1944.

This merger was followed by an equally surprising announcement in May 1944. The third and fourth largest societies – the Leeds and the Woolwich – proposed to unite, with the prospect of two smaller societies – the Liverpool Investment and the Dunfermline – joining the new society at a later stage to make a combined society of £86 million, which would have put it slightly ahead of the Abbey National. It was to be called the British Building Society and it was claimed that the combination of North and South interests would give the society the advantage of a nation-wide field of activity. Opinions varied about the reasons for the merger. Some saw it as a race for assets. Some were of the

view that the real need for amalgamations lay among the smaller range of societies. One newspaper went so far as to say that it was no secret that there had been encouragment, not to say pressure, from the Bank of England on the grounds that larger units would enable building societies to play a part in financing building programmes at cheaper rates.

This merger, however, came to nothing. The Woolwich members passed the necessary resolution, but there was opposition at the Leeds meeting and the shareholders did not give the necessary majority. The project was dropped. The Leeds' directors decided to take no further action. No doubt they had come to the conclusion that their militant members were unlikely to change their minds and were a body to be respected. Besides, the fate of the Dewsbury directors could not have escaped their notice.

A more successful move was the merger of the Leeds Provincial and Bradford Third in 1945. This created the Provincial Society with assets of nearly £29 million.

The Reconstruction Committee

With the experience of World War I to go on, and the visible evidence of destruction before their eyes, both the Government and the Building Societies Association recognised at an early stage that it was necessary to do some thinking about the ways and means of producing an adequate housing programme. The Association appointed a Committee on Post-War Reconstruction as early as 1942. It had a wide brief. Not only was it asked to consider what changes in practice and procedure appeared desirable and practicable, but also the general relationship of building societies to post-war reconstruction, with particular reference to the lines on which they might usefully and prudently participate in post-war housing developments. Lord Sankey (a former Lord Chancellor who served as President of the Association from 1940 to 1947) agreed to serve as Chairman of the Committee and the members were drawn from within and without the movement. It published an interim report on housing standards which consisted of a number of admirable but rather pious suggestions on site planning, bye-laws, design and quality of workmanship. On the question of how building societies could best participate in post-war housing the Committee came to the conclusion that nothing constructive could be put forward until the Government's own policy was known.

It was widely assumed that the great need would be for houses to rent which would certainly require to be subsidised in view of the rise of building costs. And the Committee perhaps felt that unless the government was prepared to make subsidies available to private enterprise there was little point in trying to make

any positive suggestions. The Committee did not consider how to bring owner-occupation within reach of a much larger section of the community. Too pessimistic a view was taken at this time of the possibility of a further extension of home-ownership. The need was for lower deposits and longer repayment periods, with perhaps Government guarantees and grants to ex-service men. The case for this kind of encouragement was not stated and an opportunity was lost. Too many within the movement still regarded the 10 per cent deposit and the 20-year repayment period as the keystones of prudent lending.

The Private Enterprise Sub-Committee

But if the Reconstruction Committee had little to suggest the Report on Private Enterprise Housing by a sub-committee of the Central Housing Advisory Committee* was a much more positive document. No doubt that was in no small measure due to the fact that both Sir Harold Bellman and David Smith (Halifax) were members of the sub-committee. Perhaps they and their colleagues on the Association Council preferred that recommendations on private enterprise housing should emanate from this outside body rather than from the Association's own Reconstruction Committee.

The sub-committee recommended that private enterprise should be encouraged to participate in the immediate post-war building programme. Private enterprise must produce a larger proportion of houses for letting and the participation of building societies and similar bodies was essential if this was to be achieved. When private enterprise was meeting the same needs as local authorities it should be eligible for the same subsidy.

The subsidy proposals were accepted by the Government, as also were recommendations by the sub-committee for the raising of the limit of £800 in respect of advances under the Small Dwellings Act and for the support and development of the National House Builders' Registration scheme for maintaining good standards of building.

The sub-committee's Report was also notable for a comprehensive review of private enterprise housing in the inter-war years. But in its conclusions the whole emphasis was on the need for houses for letting. It failed, like the Reconstruction Committee, to appreciate that there would be a strong demand for home-ownership.

*Now defunct, but which for many years served to advise the Minister concerned with housing. Its membership was broadly based and usually included two building society representatives.

Other Reports

Four more Reports were published in the war period of which mention should be made. The Barlow Report on the Distribution of the Industrial Population laid stress on the economic, social and strategic disadvantages of concentration of industry in relatively few densely populated areas. The remedy was the enlargement of some small towns and the creation of new ones. This led eventually to the passing of the New Towns Act in 1946.

The Scott Report on Land Utilisation in Rural Areas dealt with the rural areas where housing had been sadly neglected. Between the wars there was a general housing shortage which was not satisfied to anything like the degree that the corresponding shortage in the towns was met. The Report envisaged a resuscitation of village life and the countryside by improved housing and living conditions, and by equal economic, social and educational opportunities.

The Uthwatt Report dealt with the vexed question of compensation and betterment in relation to land use and proposed a Development Rights scheme under which the right to develop all undeveloped land would vest in the State and compensation on a global basis would be paid to landowners. This was to lead to the Town and Country Planning Act of 1947.

The fourth Report was that of the Dudley Committee on the Design of Dwellings which looked at the recommendations of the Tudor Walters Committee in the light of inter-war experience and made a number of proposals for the types of house and space arrangements required by the working-class family with children.

Government Plans

With the publication of these various Reports the Government was not short of advice on a whole range of housing and planning problems. The first decision made by the war-time Government was to erect temporary houses as soon as hostilities were over. The aim was to produce a limited number of dwellings which could be manufactured and erected with a minimum of on-site labour. Accordingly types were evolved which utilised non-traditional methods and materials, the bulk of the work being done in factories. In March 1944 the Prime Minister (Winston Churchill) stated that the first stage in housing would be the reconditioning of war-damaged houses by the end of the year, the second would be the provision of 500,000 temporary houses and the third would be the provision of 300,000 permanent houses in the first two years of peace.

But by March 1945 the Government had made significant changes in its housing plans. The number of temporary houses envisaged by the Prime

Minister had been cut back to 250,000 in the Autumn of 1944, and even this target was seen as difficult of fulfilment. There was not sufficient steel available for the original Portal House; other types were going to cost as much as permanent houses and local authorities were reluctant to make sites available which they needed for permanent houses. So the intention was to provide some temporary houses but to concentrate the main effort on permanent homes. The Government had to face criticism that its building programme was inadequate and that there were too many departments concerned with housing. The Government's answer was that the real problem was building labour which had been severely reduced by the call-up of men to the services.

In May 1945 the coalition Government resigned and a Conservative Administration was formed pending a General Election in July. This caretaker Government announced that if returned at the General Election it would introduce legislation to enable local authorities to make grants in respect of small private houses built for sale or for letting. The Exchequer would bear the whole of these grants up to the first £100 and half of any grant in excess of £100 subject to a maximum from the Exchequer of £150. Payment would be subject to conditions as to size, selling price or rent. There would be an over-riding maximum price of £1200. This promise was of no avail. A Labour Government was elected in July 1945 with a substantial majority and very different ideas on housing.

Chapter 23

YEARS OF FRUSTRATION 1945-51

The Post-War Housing Shortage

The housing achievement of the inter-war years was impressive. Although it was not until 1928 that the first million houses were built, in the following eleven years a further three million were produced. Altogether 4.3 million houses were built, of which 1.3 million were erected by local authorities and 3 million by private enterprise. The proportion of owner-occupiers in England and Wales had increased from 10 per cent in 1919 to nearly 30 per cent in 1939, although the increase was considerably less in Scotland and Northern Ireland. Building societies had financed most of the houses which were bought and the loans on new houses had been by far the major factor in building society growth.

Housing shortages had largely been overtaken by 1939; both those arising from World War I and the additional needs which came from the substantial increase in the number of separate families. There were some local shortages mainly arising from the migration of population southwards. And, although the total number of dwellings had risen to approximately 12.5 million, not everyone was well housed. There were still too many old, decrepit and out-moded dwellings. Nevertheless, the point had been reached where the main effort in future years would be directed to the replacement of the slums and the near-slums. That would mean more re-housing of poorer families in houses to let at subsidised rents.

The demands of those who could afford to buy houses appeared to have been largely satisfied and building society leaders could not conceive that there was scope for a further substantial increase in the proportion of home-owners. Indeed, Walter Harvey and David Smith voiced their fears that there might not be enough mortgages from owner-occupiers to maintain business at the levels to which societies had become accustomed in the 1930s. Both men in public speeches envisaged that it might be necessary to broaden the bases of business. Addressing the Annual Conference in 1938, Harvey said that in the search for "fresh woods and pastures new" there would probably be greater regard to industrial and business premises, blocks of residential flats and the smaller types of

rentable dwellings. These securities would offer channels for the absorption of some societies' funds.

This concern about the future level of business was soon dispersed by the consequences of war. As in World War I house building ceased; but not only were there no additions to the stock of houses, there was a considerable reduction from the extensive war damage which the country suffered. Some 200,000 houses were completely destroyed, 250,000 rendered unfit for habitation and a further 250,000 were severely damaged. Furthermore, a large number of houses were requisitioned for military and civil defence purposes or converted to offices by firms bombed out of their business premises. On the other hand, the number of families increased by some 850,000 between 1939 and 1945. By the end of the war something approaching 1.3 million houses were needed to satisfy immediate needs. Bearing in mind that housing is an on-going problem – houses go on decaying or falling out of use as dwellings and the number of families change – there was a large house-building programme ahead.

Bevan's Housing Policy

In July 1945 a Labour Government came into power with a large majority – the first Labour Government to have a majority over all other parties combined. Aneurin Bevan, a prominent left-wing member, who during the war had, on many occasions, been a severe critic of the Coalition Government, was appointed Minister of Health. He had never before held office, but soon demonstrated that he was to be reckoned as a powerful member of the Cabinet. His two main tasks at the Ministry of Health were to establish the National Health Service and to deal with the housing shortage. For, although a proposal to establish a separate Ministry of Housing had figured prominently in Labour's election manifesto, it came to nothing. Whitehall quickly convinced the Government that it would entail legislative and administrative changes which would hamper rather rather than promote the housing effort.

Bevan soon made it clear that local authorities were to be responsible for the bulk of the housing programme. This was not surprising in the light of his political philosophy. Nor was it unreasonable. If the Conservatives had been returned to power they would have likewise looked to the local authorities for much of the initial housing effort. For the view was generally held that the immediate need was for houses to let, that they would have to be subsidised and that, having regard to their inter-war experience in this field, this was a task that local authorities could best fulfil.

What aroused the wrath of both private house builders and building societies was the way in which they were relegated to a minor role. To ensure that labour

and materials were not diverted from local authority contracts the Minister decreed that private housing could only be undertaken by licence granted by a local authority. Moreover, licences must not be issued for more than one in five of the houses built in any local authority area. Where houses were built for sale, the selling price was not to exceed £1,200 (£1,300 in the London area) and houses were not to be resold within four years at more than the original selling prices. Bevan also made it clear that if local authorities were slow to promote their own housing schemes he would suspend their power to issue licences, though why the private builder should be restricted because of the lethargy of a public body was not apparent. If a local authority was failing to build houses it was reasonable to suppose that there was a case for giving the private builder more rather than less opportunity to supply the needs of the district.

Moneylenders

But it was not only the severe restrictions on private enterprise building which upset the building societies. In his first major speech on housing in the House of Commons, Bevan spoke of them as once having been engaged in building but now having become nothing but money-lending societies. He said that he did not propose to let loose their vast mass of accumulated money on to a scarcity market and to encourage people to "require mortgages that would be gravestones *(sic)* round their necks". In another part of his speech he spoke of speculative builders having in the past been supported enthusiastically and even voraciously by money-lending organisations.

The House of Commons was accustomed to Bevan's flamboyant and often vitriolic speeches. Building societies, however, were deeply shocked and resentful of the contemptuous way in which he had described their activities. They were more accustomed to the praise which their achievements so frequently elicited from Ministers and other public figures. They were highly sensitive to criticism, and Bevan had not even offered fair criticism but had dismissed them as voracious moneylenders. Building society chairmen and managers up and down the country voiced their anger and refuted the charges. The Press joined in condemnation of the offending remarks. Perhaps the *Economist* summed it up as well as anyone when it observed that Bevan's remarks were a travesty of the building societies' pre-war work, "though how far it reflects a considered judgment upon them is not clear — it may represent no more than ideological line-shooting against the societies of a type in which Mr. Bevan frequently indulged long before he took office".

Labour and Materials

The first task of Bevan and the Government was to expand the labour force and the production of building materials. The number of men engaged in the building trades had been approximately halved during the war years. Moreover, this reduced labour force included an unduly high proportion of old men and youths, so that the output of which the industry was capable had fallen far more than was suggested by the manpower figures alone. This problem had been foreseen by the war-time government and plans had been made to ensure that there would be a rapid intake into the building trades once hostilities had ceased. Those plans were successfully implemented and by 1946 the labour force had been expanded to one million, although productivity was not by any means back to the pre-war norm. Building materials were a problem too, and building operations were often held up owing to the difficulties of obtaining delivery.

It was not only house building that was demanding labour and materials. There was the need for other types of new buildings – factories, offices, schools and hospitals. There was also repair work to buildings of all kinds which had been kept to a minimum since 1939. There was a huge backlog of demand for exterior painting, internal decoration, repairs to roofs and fencing and other maintenance jobs, which even in normal times absorb a considerable amount of labour and materials. It was deemed essential that such work should be controlled, and accordingly licences were required not only for private houses but also for any repair work costing more than £10.

The housing record of the first years under Bevan was probably as good as could have been expected from any Government. It cannot be assessed solely on the number of new houses built. Account must also be taken of war-damaged houses repaired, of conversions and adaptions, and of temporary houses. Thus in 1946 220,000 additional dwellings were provided; in 1947 240,000; and in 1948 284,000. And in the latter year the building of new houses was really getting under way: 227,000 were built in that year, of which local authorities were responsible for 190,000.

The Financial Crisis of 1947

Unfortunately, troubles beset the Government, which led to curbs on the expanding house building programme. The year 1947 began badly with the coldest winter since 1880. Snow, frost, floods and storms led to an acute coal shortage and fuel crisis, the closing of factories and plants (unemployment rose to 2.75 million). The economy was in deep trouble. The American and Canadian loans made available at the end of the war were being used up far more quickly

than had been anticipated, the recovery in production and the increase in exports were both disappointing, and the drain on resources from maintaining armed forces in too many places round the world was becoming insupportable. Demands were made for a curtailment of capital expenditure, including that on housing. Bevan resisted these demands.

Then came the convertibility crisis. Under the terms of the American loan, an undertaking had been given to make sterling convertible by July 1947. Although it could have asked for postponement, the Government decided to fulfil the obligation. But everyone wanted dollars. The drain on the reserves and the remainder of the U.S. loan was such that convertibility had to be abandoned after six weeks. Further cuts and restrictions were inevitable. The meat ration was reduced, the basic petrol ration was withdrawn and foreign travel allowances were stopped. The Treasury demanded cuts in housing in order to reduce dollar payments for timber as well as to cut capital expenditure. The curbs on housing expenditure could not have much effect on the 1948 programme owing to the number of housing starts, but were designed to reduce the number of houses built in 1949 to a total of 140,000. In fact the cuts were never enforced in full but do explain why house building levelled off at about 200,000 per annum for the remaining years that Labour were in power.

Devaluation of the pound in 1949 resulted in further cuts and for a few months the issue of licences for private houses was suspended. The issue was resumed in December 1949 on a 1 in 10 basis. Later the ratio was restored to 1 in 5.

During the period from 1945-1951 in which Labour held office some one million permanent houses were built, of which 800,000 were erected by local authorities and 180,000 by private enterprise. Taking into account temporary houses, repairs and conversions, some one and a half million families were provided with homes.

Criticisms of Bevan's Policy

Taking it by and large this achievement probably surpassed any programme envisaged before the Labour Government took office. It would undoubtedly have been greater had it not been for the events of 1947 and 1949. Moreover, the shortage of building materials and fitments was a severely limiting factor as Harold Macmillan was to find in the succeeding years when as Minister of Housing he set upon the task of building 300,000 houses a year.

Bevan's critics (building societies among them) argued that a more flexible policy would have produced more houses, especially after the devaluation crisis

of 1949. That was the time to give more freedom to the private builder, the building society and the home buyer. He chose to do the opposite. Instead of leaving the private builders to shoulder some of the general housing burden, he curbed their activities along with those of the local authorities. Undoubtedly his housing policy was determined by his political philosophy. It was probably too rigid a policy. Some have said that his principal concern was the establishment of the new Health Service and that housing suffered in consequence. To some extent that may be true, but it is also true that he was determined to build houses to let and was unwilling to concede that houses built for owner-occupation would also help to reduce the housing shortage.

Plentiful Mortgage Business

Building societies were disappointed by the limited opportunities they were given to participate in the housing drive. There were two reasons. In the 1930s new houses had become the main source of mortgage business and they still hoped for it to become so again. They also had a deep conviction that they had a useful part to play in meeting the housing shortage.

They were not, however, short of mortgage business in these years. Advances for the year 1946 were £188 million, nearly double the figure for 1945. They rose to £240 million in 1947, and from 1948 to 1951 averaged £270 million a year. These were well above the record inter-war figure for 1936 of £140 million.

Part of this advance business came from the sale of houses to sitting-tenants. The scale on which rented houses were turned over to owner-occupation was far greater than occurred after World War I. Two groups of houses were involved. There were some six million houses erected before 1919 which included many well-built if somewhat outmoded houses which were eminently suitable as mortgage securities. Many of these houses were let at low rents because they had been continuously subject to rent control since 1915. The other group was some 500,000 houses built for letting between the wars, many of which, as we have seen, had been erected in the late 1930s. These had not been subject to rent control when first let, and being modern houses were even more attractive as mortgage securities, and from the point of view of the tenants were exceedingly good purchases.

Many of these modern houses were sold in blocks by their original owners to speculators specialising in selling off to tenants. Such speculators needed to offer the tenants a mortgage equal to the price, and so long as the price did not exceed 75 per cent or 80 per cent of the vacant possession value, there were many

building societies willing to make such loans. Not all, however. Notably, the Halifax stood out against 100 per cent loans, however good the bargain which the tenant was being offered. In 1949 the President of the Halifax (Algernon Denham) stated that it had always been his view that the Society had a primary duty to ensure that the borrower fortified his security by a reasonable cash stake. He said that he regretted the growing practice of making 100 per cent advances to tenant purchasers. He argued that it was beyond dispute that over-generous lending of this character stimulated the inflationary trend in house prices to the disadvantage of the house owner. Other societies were not impressed by this argument and were happy to grant as many 100 per cent loans as they were asked for. It was safe business and it was extending home-ownership on favourable terms to families who would otherwise have remained as tenants.

Just as important as sitting-tenant business was that which came from exchanges of houses already owner-occupied. After six years of near immobility there was a fairly large movement of population and a higher turnover of houses. Inflation and the housing shortage resulted in higher prices in consequence of which larger mortgage advances were required. As we have seen, prices had risen during 1944 and 1945, and at the end of the latter year were about double pre-war. They rose rapidly throughout 1946 and 1947 to approximately $2\frac{1}{4}$ times 1939 prices. Following the financial crisis of 1947 and the severe measures taken to improve the balance of payments, house prices fell slightly in 1948. They resumed their upward trend in the following year, and by the end of 1951 were about $3\frac{1}{4}$ times 1939 prices.

Did building societies fuel this price increase? This question was raised in March 1951 in a leading article in the *Financial Times*, which stated: "whereas in the inter-war period it (the building society movement) was engaged in financing the construction and purchase of new houses, its role in the post-war years had consisted much more in financing the transfer of already existing houses from one set of owners to another. The funds which the movement has so readily provided in ever-increasing volume for this purpose must clearly have played an important part in the post-war inflation of property values". But this assertion ignored the strong demand for owner-occupied houses at a time of acute shortage, the fact that half the rise had taken place by 1945 and that building costs had risen almost in parallel with house prices. Nor does it take into account that building societies, in deciding the amounts to advance on houses offered as securities, were apprehensive about a possible decline in values and had their eyes fixed firmly on 1939 values as a base figure from which they could determine a prudent lending policy.

Interest Rates and Liquidity

The mortgage rate had fallen to 4 per cent in 1945 and it remained there until (as we shall see in the next chapter) Bank Rate and the general level of interest rates began to rise in 1952. Thus, for a period of over six years the mortgage rate remained unchanged at its lowest ever level.

Hugh Dalton, the first Chancellor of the Exchequer in the 1945 Labour Government, was determined to carry on with the low interest rate policy which had been pursued before and during the war, notwithstanding that conditions were very different from the 1930s in so far as full employment and inflation were producing pressures on the economy. In October 1946 he declared that the cheap money policy should continue to be pressed resolutely home. In January 1947 he issued the Treasury 2½ per cent Stock redeemable (at the Government's option) after 1975, which came to be known as "Daltons". He also enabled local authorities to borrow from the Public Works Loan Board at 2½ per cent for housing and other purposes.

But events were moving remorselessly to produce a higher level of rates. Huge amounts of gilt-edged stocks had to be issued to compensate the holders of shares in the railway, electricity and gas companies with the Government had nationalised. By the beginning of 1948 it had become clear that the 2½ per cent line could not be held. New gilt-edged stocks were issued at 3 per cent and the cost of borrowing by local authorities was raised to that figure. By April 1948 the 2½ per cent Daltons had fallen to 75 – the holders (some building societies among them) had seen their capital diminish by one-quarter in the space of eighteen months. By May 1950 new gilt-edged issues had to be offered at 3½ per cent. The rate of interest on Saving Certificates and Defence Bonds was increased.

It was a gradual progress towards a higher level which would ultimately affect building society rates. Nevertheless, building society investment remained attractive, and despite the higher level of advances, most societies had to maintain restrictions on the intake of money until 1950 when there was a general relaxation. In 1951 there was talk of an increase in mortgage rates. One or two of the smaller societies did increase their rates for new advances to 4¼ per cent or 4½ per cent but the attitude generally was to wait and see.

Statutory Basis for Tax Arrangement

The arrangement under which building societies paid tax at a reduced rate on behalf of their shareholders and depositors had for some sixty years been based on a voluntary agreement between societies and the Inland Revenue. After the

war the Inland Revenue proposed its abolition. That proposal was firmly contested by the Association, apprehensive that the ending of the arrangement would have serious consequences for societies. Many months of discussion and negotiation ensued. Finally the Chancellor of the Exchequer (Sir Stafford Cripps) announced in 1950 that he was prepared to authorise the continuance of the arrangement for a period of five years but would propose that it be placed on a statutory basis in the following year's Finance Bill. At the same time he announced one important change, namely that henceforth sur-tax payers would have their income from building societies grossed for sur-tax purposes instead of being charged only on the amount received.

The Association and the Institute

In 1946, following the return of the Association's Secretary (Mr. Garratt-Holden) and Assistant Secretary (Mr. E.C.L. Butler) it was decided that the Institute should have its own full-time Secretary. With the concurrence of the Association and of Mr. Garratt-Holden the post was offered to Mr. Butler, an offer which he accepted.

There were two changes of note in the affairs of the Association during this period. One was the representation of district associations on the Council. The rules were amended in 1947 to provide for each of the eight district associations to elect one representative to serve on the Council. The other change was a regulation requiring every member society to carry liquid funds amounting to $7\frac{1}{2}$ per cent of total assets. Societies were given three years to comply with this requirement. Eventually some 32 small societies resigned from the Association because of their unwillingness to comply.

Chapter 24

HOUSING 1952-1960

300,000 Houses a Year

At the Conservative Party Conference held in the Autumn of 1950 the delegates demanded that if the Party were returned to power it should be pledged to build 300,000 houses a year. This demand was accepted by the Party leaders but only with reluctance, for it was a substantial advance on the Labour Government's achievements. Aneurin Bevan's official advisers had persuaded him that 200,000 houses a year was the maximum number at which it was practicable to aim. It was believed that the shortage of building materials would prove a formidable obstacle in the way of reaching the Conservative target.

However, at the General Election in 1951 it became the one really big bait to the electorate. Winston Churchill, back in office as Prime Minister, was determined that the promise should be made good, and he chose Harold Macmillan to carry out the task. Macmillan decided that the housing drive must be treated rather as a war-time operation, even if that meant disturbing, not to say upsetting, the civil servants concerned. He persuaded Sir Percy Mills, later Lord Mills, of W & T Avory Ltd to help him. Mills had served the Government during the war and was an administrator of proved character and success, well accustomed to the ways of Whitehall. Macmillan was also ably served by Ernest Marples, his Parliamentary Secretary, later Lord Marples.

Mills established regional housing boards to cut red tape and simplify procedures. The boards helped greatly in solving production problems, breaking bottlenecks and overcoming the shortages of steel, timber, cement and bricks.

All this had to be done against the background of a deteriorating economic situation. The Government were forced to make cuts in imports and to reduce capital expenditure. If it had not been for the pledge to build 300,000 houses a year, the housing programme would not have escaped the axe. Instead, the housing drive went ahead. There were no cuts and when interest rates went up, subsidies were also raised to compensate the local authorities for the greater cost of the loans made to them for housing purposes.

Controls Abolished

Having to start where his predecessor had left off, it was essential for Macmillan to base his housing strategy on the programmes of the local authorities. At the same time he sought the co-operation of private enterprise housing. In November 1951 he announced a substantial relaxation in the granting of licences; and, a year later, builders could apply for block licences, while licences were to be issued automatically for individual houses of not more than 1,000 cubic feet. Further relaxations followed and controls on all forms of building were abolished in November 1954. Having been held back so long by Bevan it took time for private builders to gear up their production of houses for sale. Nevertheless they made a useful contribution to the target of 300,000. Macmillan had aimed to reach it by 1954 but did in fact succeed in getting there in 1953, when a total of 318,000 houses was built. Of these 63,000 were built for sale. Another surge in owner-occupation had been set in train.

Development Charges Abolished

There were other steps taken by the Government which helped to produce an increased flow of houses for sale. One was the removal of the development charge. The Town & Country Planning Act of 1947 was comprised of two parts. The first embodied wide planning powers and comprehensive development plans bringing all development under control. It was designed to put land to the best use and prevent the outward sprawl from urban areas which had been an unwelcome feature of inter-war building. These provisions were generally accepted as desirable and even necessary.

The second part of the Act was far more controversial and was widely considered to be a hindrance to development generally and to housebuilding in particular. It was based on the proposals contained in the Uthwatt Report and provided that a development charge should be paid by those who received planning permission for any purpose. By way of compensation for the loss of development rights, the Act established a global fund of £300 million to be shared among owners of land. This part of the Act was resented by both landowners and house builders. Its provisions were extremely complicated. Macmillan announced in November 1952 that this part of the Act would be scrapped. *The Building Societies Gazette* observed: "It discouraged housing to a very serious degree. Over the years when house building was the most imperative need of the nation, it applied the brakes fore and aft. It kept land which ought to be developed out of the market and made it too dear for those who wished to buy and build. Its disappearance will encourage house building and

give help to would-be home-owners at a time when they most need it to offset the high costs of building . . . watching the operation of the system in its earlier stages surveyors, land agents and the legal profession gave warnings from time to time of what was happening. Now, at the end of five years, the effect is apparent to everyone associated with land and housing".

Rents and Repairs

Macmillan also wanted to bring about a re-orientation of official housing policy. He saw that there was a great danger of many houses falling into decay through lack of repairs and maintenance. The controls on rents were preventing landlords from doing the necessary work. He therefore allowed landlords to increase rents by an amount related to the increase in maintenance costs, but they first had to show that their houses were fit and in a good state of repair; and that they had spent money on making them so. The tenant was protected; if he was not satisfied with the state of his house he could apply to the local authority for a certificate of disrepair. Macmillan also sought to encourage landlords to improve their houses by allowing them to add 8 per cent of the capital cost to the rent charged to the tenant.

In 1956 the Housing Subsidies Act reduced the subsidies payable by the Exchequer for normal housing needs and gave the Minister power to abolish them, which he did in November 1956, except for dwellings built for old people and single persons. Local authorities were encouraged to concentrate once more on slum clearance for which the subsidies were not reduced. These steps led to a decline in local authority house-building.

In 1957 a further and more serious attempt was made to deal with rents in the private sector. The Rent Act of that year freed from control the better privately owned houses and permitted rents for the rest to rise to a new ceiling. One consequence of this was that many of the tenants living in houses freed from control decide to buy houses rather than pay higher rents.

Thus rents were moving in favour of the house-builders and the building societies. Home-ownership was becoming more attractive and local authorities were concentrating on slum clearance and special needs.

The Tripartite Guarantee

Another form of encouragement was given to owner-occupation by Macmillan in 1954 when he reached agreement with the Building Societies Association on a form of guarantee to enable 95 per cent advances to be made on houses valued at up to £2,000 and built after 1918; and 90 per cent advances on houses valued at up to £2,500 and built either before or after 1918. The guarantee was

tripartite, any losses resulting from the building society having made a larger than normal advance being shared equally by the Government, the local authority and the society. In the following year the two schemes were merged and the new arrangement provided for advances up to 95 per cent on houses built after 1918, and 90 per cent on houses built before, the limit in each case being a value of £2,500.

The terms of the guarantee were favourable to the building societies as the normal advance was fixed at 66⅔ per cent and the liability continued until the debt was reduced to 50 per cent. The scheme proved acceptable to many more local authorities than had been willing to operate the inter-war arrangements. A good deal of business was done with the aid of the guarantees although eventually the extension to 95 per cent advances of the guarantees available at a single premium from insurance companies led to this form of guarantee superseding the tripartite form. Administratively, it was simpler for a building society to deal with one insurance company rather than a variety of local authorities; and alternative arrangements were necessary in any event for those areas where the local authority was not willing to give the guarantee.

The House Purchase and Housing Act 1959

But the most important negotiations with the Government took place towards the end of the decade. Following the Rent Act of 1957, the Ministry of Housing decided that one way of preserving older houses would be to encourage their transfer from landlords to owner-occupiers. In that way the occupier would have every inducement to maintain and improve his property. Too many houses were being neglected because the landlords were not prepared to lay out money or sometimes because the tenant resisted improvements. But in order to encourage the purchase of the older houses it was desirable that mortgage facilities should be available on reasonably generous terms. With the increase in house building, societies had tended to concentrate their lending on newly built houses. Houses built before 1919 were treated with some caution, advances were of a lower proportion and repayment terms were shorter. This was a reasonable attitude. After all this type of house was often lacking a bathroom or hot water or had an outside w.c. There was a good flow of business from the new houses; there was also the stock of modern style inter-war houses. Why should building societies saddle themselves with third-class securities?

The Ministry approached the Association to see whether some arrangement could be made to ensure that loans were available for the older houses. At that time the demand for mortgages was high and building societies were finding it difficult to meet borrowers' needs. The Government therefore agreed to make

funds available which building societies could borrow provided that they made advances on pre-1919 houses. The Government at first wanted societies to agree to make loans of 100 per cent but settled for advances of 95 per cent, the excess advance over 75 per cent being covered by an insurance guarantee policy. The scheme was to apply to houses of an estimated value of £2,500 (£3,000 in the London area). A society making such advances could take up loans from the Government at monthly intervals, if desired, to reimburse itself. The Government loans were repayable by equal half-yearly instalments spread over a period of 20 years. The rate of interest payable on the Government loans was one-half less than that charged to the borrowers. Alexander Meikle, then Chairman of the Association, who was mainly responsible for negotiating the agreement, summed up its effect thus; "Provide the building societies with the funds they need for loans to purchasers of the older houses and that will take care of them. The societies' own funds thereby conserved become available for the more modern and new houses, and so everybody benefits all along the line".

Trustee Status

There was one other important term of the agreement. For some years the Association had been seeking trustee status for monies placed on deposit with societies. Meikle and his colleagues argued that if the Government was prepared to lend money to societies they could hardly do so without acknowledging the security afforded to their loans. This was conceded by the Government and it was agreed that societies with total assets of not less than £500,000 fulfilling certain conditions as to liquidity and reserves should be "designated societies". Such societies would be accorded trustee status and only those societies would be eligible to participate in the loans scheme and be able to borrow money from the Government.

The minimum asset figure of £500,000 excluded some members of the Association, and there was a certain amount of dissatisfaction among those who were excluded. The Association had tried to persuade the Government to accept a lower figure, but it was argued that the smaller societies might not always have a wide enough spread of assets and liabilities to ensure the maintenance at all times of a stable liquid position.

Of the arrangement generally there were other criticisms voiced by building societies. Some thought the ½ per cent margin was too low. Others were fearful that it might result in unjustifiable inflation of the price of pre-1919 properties and the attempted sale of properties likely to be included in slum clearance areas or scheduled within a short time as unfit for habitation. Some were fearful that

the acceptance of loans from the Government would in some way prejudice the independence of the movement.

Nevertheless, the movement as a whole was delighted that Trustee Status had been granted and most "designated societies" participated in the loans scheme which operated until July 1961, when the then Chancellor of the Exchequer (Selwyn Lloyd) faced with another financial crisis announced its termination as one of his emergency measures. By then some £100 million had been advanced to societies by the Exchequer.

Buoyant Years for Home-Ownership

With the freeing of the house-builder from the licensing system, building for sale increased throughout the years to 1960. Over 100,000 were built by private enterprise in 1954 and thereafter the number increased gradually to 170,000 in 1960. By this time the local authorities' total had declined from 239,000 houses in 1952 to 128,000.

House prices held steady throughout the 1950s following upon the rapid rise in the 1940s. The total increase from 1950 to 1960 was no more than 10 per cent. In the same period the index of average earnings doubled and this factor made for a ready sale of houses. The raising of rents undoubtedly encouraged families to buy either as sitting tenants or as first-time purchasers of vacant-possession houses. The number of houses in the private-rented sector continued to decline as landlords sold.

Building society mortgage advances had been steady at around £267 million from 1948 to 1952. From 1953 onwards they began to rise reaching £374 million by 1957 and £560 million by 1960. With house prices stable, this represented a real expansion; the number of borrowers increased from 1.5 million in 1950 to 2.35 million in 1960. By the end of the decade the proportion of houses in owner-occupation in Great Britain was 42 per cent.

Chapter 25

INTEREST RATES 1952-60

Interest rate variations in the 1950s were modest. The share rate never rose above 3½ per cent and the highest mortgage rate was 6 per cent. Yet the changes which had to be made – especially those in an upward direction – created just as much anxiety as the more spectacular rises of later years.

After living for 20 years with a 2 per cent Bank Rate (apart from a short period in 1939 and early 1940), and having during those years always had more funds offered to them than they knew what to do with, building societies found they were moving into a different world when after the election in 1951 the new Chancellor (R.A. Butler) – later Lord Butler – announced "that the struggle against inflation demanded the use of more direct and active monetary policy than had been the system of mere guidance to the banks employed since the war". The 2 per cent Bank Rate had been quite ineffective and the requirements of the money market had been supplied at too low a rate. Butler raised the Bank Rate to 2½ per cent in November 1951, a symbolic rather than effective measure. It was a different matter when he raised it to 4 per cent in March 1952. It foreshadowed tighter and dearer money.

After this rise in Bank Rate the Association had little option but to recommend societies to increase the share rate to 2½ per cent and the mortgage rate to 4½ per cent. Most societies followed the recommendation although the Halifax (still over 20 per cent liquid) remained at 2¼ per cent, kept its existing mortgages at 4 per cent but charged 4½ per cent for new loans. This was the beginning of an attempt by the Halifax to break away from the rates charged by the other large societies. It was an endeavour to pay less to investors and to charge less to borrowers. It was based on the expectation that the size of the society, its body of loyal savers in the North of England and its network of branches and agencies would enable it to maintain a good inflow of money in uncompetitive conditions. The experiment, as we shall see, did not succeed. And no large society has ever since attempted to pay less to investors than its main competitors.

1955 – An Anxious Year

There was no further change in rates until 1955. Bank Rate was reduced to $3\frac{1}{2}$ per cent in September 1953 and to 3 per cent in May 1954. The dearer money policy was not much in evidence and building societies experienced good years in both 1953 and 1954. Money flowed in quite well, advances increased and societies' liquidity ratios improved.

The next year – 1955 – was an anxious year. Bank Rate rose to $3\frac{1}{2}$ per cent in January and then to $4\frac{1}{2}$ per cent in February. The second quarter of the year saw a falling off in receipts from investors and a persistent rise in withdrawals. Some societies suffered more than others but for the movement as a whole investment receipts fell by some 8 per cent and withdrawals rose by 27 per cent compared with the second quarter of 1954. The Association was reluctant to recommend an increase in rates, and at the beginning of July, although admitting that the amount available for new loans had been less than in the corresponding period of the previous year, in consequence of which some societies had found it necessary to impose restrictions on lending, nevertheless recommended that no change be made. The Council stated that it had always sought to avoid frequent changes in interest rates and was of the opinion that the present trends were not sufficiently established to justify changes in building society rates. It added that it adhered to its long declared policy of keeping the cost of home-ownership as low as possible.

Unfortunately for the Council, on the same day as this no-change decision was made, the Chancellor announced that the interest rate charged on loans made by local authorities for house-purchase was to be raised by one-half per cent. That and the steadily worsening internal situation prompted a number of societies to give notice of increases. At a special Council meeting at the end of July 1955 it was decided that the inevitable must be accepted. A recommendation was made to increase the share rate to not more than 3 per cent and to increase the mortgage rate on both current and new mortgages to a minimum of 5 per cent. Most societies followed these recommendations, the large London societies establishing a new mortgage rate of $5\frac{1}{4}$ per cent. The Halifax contented itself by raising the share rate to $2\frac{3}{4}$ per cent and the mortgage rate to 5 per cent.

The new rates quickly rectified the money-flow and for the rest of the year the net gain in funds was such that societies were able to produce figures for the whole year which in no way reflected the set-back which had occurred in the middle months.

The year 1955 undoubtedly marked a turning point for building societies. It was the first post-war year in which they had to suffer a marked fall in net investment receipts. There was evidence that with the growth of their funds they

had attracted investors who were more interest-rate conscious than the smaller savers on whom they had formerly relied. It was also becoming clear that interest rates had a new importance and that although societies might say their rates were not related to Bank Rate, they could not remain immune to a rising trend of interest rates of which a rising Bank Rate might well be the indicator. The movement was still concerned not to impede the spread of home-ownership; and the fear of raising mortgage rates made it reluctant to raise investment rates until events compelled a rise. The result was that from now onwards the position of equilibrium where funds were adequate to meet mortgage demands was rarely reached. Restrictions on the amount of mortgage lending were to become a normal feature of business.

Mortgages at 6 Per Cent

From the building society standpoint there was worse to come in 1956. The problems of the balance of trade and the currency reserves were still harassing the Chancellor. Despite measures taken in an emergency budget in October 1955 the financial situation of the country was still giving concern when soon afterwards Mr. Macmillan took over from Mr. Butler at the Treasury. The rate of inflation (though still low judged by later years) was greater than in competitor countries and was affecting our export performance. So in February 1956 further measures were taken to dampen down demand, discourage imports and diminish speculation against the pound. One of the measures was a further rise in Bank Rate from $4\frac{1}{2}$ per cent to $5\frac{1}{2}$ per cent.

It did not take long for the impact of that rise to be reflected in the building societies' receipts and withdrawals. Local authorities were now inviting loans from the public at a gross rate of interest which compared favourably with that offered by building societies and which made great appeal to the person paying little or no tax. The hire-purchase companies were offering attractive rates too, and moreover spending liberally on advertising. Then the rise in Bank Rate and the increasing competition were followed by Macmillan's "Savings Budget" in which he announced the plan for Premium Bonds (to be inaugurated at the beginning of 1957) and alterations in terms to make more attractive to the public Government savings media such as saving certificates, defence bonds and savings bank deposits.

The Association Council was unwilling to raise rates hoping that the 3 per cent share rate could be held, thus avoiding a further rise in the mortgage rate. Some societies, fearful of a repetition of the previous years experience, decided to raise the investment rate but the deciding factor was the decision of the Halifax to give notice at the beginning of June that it was proposing to increase its share

rate from $2\frac{3}{4}$ to $3\frac{1}{2}$ per cent and to increase its mortgage rate for new loans to 6 per cent. Existing mortgages were to be increased to $5\frac{3}{4}$ per cent from December* Faced with this turn-about by the Halifax from paying less than the other leading societies to paying one-half per cent more, the Council was left with no option but to recommend other societies to move $3\frac{1}{2}$ per cent and 6 per cent. It would have happened anyway; the Halifax merely advanced the inevitable by a few weeks.

The Halifax had made a determined and persistent effort to place itself in a position where it could attract money while paying a rate of interest slightly less than the rest of the movement. It had paid $\frac{1}{4}$ per cent less for several years when money was flowing easily to building societies; and throughout the year 1955 when interest rates were moving up it continued to pay a quarter per cent less. In 1955 it did very well, increasing its assets by over 11 per cent. But the first half of 1956 produced a serious diminution in the Society's net inflow of money. Compared with a net increase of £12 million in the first half of 1955 the net increase for the corresponding half of 1956 was no more than £3 million. On the assumption of a progressive deterioration over the six months this would suggest that by the time the decision to go to $3\frac{1}{2}$ per cent was made the monthly net balance was showing an outflow rather than an inflow. Hence the decision to raise the share rate by three-quarters per cent.

Building societies did not like the idea of raising mortgage rates to 6 per cent. It meant that some existing borrowers had now had their interest charges raised by 50 per cent. It meant, if they did not increase their payments, that their loans would be extended in time. Societies were anxious, too, about the effect on new purchasers. Would the higher cost of mortgages prevent many families from buying? Would there be a slump in house sales and in house prices? Experience has shown that a rise in the mortgage interest rate does deter some families. In 1956, however, with the rise in earnings which had taken place there were still enough buyers above the effective demand level to maintain house sales and house prices.

Bank Rate at 7 Per Cent

Once the nettle of a 6 per cent mortgage rate had been firmly grasped there was little repercussion. Borrowers both new and old accepted that in the changed conditions it was a reasonable rate. The hesitations of the Association Council indicated that building societies were moving with reluctance and the Press

*The Halifax had also given notice to resign from the Association – see next chapter.

asserted that it was necessary for building society rates to rise. In February 1957 Bank Rate was reduced to 5 per cent, but at the time of the reduction it was made clear that this implied no change in policy, merely an adjustment to market conditions. There was certainly no inclination on the part of building societies to reduce rates in the face of the competition from the National Savings movement.

There were expectations among city men that further reductions in Bank Rate might be made in the course of the year. That was not to be. The Autumn saw yet another run on sterling. This was due to India and other overseas sterling countries running down balances held in this country in order to finance their own development programmes; other holders of sterling had also been selling pounds to buy German marks. Bank Rate was raised to 7 per cent on 19 September 1957. This was an unprecedented rise in peace time. It sent shock waves throughout the city. And although building societies had been at pains to dissociate movements in Bank Rate and their own rates, they did ask themselves what effect it was going to have on their own business.

The joint-stock banks' deposit rate automatically went up and the borrowing rates of the local authorities and hire-purchase companies were also increased. An increasing number of small and medium sized societies in London began to offer 4 per cent (some London societies had long found it necessary to pay something extra in order to live alongside the three large London societies). For the rest of the movement, however, the money flow remained reasonably stable and there was a general disposition to accept a lower tempo of business in preference to higher rates.

Building societies held on. 1957 results were good and the amount advanced was well above that for the previous year. Bank Rate was reduced to 6 per cent in March 1958 and with that came hope that by holding on building societies could avoid any further increase. By August the Bank Rate was down to $4\frac{1}{2}$ per cent and the popular Press began to urge a cut in the rate of interest charged to borrowers. The Association Council issued a statement in which it pointed out that a reduction in the mortgage rate could not take place until societies had first lowered rates to investors, and that could not take place until there had been a sufficient reduction in the general level of interest rates rates and those of the movements' competitors. Once again the Halifax decided to go it alone and announced that with effect from 1st December 1958 it would reduce the mortgage rate for both new and existing borrowers to $5\frac{1}{2}$ per cent and the share rate to $3\frac{1}{4}$ per cent. If it was hoped by this decision to bring about a general reduction the Halifax was disappointed. The rest of the movement was content to remain at $3\frac{1}{2}$ per cent. Bank Rate was reduced to 4 per cent in November 1958 and in the spring of 1959 the inflow of money began to show a marked increase. Some

societies experienced an almost embarrassing flood of money. The Leicester Permanent and the Newcastle upon Tyne Permanent dropped their lending rate to $5\frac{1}{2}$ per cent in March. By May the Council decided that the time had come for a change and recommended societies to lower rates to $5\frac{1}{2}$ per cent and $3\frac{1}{4}$ as soon as practicable.

By that time the Halifax had been operating on $3\frac{1}{4}$ for six months. At the Halifax Annual Meeting in 1960 Denham admitted that the restoration of parity in June 1959 had led to an increase in the Halifax inflow. This was the last serious effort which the society made to operate at a lower rate than its competitors. On two occasions in the 1960s the Halifax announced reductions in rates, but one was overtaken by a reduction in the recommended rate, and the other was ostensibly to protect its reserve ratio.

The improved flow of money might not have been sufficient at this juncture to bring about this reduction to $3\frac{1}{4}$ and $5\frac{1}{2}$ per cent as the demand for mortgages was strong enough to absorb all the funds. There were other factors which contributed to the decision. One was that many societies when raising mortgage rates to 5 per cent and later 6 per cent had promised their borrowers that the rate would be reduced as soon as conditions made this possible.; and they were anxious to demonstrate that they were ready to fulfil those promises. Another factor was the advent of trustee status; some societies were happy to protect their reserve ratios by expanding rather more slowly and were therefore willing to agree to lower investment rates. There was also another consideration in connection with the House Purchase and Housing Act. Loans under the Government scheme for older houses had to be made at the rate recommended by the Association. The Council felt that it would be in a most invidious position if at the start of the scheme it was recommending a lending rate of 6 per cent when the Halifax had been lending at $5\frac{1}{2}$ per cent for some months.

Back to 6 Per Cent

The rates were to remain unchanged for a year. After the change in 1959 money continued to come in well for the rest of the year and mortgage advances took a record leap forward to end at £517 million – an increase of £140 million over 1958. There was some discussion over the question of recommended rates. The *Economist* thought that the Association should "reconsider the adhesive that now holds this great mutual movement together – recommendation of given rates on shares and deposits". The *Gazette* in a leading article stated that recommendations were not always adhesive but sometimes "disruptive". There was some feeling on the part of provincial societies over the claim of the smaller Metropolitan societies that they had a special problem and were compelled to

offer and charge slightly higher rates. The recommended rates of May 1959 had by no means been generally adopted. Some 140 societies (including the hard core of Metropolitan societies) had remained at $3\frac{1}{2}$ per cent. They had not found it practicable to do otherwise. Many of them had reduced their mortgage rate to $5\frac{1}{2}$ per cent and were thus working on a smaller margin. Some were of the opinion that the rates should not have been reduced in 1959 in view of the heavy demand for mortgages which all societies were experiencing.

By April 1960 it was felt by many that the Council was dragging its feet and that a move back to $3\frac{1}{2}$ per cent and 6 per cent was fully justified. Bank Rate had been raised to 5 per cent in January. The limits on holdings of Saving Certificates and Defence Bonds had been raised in the Budget. There had been a significant fall in net investment receipts; from £21 million in January to £11 million in April. At the Annual Conference in May it was clear that a decision could no longer be delayed and it was agreed to recommend a return to $3\frac{1}{2}$ per cent and 6 per cent from 1st July.

Thus the decade closed with interest rates at their highest although these rates were to look modest besides those of the sixties and seventies. The significance of the changes which took place in the fifties was the gradual but definite move to an acceptance of the recommendations of the Association Council. The Halifax was the main deviant; and the small societies in London (not without some grumbling on the part of provincial societies) gradually established a convention that they were obliged to offer a $\frac{1}{4}$ per cent more for share investments. These London societies had two options open to them; either to work on a smaller margin or charge more for mortgages. The strong demand for mortgages in the second half of the decade and the inability of the larger societies to meet those demands enabled the smaller societies to transact sound business at $\frac{1}{4}$ per cent or $\frac{1}{2}$ per cent more than the recommended mortgage interest rate if they so desired.

There is no doubt that on the whole the recommended rates were pitched below what the house market would have stood. The building society tradition of encouraging the home-owner gave him the advantages of both capital appreciation and a favourable interest rate.

Chapter 26

FORTUNES AND MISFORTUNES 1952-60

The years from 1952 to 1960 were, as we have seen in Chapter 24, encouraging and expansive for building societies. If the progress in actual figures seems modest compared with the astronomical increases of recent years, nevertheless the increase of business in the 1950s was of great importance. It marked the resumption of building for sale and the beginning of a further and considerable extension of owner-occupation which to date has raised the total number of occupied houses to well over 50 per cent. By 1960 the total assets of the movement had risen to £3,165 million and the amount outstanding on mortgage was £2,647 million. The number of societies had continued to decline; from 807 in 1951 to 726 in 1960. The large societies continued to maintain their share of total assets.

The leading societies were as follows:—

1950	£1,000	1960	£1,000
Halifax	165,487	Halifax	490,544
Abbey National	122,158	Abbey National	388,724
Co-operative Permanent	63,629	Co-operative Permanent	239,257
Woolwich	63,367	Woolwich	178,374
Leeds Permanent	54,535	Leeds Permanent	138,128
Provincial	42,334	Provincial	90,576
Burnley	29,578	Alliance	76,588
Temperance Permanent	25,911	Burnley	66,849
Leicester Permanent	23,875	Leicester Permanent	68,512
Alliance	23,719	Leek & Moorlands	63,329

The Association

Although the 1939 Act had given statutory effect to a substantial part of the contents of the Code of Ethics, the Council of the Building Societies Association retained an itch to restrict still further the terms of business, especially in connection with the granting of mortgages. The 1939 Act had dealt stringently with the conditions under which builders' pools could be operated, and with the various types of collateral security which a building society was permitted to accept. So far as builders' pools were concerned, the requirements were such that

by the early 1950s it was clear that this form of alliance between builder and building society was as dead as the dodo. Loans would therefore be made on newly built houses on more or less the same terms as applied to existing houses. Societies could decide what repayment term they would allow; were able to determine their own maximum advance; pay commission to estate agents for the introduction of mortgage business; and lend 100 per cent of price to sitting tenants.

In short, given a surplus of funds and a limited amount of mortgage business, there was still plenty of room for competitive practices. Some of these had begun to show up by the beginning of the decade: longer repayment terms; acceptance of transfers from other societies without reference to those other societies; highly competitive offers of commission; and competitive terms to attract sitting-tenant business. In the early fifties, before the private builders had started to gear up under Macmillan's housing drive, it was mortgages, not funds, which were in short supply; and it was mortgage lending which the Council sought to protect from unsound or risky terms. Representatives of a group of leading societies (including those represented on the Council) and representatives from District Associations met in February 1951 to consider the adoption of a voluntary agreement which all members of the Association would be urged to sign.

In the end, recommended terms of business were sent to societies with a strong request for societies to agree to them. But there was no intention on the part of the Council to enforce the recommendations in the same way that they had tried to make the Code of Ethics binding on societies. What did emerge was a consensus on some practices: for example, reference to the other society where a borrower applied to transfer his mortgage; and a maximum repayment of 25 years. But when at the end of 1954 the Co-operative Permanent announced that it was prepared to grant mortgages repayable over a 35-year term, that consensus was rudely shattered, and criticisms were strongly voiced by several leaders of the movement.

What did emerge from the attempts of the Association to regulate business was the interest rates undertaking, under which societies subscribing to the undertaking agreed to give to the Association one month's notice of any intention to depart from the rates recommended by the Association.

Collective Advertising

Another innovation of the 1950s was the introduction of collective advertising. This was a subject which had been discussed for many years. Its advocates argued that all societies would benefit from publicity put out by the Association to make known to the public what building societies had to offer in the savings

and home-ownership fields. Many remained unconvinced. There were those among the larger societies who felt that their contributions to a collective scheme would benefit the smaller societies much more than themselves. Among the smaller and medium societies there were those who thought that the larger societies with substantial advertising budgets of their own would be able to capitalise on a collective scheme by concurrent or follow-up advertisements. Several times the Council considered the possibility of introducing a collective scheme; and on each occasion it became clear that not enough support would be forthcoming to justify going ahead.

What really brought about a sufficient increase of support was the initiative taken by the Metropolitan District Association in 1956. The members of that Association agreed to subscribe the cost of a series of advertisements in the then three London evening newspapers (the *Evening News*, *Evening Standard* and *Star*). These advertisements explained the facilities for savings and investments afforded by building societies and invited readers to write to the Secretary of the Association for a list of members. The response was good and the campaign was regarded as highly successful. This practical demonstration undoubtedly had a decisive influence in bringing about a further consideration of the advisibility of embarking on collective advertising by the parent Association. This time enough support was forthcoming. In 1957 it was agreed to launch a national scheme and it has now become an integral part of the Association's activities.

The Halifax Resignation

One of the more curious episodes in the affairs of the Association was that leading to the resignation of the Halifax in 1956. Algernon Denham, a director of the Halifax since 1922, became President in 1945, an office he held until shortly before his death in 1961. By the 1950s he was firmly in command at Halifax and seemed to have a strong desire to make his influence felt in the building society movement. In 1955 he began to express dissatisfaction with some of the ways in which other societies were conducting their business. In particular he took exception to the acceptance of deposit monies from limited companies. He was of the opinion that such deposits were placed with building societies only because they were offering higher rates than were available from banks and other financial institutions. The monies were all too likely to be withdrawn when higher rates were offered elsewhere. It was therefore volatile and dangerous money, especially when the companies were permitted to invest large sums.

Denham went so far as to demand that every member of the Association Council should give a personal undertaking that the society with which he was

associated would not accept any investment of more than £5,000 from a limited company whatever the circumstances and however long the period. The Council replied that it was out of the question for its members to give such an undertaking since they served in a personal capacity and the policy of each society rested with the board of that society. The Council also pointed out that Denham had greatly exaggerated the amount of money which had been or was being taken from limited companies. Their investigations had shown that the practice was followed to only a limited extent and was not of material importance, the total amount of such monies representing less than 5 per cent of total deposits (i.e. about one-half per cent of total assets).

At the time of this attack on company deposits, the General Manager of the Halifax (Fred Bentley) was the Deputy Chairman of the Association. Denham chose not to make the Halifax views known through its representative on the Council but by means of his own personal statements and speeches. And he tended to make rash statements. For example he declared "For the past decade, during which the movement has experienced phenomenal growth, we have consistently practised restraint in our operations and endeavoured to discourage an expansionist policy". To which the Association roundly replied "The Halifax has been much advertised as the largest in the world and it has achieved that position by pursuing over many years a policy of determined expansion. During the last year alone its assets increased by $11\frac{1}{4}$ per cent, being more than the average for all building societies".

The situation was personally embarrassing for Bentley. He had accepted the Deputy-Chairmanship of the Council with the full approval of the Halifax Board. When there was talk in the Halifax boardroom of possible resignation from the Association, he made it clear that such a step (or even the threat of it) would make his appointment untenable. Moreover, he had been nominated to take office as Chairman of the Association in May 1956, and that proposal had also been endorsed earlier in the year by the Halifax Board. Then, on the eve of the Association's Annual Conference in May, at which Bentley was due to be elected to the Chair, the Halifax Board, having received a few days earlier the Association's decision that it could not make any recommendations on the restriction of limited company deposits, gave notice of resignation.

Bentley failed to persuade Denham to withdraw the threat to leave the Association. He was in a difficult and embarrassing position. Should he withdraw from office in the Association? Or should he resign from his office as General Manager of the Halifax? It was impracticable to act as Chairman of the Association whilst serving as the chief executive officer of a non-member society. Could he serve as Chairman even if he resigned from the Halifax service? No

precedent existed for a Chairman who did not belong to a member society. However, Bentley was assured by his colleagues on the Council that he would have their full support if he were to resign from the Halifax and agree to serve as Chairman. And that was what he did.

The Halifax resigned from the Association with effect from 30th June and (as we saw in the last chapter) announced at the same time an increase in interest rates which forced the Council into recommending similar action by other societies. Thus, under Denham, the Halifax pursued policies which veered from excessive caution to competitive aggression and, in relation to the Association, differed markedly from those which Bentley advocated. There is little doubt that not only was Bentley reluctant to forgo the honour of serving as Chairman of the Council, but that he was glad to escape from Denham's dominance.

Some months later Bentley was able to contest an election for directors at the Annual General Meeting, and, with the aid of a large band of supporters, secured a seat on the Halifax Board. Thus he was able to resume his long association with the Society. It was not until after Denham's death in 1961 that there could be any hope of persuading the Halifax to rejoin the Association. It did so in 1964.

Term Shares

Term shares – that is, money placed with a building society for a fixed period (usually of one to four years) on which the society pays a higher rate of interest than on ordinary share money – have gained wide acceptance in the 1970s as a means of providing societies with a tranche of firm and stable investments.

In the 1950s there was great controversy over the introduction of term shares by one or two enterprising societies. Some of the earliest so-called term shares were not really for a fixed term. Instead of money being lodged for a fixed term of years it was accepted subject to a rather longer term of notice than was required for ordinary accounts – say three or six months instead of the usual one month. In 1956 the Hastings and Thanet instituted a new share paying one-quarter per cent above the normal rate and subject to six months' notice. In January 1958, however, the Leicester Permanent introduced a term share that really was a term share as we know it to-day. It was for three years, a maximum of £2,500 from any one investor, and a fixed rate of 4 per cent which was $\frac{1}{2}$ per cent above the ordinary share rate. The Leicester Permanent's example was followed by others. In general the rate was not variable but fixed for the whole term.

The few societies who issued such shares were subjected to a good deal of criticism. Some saw it as putting up the cost of obtaining money, were afraid

there would be enormous transfers from existing accounts and considered the offer of a fixed rate was highly dangerous as interest rates might fall. Others simply opposed the term share (and continued to do so for many years) merely on the ground that it was against the traditional policy of providing freely available withdrawal facilities. Algernon Denham said, "it would be foolish to tamper with a structure which not only has stood the test of many years but also provides the prudent investor with a combination of facilities which he cannot readily obtain elsewhere". Denham was by no means alone in thinking along these lines about term shares.

Suspect Societies

The 1950s brought some anxieties to building societies owing to the activities of a number of comparatively small societies offering in the early part of the decade a slightly higher rate of interest to investors than that recommended by the Association and in the later years considerably more – as much as $4\frac{1}{2}$ per cent and 5 per cent when the recommended rate was $3\frac{1}{4}$ or $3\frac{1}{2}$ per cent. These societies, some of which were growing fairly rapidly, were suspected (and not without reason) of using their funds to make loans on blocks of flats, rent-controlled houses bought for re-sale to sitting-tenants or with vacant possession and on commercial properties. It was also believed that valuations were obtained which were too accommodating, advances were higher than prudence dictated, and that all too often the directors and senior officers of the society were financially interested in the transactions. The Registrar gave warning about these activities in 1955, and the *Investors Chronicle* carried an article in December 1955 drawing attention to the dangers of investing in such societies and instancing one which having assets of less than £5,000 in 1949 had increased those assets to over £600,000 in six years. There were other instances of this kind of mushroom growth.

In 1955 the Registrar made orders against some of these societies prohibiting them from inviting subscriptions for shares or money on deposit. One of these was the Exeter Benefit where the accounts for 1954 revealed a large increase in the number of mortgages upwards of twelve months in arrear. The Registrar had obtained valuations for some of the properties where default had taken place and was compelled to take action. Press publicity resulted in demand for withdrawals to an extent which could not be met. This society was a member of the Association. The Co-operative Permanent stepped in and took a transfer of the engagements of the society and the Association was thus relieved of any embarrassment arising from the failure of a member society.

But other suspect societies carried on their activities. Although the Registrar

kept a watchful eye on them, so long as they were not obviously in trouble his powers were limited. The *Gazette* observed in May 1956 that a situation which allowed any four people regardless of background, experience or financial standing to fill up a form, pay a fee of £10 and send two copies of its Rules to the Registrar and thereafter begin to invite investments from the public was highly dangerous. Most of the societies offering high rates of interest operated in London and severely affected the smaller London Societies.

Scottish Amicable

Matters came to a head with the failure of the State Building Society in 1950. But before that happened there was another failure on the part of an Association member. The society was the Scottish Amicable. This was a well-conducted and sound society whose only trouble was that it had made investments in undated and long-dated gilt-edged securities which had fallen in value owing to the rise of interest' rates which had taken place since 1952. Press comment drew attention to the fact that the depreciation exceeded the reserve funds of the society. This was a society with assets exceeding £25 million and the Press article led to a flood of withdrawal notices which the society was unable to meet. Again the Co-operative Permanent stepped in and took over the society.

The State Affair

The State Building Society was one of the suspect societies which had attracted considerable funds by offering a high rate of interest to investors. At the end of 1952 its assets amounted to no more than £560,000; by September 1959 they were over £15 million. Since early 1957 it had made substantial advances to the Jasper group of companies – so much so that by September 1959 the outstanding balances to that group amounted to £7.7 million, rather more than half the loans due to the State. Grunwald the solicitor to the State and Murray its Managing Director were involved in these transactions. Take-over bids were made for property companies with bridging finance from banks, from clients of Grunwald and frequently from the State. When Murray had arranged for the State to participate in a deal of this kind, the money had to be sent to Grunwald and used for the purchase of control of the company being taken over. The funds of the Society were thus used before Grunwald was in a position to arrange for the corresponding mortgages. After the acquisition was completed, legal charges on the properties of the newly acquired company were executed in favour of the State.

The Society had of course no power to invest in ordinary shares of property companies and the use of the Society's funds for bridging finance without the

security of freehold or leasehold estate was contrary to the rules of the Society and a contravention of the Building Societies Acts. The Society was acting quite improperly but if all went well the mortgages were in due course provided. But what happened if the group committed itself to acquire control of a company without having enough finance to complete the whole transaction? This is what happened in the case of the bid which the Jasper group made for the Lintang company. The take-over bid in that case followed the same pattern as previous bids, although the amounts involved were much larger. The State provided £3.25 million which, if all went well, was later to be secured on the two main properties owned by Lintang. But things did not go well. The amount involved for the purchase of all the Lintang shares and for the purchase of another company which Lintang had contracted to buy for nearly £3 million involved something over £11 million. Grunwald and Murray had over-reached themselves and the State had parted with £3.25 million for which it had no security. The money had been used to buy the controlling interest in Lintang from the principal shareholders and the shares so bought had then been charged to a bank to obtain money to purchase the remaining shares. A complex tangle of entitlements to shares and monies resulted. Murray and Grunwald were sent to prison for five years. The Registrar secured the appointment of a new board of directors headed by Lord Reith and J.H. Robertson, a former General Manager of the Abbey National, was persuaded to act as Manager. Lord Reith and J.H. Robertson set about the task of putting the affairs of the State in order and recovering the £3.25 million. In the end they were successful and the shareholders eventually received 21s. in the pound.

The 1960 Act

The State affair and the unsatisfactory conduct of a number of other societies indicated that legislation was needed to deal with the abuses which had been revealed. Accordingly the 1960 Act was enacted. Its main effects can be summarised thus:

(1)   to ensure that societies would make at least 90 per cent of their advances on owner-occupied houses

(2)   to ensure that proper standards of accounting and audit were maintained

(3)   to ensure that members of a society had an adequate opportunity of expressing their views

(4)   to ensure that proper standards were maintained by societies in advertising for funds

(5)   to impose more stringent conditions before new societies could be formed and to apply similar conditions where small and perhaps moribund societies were taken over

(6)   to give greater powers to the Registrar to deal with a society which got into difficulties or abused its position

(7)   to ensure independent and skilled assessment of securities.

A fuller examination of the more important provisions of the Act is made in the next chapter.

Chapter 27

THE BUILDING SOCIETIES ACT 1960

The 1960 Act imposed restrictions on building society operations, enhanced the powers of the Chief Registrar and provided members of societies with greater opportunities to take action if they were dissatisfied with the way in which their society was conducted.

Mortgage Advances

Building societies, so long as they made advances on freehold or leasehold security, had had complete freedom to choose the kind of property on which their loans were secured. As we have seen, in the latter half of the nineteenth century societies had lent much of their money on rented properties, shops and even industrial premises. Even when lending to owner-occupiers was growing fast in the inter-war years and after World War II, societies did not regard themselves as in any way inhibited from considering other types of security. It was not until the 1950s that the activities of the 'suspect' societies, using their funds for speculative purposes, began to change attitudes. Apart from the dangers inherent in the abuses which were going on there was also a growing feeling that as it was difficult to find enough money to meet the demand for loans from house-buyers, societies ought not to divert their resources to other kinds of property.

When the 1960 Bill was drawn up it was generally agreed that something must be done to limit loans on non-owner-occupied property. It was decided therefore to divide loans into two classes: special advances and normal advances. Special advances were defined as loans to corporate bodies (i.e. commercial loans) and loans to individuals where the amount exceeded £5,000 or was such that it would bring the total indebtedness (including any outstanding loans) to over £5,000. And societies were prohibited from lending more than 10 per cent of their total loans in the form of special advances. At least 90 per cent of their lending would thus take the form of normal advances, namely loans not exceeding £5,000 made to individuals. This did not prevent a society from lending an individual up to £5,000 on rented or even commercial property, but as there was little demand for small loans of this kind the effect of the restrictions

was to ensure that in future the bulk of a society's lending would be on owner-occupied houses. And, after the Act came into force, societies were generally anxious to report to their members that their special advances were far below the statutory ten per cent.

So the provisions of the Act, coupled with public opinion and the changing philosophy of building societies themselves, has resulted in socities being regarded and regarding themselves as institutions, raising funds not to lend on freehold and leasehold security, but more narrowly on owner-occupied freehold and leasehold security.

Special advances are occasionally made, but are now mainly to accommodate the purchases of higher priced houses where the loan required is above the limit for a normal advance. The Chief Registrar was given power to increase the £5,000 limit. The first occasion on which he did so was in 1963 when he raised it to £7,000; with the continual rise in house prices he has raised it on several further occasions. It stands in 1980 at £25,000.

The Chief Registrar is also given power to authorise a building society to exceed the 10 per cent limit for special advances if it proposes to make advances on newly constructed dwelling houses or flats which are to be let to tenants. This power was used when the Housing Corporation was established in 1964 and building societies were asked to make loans to housing societies sponsored by the Corporation.

Mortgage Valuations

One of the most warmly contested clauses of the Act was that relating to the making of mortgage reports and valuations. For it was proposed that no director, manager or secretary of a society should be permitted to undertake such reports for his society. There were many societies where it was the practice for directors, if not managers, to carry out inspections and report on properties. Many were qualified members of the Chartered Surveyors and other professional bodies who thus supplemented their directors' fees by the payments they received for their valuations. They did not look kindly upon the proposal that they should be excluded. In the end a compromise was reached whereby those who were in office at the commencement of the Act were permitted to undertake valuations for a period of ten years, subject to approval by special resolution at each Annual General Meeting. Directors and officers appointed after the commencement of the Act were not eligible to make reports and valuations. And with the passing of the ten years every report must now be made by an independent person.

New Societies

Steps were taken to ensure that new societies, if formed, would not be promoted by persons without a stake in the society. The Act provided that there must be a minimum of ten founding members who must each invest £500 which was not to be withdrawn or transferred within the first five years. Nor may a new society advertise without the permission of the Chief Registrar, and the Act lays down conditions which must be fulfilled before the Chief Registrar's permission is given.

Chief Registrar's Control Over Societies

The Chief Registrar's control over societies as provided in previous legislation was greatly strengthened by the 1960 Act. If he is not satisfied with the conduct of a society he can now order an inspection or call a meeting of members on his own initiative without having to wait for a member or members to call upon him to take action. He can now not only prevent a society from inviting investments (as provided by the Prevention of Fraud (Investment) Act) but also prohibit it from accepting investments even where they have not been invited. He may prohibit advertisements of all descriptions or specific advertisements. He may also restrict the activities of a small society where there has been a change in the scale or character of the business carried on.

Investment of Liquid Funds

Building societies must carry a certain amount of liquid funds. They are required to maintain a minimum of $7\frac{1}{2}$ per cent to be eligible for Trustee Status and as a condition of membership of the Association. That means in practice that they must carry more than the minimum to avoid the danger of falling below it: Liquidity must be held in cash, local authority loans, Treasury bills and gilt-edged. The investment of these liquid funds calls for prudent management. The case of the Scottish Amicable showed what may happen if monies are invested in long term securities; they can depreciate in value to the point where a society not only becomes illiquid but insolvent. Liquidity should never be sacrificed to the maximisation of income.

Under the Act the Chief Registrar has prescribed rules for investment which provide a framework within which each society is required to build up its portfolio. At least $7\frac{1}{2}$ per cent of its assets must be invested in securities maturing within five years before a society can hold any longer maturing stocks. If $7\frac{1}{2}$ per cent is so held, then a further $7\frac{1}{2}$ per cent can be held in securities maturing within 15 years. Only after 15 per cent is thus held can funds be invested in

securities with more than fifteen years to run. There is also an over-riding ban on local government securities maturing in more than five years and on other securities maturing in more than twenty-five years. So far as cash is concerned, that must be placed with one or more of the banks authorised by the Chief Registrar to hold the funds of a building society.

Societies in Difficulties

With all the legislation in the world, competent auditors and a vigilant Chief Registrar, societies do get into difficulties from time to time. Someone connected with the society is often responsible, but that is not always the case. The Derbyshire Society was certainly not to blame when the collapse of Rolls-Royce, on which the town of Derby was heavily dependent for employment, caused a run on the Society by investors who feared that its borrowers would be unable to meet their mortgage payments. The 1960 Act provided a means of assistance in just such a case by enabling the Chief Registrar to authorise another building society to lend money to the one in difficulties. That was done in the case of the Derbyshire, to which the Halifax agreed to lend £1 million and to which other large societies also agreed to lend if necessary. This action and the knowledge that it was being taken quickly restored confidence.

Loans have also been authorised in one or two cases where one society was being taken over by another and larger society. In 1976 the North London Building Society announced that it was proposing to transfer its engagements to the Cheltenham and Gloucester Society. Shareholders were informed that the high interest rates, which had been paid on investments of over £5,000, would not be maintained once the transfer took place. This brought a spate of withdrawal notices, and pending the transfer of engagements the Cheltenham & Gloucester was authorised to, and did in fact lend £500,000 to the North London to enable it to meet the demands of investors.

Guarantee Funds

The Act also provided that building societies could set up a guarantee fund to meet losses incurred by investors or depositors in a society participating in sub-scribing to such a fund. The fund could be established through an insurance com-pany; or by means of a joint fund built up between a number of societies; or in any other way which the Chief Registrar approved. The Treasury gave con-sideration to the setting up of a compulsory scheme, but finally decided against it. The Government expressed the hope that societies would get together and devise a fund of their own. The Economic Secretary to the Treasury said, "We

think it likely that in fact this will be such an attractive idea that societies will feature this aspect, if they join together, in their advertisements and in other ways in order to show potential investors that they are societies which exercise these powers".

The pros and cons were thereupon considered by the Council. Two considerations seem to have influenced their decision to do nothing. The first was the fact that a considerable group of smaller member societies (especially in the London area) were paying a $\frac{1}{4}$ per cent more than other societies. Why should the larger societies guarantee the investors of societies paying higher rates of interest? With a guarantee an investor could invest with impunity in the most obscure society. The other was a belief that the standards required of members by the Association, coupled with the strict requirements of the new Act, were such that there was now little fear of a member society losing its investor's money.*

Members' Rights

(1) Inspection of Register of Members

Until the 1960 Act was passed members of a building society, unlike those of a company, had no right to inspect the register of members and therefore no opportunity to communicate with fellow members should they wish to do so. Building societies regarded their members as investors and customers whose affairs were to be regarded as private and confidential. The Association looked upon proposals to open up the registers with some apprehension. In the end, the right to inspect the register was given, but subject to severe restrictions. Only if there were clear signs of trouble was a member given an automatic right to consult the register for the purpose of communicating with other members. If an order had been made against the society prohibiting it from inviting or accepting investors; if withdrawal notices had not been met after six months had elapsed; or if no interest or dividends had been paid in the previous financial year: then the member must be given access to the register.

Where none of these three circumstances appertains, a member wishing to inspect the register must make written application to the Chief Registrar. The Chief Registrar, if he is satisfied that the applicant wishes to communicate with other members on a subject relating to the affairs of the society and having regard to the interests of the members as a whole and to all other circumstances, may if he so thinks fit direct that the member shall have the right to obtain from the register the names and addresses of members. But first the society must be given the opportunity of making representations to the Chief Registrar. And, if

*But see Chapter 33.

requested to do so, by either the applicant or the society, the Chief Registrar must afford a hearing by both parties.

Such a hearing was held in 1964 when a member of the Co-operative Permanent wished to communicate with the members of that Society. He wished to propose an alteration of rules requiring the Board of the Society to disclose, in the Annual Report, the number of Board meetings held in the year, the number attended by each director and the amount of remuneration paid to each director. The Chief Registrar (Mr. S.D. Musson) dismissed the application. He said "building societies by and large regard the register of members as confidential and it appears to me that Parliament only intended to displace this confidence in the exceptional circumstances mentioned in subsection (1) of section 63 where a society is in grave difficulties or under subsection (2) in any other circumstances where the Chief Registrar considered it was right that the register should be made available to a member or members. I have to decide each application under the subsection on its own facts but in my view the circumstances have to be exceptional and of real importance to the running of the society. I consider that I should regard the words "its affairs" as intended to refer mainly to the society's finances, its business activities and the manner in which it carries on its business and I do not consider the type of amendments to the rules which the Applicant seeks in the circumstances of this case as within the ambits of the type of case where Parliament intended that a direction should be given under the section". He added "with due respect to the Applicant I can only describe his proposed alterations as trivial and unusual".

This is the only case which the Chief Registrar has had to hear and decide. From his remarks it seems that a direction enabling a member to inspect the register of a society will not lightly be given.*

(2)   *Meeting of Members*

The Act makes detailed provisions for enabling members to exercise their rights; ensuring that annual meetings are held; and that the rules of a society make adequate provision for requisitioning meetings, notices, procedures, voting rights and the right to demand a poll and appoint proxies.

(3)   *Special Resolutions*

Provision was also made to enable a member to propose a special resolution at a

*It has however been given to two members of the Anglia Hastings & Thanet Building Society by the Chief Registrar's direction (April 1979). The two members were permitted to obtain from the register of the society the names and addresses of members for the purpose of communicating with them on two subjects – the composition of the Board of directors and the rules of the Society relating to the Board of directors. The period of access was limited to 12 months and the two members were not to disclose the names and addresses to any other person. The Chief Registrar was then Mr. Keith Brading.

meeting of his society. A special resolution is required for an alteration of rules; for the approval of a union with another society or a transfer of engagements from one society to another; a change of name; or the winding-up of a society. A number of societies have been subjected to special resolutions submitted by members proposing alteration to rules, some of which have been of a trivial nature. It does provide, however, a means whereby a member can put forward changes which he thinks are desirable.

Consolidating Act

In 1962 the legislation contained in the various Building Societies Acts was consolidated in the Building Societies Act 1962. References made earlier refer to that Act, not the Act of 1960.

Chapter 28

INTERLUDE 1961-1964

After the State affair and the passing of the 1960 Act, up to the advent of a Labour Government in 1964, building societies enjoyed a relatively peaceful four years. Societies and the Association were digesting the provisions of the new Act. Rules had to be altered to conform to some of the requirements of the Act. There was a new form of Annual Statement to prepare for members and a new form of Annual Return to prepare for the Chief Registrar. There were new regulations regarding the investment of funds in gilt-edged and other authorised securities. But though it was something of an interlude it was not without interest. There were some important developments in housing, interest rate changes took place and mortgage advances rose sharply.

Housing

In July 1961 the Government, faced once again with the necessity of cutting down expenditure and of taking other measures to deal with the outflow of short-term funds and to restore confidence in the pound, decided to end the House Purchase Scheme for older houses. When the Scheme was finally wound up some £92 million had been loaned to societies by the Government, and the money had been used to provide nearly 90,000 mortgages. The underlying concept of promoting the sale of older houses and encouraging their improvement was a sound one and it was a pity that the arrangement was so abruptly ended. It supplemented building society funds at a time when demand for loans was high, and its termination meant that there was no longer an inducement for building societies to give older dwellings as much consideration as newer houses.

1961 saw yet another Housing Act, the main purpose of which was to introduce a new principle into the subsidy system for local authority houses. The Act provided for subsidies at two basic rates of £24 and £8 per house, and the rate payable in the case of any particular authority was determined by reference to the state of its housing revenue account. The 1961 Act also increased the permitted return on a landlord's expenditure for improvement work from 8 per cent

to $12\frac{1}{2}$ per cent. And it established a fund of £25 million for making advances to housing associations to provide cost-rent and co-ownership housing.

This £25 million fund was in the nature of an experiment and, following the successful way the funds were used, it was decided in 1964 to set up the Housing Corporation to do the same job on a much larger scale. When the Corporation was established in 1964 building societies were invited to co-operate by making loans on first mortgages, the balance of the expenditure by housing societies being provided on second mortgages from the Corporation's funds. The initial sum allocated to the Housing Corporation was £100 million and the Association indicated that building societies would provide a further £200 million.*

So far as owner-occupation was concerned, by far the most important event was the ending of Schedule A. The Chancellor (Selwyn Lloyd) announced in the course of his Budget speech in 1962 that he proposed to end this tax on house-owners in the following year. Schedule A tax was payable on the assumed investment value of the house determined by the value for rating purposes. It was what is known as an 'imputed' income: the value to the occupant of living in his house instead of having to pay rent. Rateable values had not been revised and therefore the house-owner was by no means taxed on the true value of his house. But new rating valuations were to come into force in 1963 which would have meant a considerable (though by no means unjustifiable) increase in Schedule A charges. The Government, which had long resisted demands for the abolition of Schedule A, were unwilling to face the sudden trebling or even quadrupling of the tax. Rather than do that they brought it to an end. "After all", said Mr. Selwyn Lloyd, "it is only a notional income". The abolition saved the Government the problems it would have had in bringing the level of assessments up to date. House-owners rejoiced and building societies were delighted with this further encouragement to home buying. Yet it has to be admitted that there were no rational or logical grounds for the abolition of Schedule A. True, there was a real difficulty caused by the long period in which rating values had remained unchanged, and the sharp increases which would have had to be made on the 1963 rating revision. This could have been overcome by increasing the Schedule A assessments gradually over, say, a five-year period.

Interest Rates

The increase in the share rate to $3\frac{1}{2}$ per cent in July 1960 had arrested the decline in net receipts but had not produced a marked improvement. It was

*See Chapter 31.

clearly too small a rise, but there was again the greatest reluctance to raise mortgage rates in order to get an adequate flow of money. By June 1961 the slide had gone far enough to force a recommendation from the Council that the share rate should be raised to $3\frac{3}{4}$ per cent and the mortgage rate to $6\frac{1}{2}$ per cent with effect from 1st October. It was just as well that this decision was made and announced in June. For in July the economic difficulties which had led to the Chancellor terminating in 1959 House Purchase arrangements also prompted an increase in Bank Rate from 5 per cent to 7 per cent.

By the following April 1962 Bank Rate had been reduced in successive stages to $4\frac{1}{2}$ per cent and the movement was being subjected to Press comment and criticism because it was not reducing rates. The Chairman of the Council (C.J. Dunham) led a vigorous campaign to emphasise the demand for mortgages, the need to pay enough to investors in order to raise adequate funds and the probability that interest rates would not be reduced during 1962. Charles Hill (now Lord Hill), the Minister of Housing and Local Government joined in, saying, "there is room for more vigorous effort by the building society movement to explain to the public just what are the facts as regards the way it has to raise money and the way it has to lend it. And about the difference between short-term bankers' money and long-term investment money and about having to have so much liquidity".

There was still a widespread feeling that building societies ought to reduce rates as soon as Bank Rate began to fall regardless of the fact that for ten years societies had not been able to meet fully the demand for loans. In these ten years (and for long afterwards) the movement never attained the point of equilibrium where the inflow of money was just about matched by the demand for mortgages. And the reason was that there were always pressures to hold down or bring down the mortgage rate. It must be admitted that after many years of $4\frac{1}{2}$ per cent and 5 per cent mortgages there were many within the building society movement who were in sympathy with these outside voices, believing that high mortgage rates would discourage owner-occupation.

In September 1963 the Halifax (still outside the Association) announced that from 1st February 1963 it would reduce the mortgage rate to 6 per cent and the share rate to $3\frac{1}{2}$ per cent. The Association remained firm until January 1963 when the improved flow of funds prompted a similar recommendation to reduce to $3\frac{1}{2}$ per cent and 6 per cent from April 1963. In the following October the Halifax took the movement completely by surprise by announcing a further reduction of $\frac{1}{4}$ per cent in their rates to take effect from 1st February 1964. The Halifax board gave as the reason for this reduction that the society had been growing too fast and in consequence its reserve ratio was falling. By reducing

the share rate the inflow of money would be discouraged, mortgage demand would be increased, and the liquidity ratio (then about 20 per cent) would ease, and the fall in the reserve ratio would be arrested. Whether this was an attempt to lead the movement in another general reduction is not clear. If it was, it did not succeed as the Association made no recommendation to reduce rates. By February 1964 rates were hardening and the Halifax announced that it would revert to $3\frac{1}{2}$ per cent and 6 per cent from 1st April 1964, i.e. only two months after the reductions to $3\frac{1}{4}$ and $5\frac{3}{4}$ per cent. The society claimed (somewhat unconvincingly) that the period of lower rates had done what was needed in relation to reserves and liquidity.

The Association

At the Association's Annual Conference in 1961 the question of the composition of the Council was raised once again. Mr. A.G.C. Trollope put forward on behalf of the Metropolitan Association a motion that the Council be invited to submit proposals to the 1962 Annual Meeting to provide (a) that approximately half the members of the Council should be elected by district associations (without increasing the total number of members of the Council), and (b) that an appropriate age should be fixed for retirement from the Council. Mr. Trollope said that the sole intention of the Metropolitan Association was to effect a change which would appear to be more closely in harmony with the increased stature and importance of district associations. A change in the method of election and an age limit were necessary so as to ensure a better opportunity for a more representative and less entrenched body. The resolution was carried by an overwhelming majority after Mr. Trollope had agreed that the resolution should cover any other proposals for change which the Council might decide to put forward. Accordingly the Council brought before the 1962 Conference a series of proposals, including provision for 18 nationally elected and 16 district association members. The latter figure represented an increase of six, giving two representatives to each of the six largest district associations. It was also proposed that the retirement age should be 70. A third proposal was that the permitted number of co-opted members should be reduced from six to four. On voting, the proposal to increase the number of district association members failed to obtain the necessary three-fourths majority, although there was a considerable majority in favour. The other two proposals on retirement age and the number of co-opted members were carried.

Increase in Mortgage Advances

The number of houses built for sale in the years from 1961-1963 remained steady at around 175,000 per annum and increased sharply to 221,000 in

1964. House prices continued to increase steadily at about 6-7 per cent per annum. As a result total mortgage advances increased each year, and in 1964 for the first time over £1,000 million was advanced. By the end of that year total assets of the movement amounted to £4,862 million.

Chapter 29

THE LABOUR GOVERNMENT AND HOUSING 1964-70

Ways and means of tackling the housing shortage featured prominently in the Labour Party's manifesto for the 1964 election and promises of cheaper housing were dangled before the electorate. There were to be lower interest rates for future owner-occupiers, and, possibly, for existing house buyers. 100 per cent mortgages were to be made available and Government funds provided for building societies to facilitate once more the making of loans on older houses. The Rent Act of 1957 was to be repealed; an end made to further decontrol; security of tenure provided; and machinery established for setting rents on a fair basis. Steps were to be taken to stamp out jerry building, introduce leasehold enfranchisement and encourage the modernisation of older houses. A land commission was to be set up in order to end the competitive scramble for building land.

The manifesto also stated that labour would increase the building of houses for rent and for sale. 400,000 houses per annum was regarded as a reasonable target, but the party did not intend to have an auction on housing figures.

The promise of lower interest rates aroused a great deal of discussion during the run-up to the election. George Brown (now Lord George Brown) was reported as saying that mortgages would be granted at 3 per cent. The shadow Minister of Housing, Michael Stewart (now Lord Stewart) did not go as far as that but he did state specifically "a policy of lower interest rates will apply not only to the housing programmes of local authorities but also to mortgage loans to intending purchasers – whatever the institution from which they borrow – local authorities, building societies, etc. – that institution will receive Government aid so that it can lend on fair and reasonable terms".

Richard Crossman

When the Labour Cabinet was formed Michael Stewart and Richard Crossman exchanged roles, Crossman, (who had been shadow Minister of Education and firmly expected to go to the Education Ministry) becoming Minister of Housing and Local Government. Like Aneurin Bevan, he was a left-winger but from a middle-class background. He had earned his living as journalist and writer, and

like all but three of his colleagues he was a Cabinet Minister for the first time. Nor had he held office of any kind before. He had a keen, questioning mind if not always good judgment. He went about his tasks as Minister of Housing with enthusiasm, and soon displayed a desire to co-operate with building societies and to convince them that he was in full sympathy with owner-occupation. It was all very different from 1945.

The Rent Act 1965

Crossman's first priority in housing was to repeal the 1957 Rent Act and extend the scope of rent control and of protection from eviction. Accordingly, control was extended to all but luxury accommodation. Dwellings which had been controlled under previous Acts remained controlled, but those houses and flats now brought within the Acts were to be known as regulated tenancies. It was to these that the new concept of a "fair rent" was to apply. This fair rent was to be determined by a rent officer, having regard to the age, character and locality of the dwelling and to its state of repair; but scarcity value was not to be taken into account. Either the landlord or the tenant could apply to the rent officer for a determination of the fair rent; if either party objected to the rent fixed by the rent officer he then referred the matter to a rent assessment committee.

It was by the introduction of the fair rent (which was not closely defined and left a good deal to the common sense of the rent officers and the rent assessment committees) that Crossman showed he was not a doctrinaire and that he was prepared to employ a pragmatic approach to the problems of housing.

The Land Commission

Although the responsibility for the legislation setting up the Land Commission was not directly that of Crossman, the main objects of the Commission were directly related to the general housing plan. One was to secure that the right land was available for the regional and local plans. It was expected that land would be made available for housing at lower than market prices, and a special form of tenure known as "Crownhold" was to be introduced. The Land Commission was given the power to acquire land compulsorily and hold it for release for housing and other uses. The other main object was to ensure that a substantial part of the development value created by the community went not into the pocket of the fortunate landowner but to the community itself. The Land Commission was to collect a levy of 40 per cent on development value.

Crossman, himself, was always unhappy about the Land Commission. The Act establishing it was not passed until 1967, but in June 1966 Crossman

remarks in his Diary; "The Land Commission? I am trying to make it relevant so that it can do something useful in providing land for private-enterprise builders during the next five years. But, frankly, we don't need the cumbrous machinery of a Land Commission. It will cause nothing but disillusionment when it is on the Statute Book".* He also observed that the betterment levy could have been collected far more cheaply by the Treasury as part of capital gains†.

The Land Commission signally failed to make land available for house builders. It was, as Crossman predicted, a cumbrous machine. And it was abolished when the Conservatives were returned to power in 1970. As Crossman had suggested, development values were dealt with by way of profits and capital gains taxes and by a development tax.

The Housing Programme 1965-70

The Government, endeavouring to get away from the *ad hoc* economic policies which had been pursued throughout the 1950s, established the Department of Economic Affairs whose central functions was to be the preparation and implementation of a National Plan. That Plan was published in September 1965 and envisaged a 25 per cent increase in national output over the period to 1970. The implications for the various sectors of the economy were worked out in some detail. So far as housing was concerned, the Plan provided that it should have a much greater priority than it had had for many years. It was left to Crossman to draw up the details and to that end he began to prepare a White Paper setting out *his* programme for the years to 1970.

In 1964 383,000 houses had been completed in the United Kingdom. His objective was to reach a half million houses by 1970. Within that total he wanted to ensure a proper balance between building for owner-occupation and building by local authorities for letting. He acknowledged that there was a large and increasing demand for homeownership. The housing plan must meet that demand and also take account of what was probably an even larger suppressed demand for owner-occupation among the many families who could not quite afford a mortgage on current terms.

At the same time Crossman argued that it would be criminal not to allow for an even faster growth of building to let. There were too many families living in bad housing conditions – families which could only afford to rent and who in most cases could not afford to pay an economic rent. In particular the conditions of housing in the big cities made the provision of a large pool of houses to let in those cities at rents below the profitable level an urgent social necessity. Despite

*Crossman Diaries Vol. 1 p. 533.
†*Ibid. p. 560.*

these needs house building by local authorities had been running at low levels. In England and Wales they had erected 221,000 houses in 1954. From then on, there had been a steady decline to 98,000 and thereafter only a modest increase to 126,000 in 1964.

Crossman felt that local authority housing should rise to 250,000 by 1970. In other words he was planning for parity between local authority and owner-occupation housing to be reached by 1970. That meant a much greater increase in local authority than in private sector house building. Given that the resources of the building industry would be hard pressed to increase total output to 500,000 by 1970, it might even be necessary to impose some limits on the private sector since that sector was already in sight of producing 250,000 houses per annum.

Negotiations with the Building Societies

If the balance was to be what Crossman thought was needed, then it called for co-operation between those concerned with housebuilding and housing finance. Discussions were therefore begun with the building societies to enlist their agreement and support. After their rather discomforting experience with Aneurin Bevin, the members of the Association Council were agreeably surprised to be closely consulted by Crossman. But they were wary, too. The point that they found difficult to swallow was that they might be called upon to restrict mortgage lending if they found that new houses for sale were in such demand that the annual rate of production for the United Kingdom as a whole was likely to go up beyond the 250,000 target figure before 1970. With the total at 221,000 for 1964 (an increase of 44,000 on the previous year) this seemed quite likely. Were mortgages to be refused, private house builders discouraged and perhaps newly built houses left unsold? This prospect aroused opposition and at the August meeting of the Council when the issue came up for decision it was turned down. Crossman writes in his Diary*: "I had received one surprising and very bad piece of news, namely that the Council of the Building Societies Federation (sic) had considered my national housing plan and had unreservedly turned it down. This was the worst blow I had received since becoming Minister. The last meeting I had with them, just before Parliament broke up, was first-rate and indeed I felt confident that everyone present would go back and recommend the Council to accept the plan in principle and help me to work out its detail".

However, those who had been closely involved in the negotiations, led by

*Vol. 1. p. 313.

Donald Gould (the then Chairman of the Council), decided that further efforts should be made. They called together the ten largest societies in September and gained their acceptance in principle of the plan. The Council then reversed its decision of August and decided to give support to the plan. The Deputy-Chairman of the Council (Gilbert Anderson) later gave his views on the question of co-operation by saying that he and others did not think it would be good tactics to say to any Government that they foresaw so many difficulties that they did not wish to co-operate. Ministers and senior Civil Servants would suggest writing off the movement as unimaginative and rather stupid. Building societies maintained that they were non-political and whether or not there was a change of Government the scheme was likely to go on and it would be irretrievably damaging to the movement if it was to co-operate with another Government having rejected this one.

This was the real issue for the building societies – whether to agree to co-operate. There are always two views on this question. There are those who believe that the movement is of such importance in housing finance that it should at all times be consulted and be allowed to use its funds to help a Government's housing efforts. When a Government does come along and propose a new scheme or plan (as in 1959 and now again in 1964) there are those who automatically recoil from anything which threatens the freedom or independence of building societies. The "thin end of the wedge" is to them a terrifying weapon. As we shall see in the next chapter these fears were not assuaged by the Government's attitude to building societies on the subject of interest rates.

What of the merits of the plan? In the circumstances there was probably a need for an increase in building to rent, which only local authorities could supply. There was room for argument about how many more subsidised houses should be built. Crossman himself admitted it was a matter of judgment. But what most building societies felt was that houses built for sale helped to solve the housing shortage because many of those who bought new houses left older accommodation which could be purchased by less well-off families; what is known as the filtering-up process. Crossman proposed a fifty-fifty basis and the building societies at once saw the possibility, if all went well with the house-building programme, of this meaning a curb on the private sector and their own lending. If however demand fell off, how would the Minister succeed in putting a floor to house sales and lending? If Crossman's ideas were commendable there were many doubts as to how they would work out in practice.

The Plan Abandoned

In the event, the economic and financial problems which confronted the Government put an end to the great expectations which the National Plan had

raised. The balance of payments seemed likely to be worse in 1966 than in 1965. In July 1966 the Bank Rate was raised by 1 per cent, special deposits were called for from the banks and deflationary measures reducing demand by £500 million were announced. It was the biggest deflationary package ever and was accompanied by a six-month standstill on wages, salaries and dividends. Prices, with certain exceptions, were also to be frozen.

These measures succeeded in reducing imports but exports did not rise. Output stagnated and unemployment rose. In May 1967 another massive run on the pound began and the situation was not helped by the Six Day War in the Middle East which began in June and led to a temporary embargo on oil to the United States and the United Kingdom. The closure of the Suez Canal added to the difficulties. The financial crisis became acute in the Autumn and finally led to devaluation of the pound from $2.80 to $2.40. Then came more deflationary measures: Bank Rate up by $1\frac{1}{2}$ per cent to 8 per cent; restrictions on bank lending and hire purchase; and severe cuts in defence and other public expenditure. The Government went so far as to reimpose prescription charges, postpone the school-leaving age rise to sixteen and discontinue free milk in secondary schools.

The National Plan was now in ruins and the Housing Programme had also gone by the board. There was no hope of attaining the target of 500,000 houses by 1970. The highest figure was that of 1968 when 425,000 houses were erected, an increase of 10,000 over 1967 and of 20,000 over 1966. In 1969 the figure fell to 378,000 and in 1970 to 362,000. These falls were due mainly to a sharp drop in the building of houses for sale. Higher interest rates and the deflationary measures had reduced demand and created difficulties for the private housebuilder. Local authority housing fell, too, from 1968 although not as sharply with the result that in 1970 one of Crossman's aims had been achieved — the two housing sectors achieved parity, but at roughly 80,000 below the figure of 250,000 envisaged for each.

Measures to Implement the Housing Programme

The Housing Plan failed in its grand design to build more houses but some of the measures which were taken to implement it must be recorded. Control of less essential building was imposed by a system of controls on office development in London and Birmingham and a licensing system for privately sponsored construction projects to the value of over £100,000 outside the development districts. These restrictions were made partly because too many office buildings were being erected and partly to give priority to housing, industrial buildings, educational buildings and hospitals.

Local authorities were to be encouraged to take full advantage of industrialised building. It was hoped that local authorities would get together and provide large contracts which would enable contractors to provide houses using industrial methods approved by the National Building Agency and thus increase output and lower costs. The results were disappointing.

The most important step taken in connection with local authority housing was the reorganisation of the subsidy system. Under the Housing Subsidies Act of 1967 subsidies were made available on the 'approved cost' of each scheme, the amount of the subsidy representing the difference between 4 per cent interest on this 'approved cost' and the annual loan charges for 60 years. Thus as interest rates rose the amount of the subsidy would rise. This was a reversion to the subsidy principle of the 1919 Act; the local authority's cost was limited and the rest was borne by the Exchequer. To avoid an undue burden being placed on the Exchequer through extravagance or over-pricing the Ministry introduced the concept of the "cost yardstick" which set the maximum cost of dwellings approved for Exchequer subsidy. This new form of subsidy was a direct encouragement to local authorities.

The Option Mortgage and 100 per cent Loans

The hopes of the Government that they would be able to reduce the cost of house-purchase to new, if not to existing borrowers, had to be put on one side after the election. Interest rates were on the way up and the financial crisis necessitated deferment of the commitment. But, in 1967, provision for an option mortgage scheme was included in the Housing Subsidies Act. This gave house purchasers the opportunity to opt for a subsidy in place of income tax relief on mortgage interest. It was therefore of direct appeal to borrowers on low incomes who would in the ordinary way obtain little or no tax relief. The relief took the form of a 2 per cent reduction in the mortgage interest rate but provision has since been made for this relief to be raised when higher interest rates are being charged by lenders. It rises to 3.9 per cent when the interest rate is 13 per cent.

The scheme was hammered out at discussions between the Ministry and the Building Societies Association. The Ministry wanted to adopt a complicated scheme which the building society representatives strongly opposed. In the end the simpler proposals of the latter prevailed.

Accompanying the option mortgage proposals was another for 100 per cent loans to be guaranteed jointly by the Government and insurance companies. These 100 per cent loans were to be available only to those taking out option mortgages and buying houses where the valuation or purchase price was not

more than £5,000.* Option Mortgages were available from 1st January 1968 and the 100 per cent loan scheme commenced on 1st April 1968.

Protection for House-Buyers

The National House Builders Registration Council was established in 1936. It was not solely a builders' organisation; building societies, architects and others were represented on the governing body. Its purpose was to set standards and to control by inspection and certification the houses erected by house building firms subscribing to the scheme. Over the years the number of firms working under the Council had been disappointing. The Ministry encouraged the Council to raise its required building standards and improve the protection offered to a purchaser of a certified house. But only about 30 per cent of all new private houses were covered by the scheme.

The Registration Council and the Building Societies Association discussed the possibility of making adherence to the scheme a condition for a building society advance on a new house. The Government was determined to ensure that houses were built to acceptable standards and purchasers protected against shoddy work. If necessary it was prepared to bring in a compulsory scheme but preferred that it should be done on a voluntary basis. Pressure was gently but firmly exerted by the Ministry on both bodies. The issue was resolved by the Association recommending to its members that from 1st September 1968 no advance should be made on a new house unless it was certified by the N.H.B.R.C. or had been erected under the supervision of an architect. Local authorities were asked by the Ministry to restrict their loans on new houses in the same way. Once this had been done, house builders throughout the country rushed to join the certification scheme.

*The limit for option mortgages is now £25,000 and that for 100 per cent loans is £14,000 (April 1980)

Chapter 30

THE LABOUR GOVERNMENT AND INTEREST RATES 1964-70

The Labour Party's manifesto for the 1964 election held out the prospect of lower interest rates for intending owner-occupiers. It promised that lending organisations would receive Government aid to enable them to make loans available on easier terms. Once the election was over and Labour was in office, building societies were eager to learn how the Government intended to fulfil this promise. Would they abolish or substantially reduce societies' taxation? Or would they pay a subsidy for new mortgages? Or would they make Government money available at a low rate for on-lending?

In its early days the Government had more pressing financial problems to face. There was a serious balance of payments deficit to deal with and a heavy run on the pound which necessitated a 7 per cent Bank Rate and support from the U.S. and E.E.C. Central Banks. Taxation was increased to cover the cost of higher old-age pensions and social security benefits and also the cost of the abolition of prescription charges. Crossman told the House of Commons that the Government was obliged to defer plans for cheap mortgages although it in no way withdrew from the commitment.

The First Confrontation

But while the prospect of cheaper mortgages was deferred, the immediate question was whether there should be a rise in building societies' mortgage rates. The 6 per cent rate which had been fixed in April 1963 had held through that year and 1964. By October 1964 interest rates generally had risen and building societies found that the inflow of money was tailing off. It was felt that an increase in investors' rates might be required, with a consequent increase in mortgage rates.

From the Government's point of view this was an unwelcome prospect. It was one thing to defer prospects of cheaper mortgages, another to have to contemplate an immediate rise in rates to both existing and new borrowers. Accordingly the Chancellor and Crossman met representatives of the Council on 30th October to ask them not to raise their rates. Crossman wrote in his Diaries: "It

was a curious sensation to feel that we were speaking for Her Majesty's Government and telling this vast organisation not to raise its interest rates when it intended to do so. Of course they replied that if they didn't raise the interest rates and get the money in there we would be fewer house built and there might be a sudden upsurge of unemployment in the building industry. Nevertheless, we kept the instructions very strong".* At the following meeting of the Council in November it was recommended that there should be no immediate increase in rates. The Chancellor had been informed of the Association's willingness to assist the Government to keep costs and prices steady but that increased tax burdens compelled the Council to give continued thought to how long building societies could maintain their present rate of interest on mortgages. Another meeting with the Chancellor and Crossman took place on 9th December. Crossman noted: "Since the economic situation is still not very good and there is continued lack of confidence, there is, of course, pressure on the societies to raise the rate and the Chancellor had to plead even more strongly with them to hold back and to urge them at least to postpone the decision until after Christmas. It was obvious we were fighting against the tide".†

Building societies too were fighting against the tide. Some societies were by now experiencing a high level of withdrawals. And all of them were concerned about narrowing margins. But with the Chancellor apparently reconciled to an increase after Christmas the Council decided at its December meeting that it would recommend a new rate structure at its January meeting. In the meantime the Leicester Permanent decided to increase its share rate from 3½ per cent to 3¾ per cent from 1st January 1965 but deferred a decision on mortgage rates until after the January Council meeting. The *Gazette* commented "What is extraordinary is not that the Leicester Permanent found it necessary to make the change a month or so earlier than other societies: it is extraordinary that all societies put their own needs on one side for so long in the interest of the movement and the country".

In January 1965 the Council recommended that the share rate should be raised from 3½ per cent to 3¾ per cent and that the mortgage rate for both new and existing borrowers should be increased from 6 to 6¼ per cent. The Council also recommended that, wherever possible, societies should allow borrowers to continue their existing payments. Although the Chancellor had indicated that he was resigned to this increase, nevertheless he made it clear in the House of Commons a few days later that in his view there was at that moment no case for an upward change in rates. He based his opinion on three grounds. The first was that the

*Crossman op. cit. Vol. 1 p.39.
†Ibid. Vol. 1 p.92.

building societies had said that this was to be a long-term increase yet it was apparently based on a temporary increase in the Bank Rate. The second was that most societies were well above the reserve ratio necessary to qualify for trustee status, by which he implied that they could therefore raise the investment rate if they felt that necessary without raising the mortgage rate. And thirdly he said that societies would benefit from the new corporation tax and would be able to add substantially to their working margins and reserves.

The Association was quick to refute these arguments. It had never been stated that there was to be a long-term increase in rates; they were based on a level which would equate the supply of funds with demands for mortgages and the duration of the new structure would depend on the success of societies in attracting funds from the public. On the point made about running down reserve ratios the Association declared firmly that as financial institutions societies could not hazard the confidence of their investors and long practical experience had shown that this was best achieved by maintaining a sound reserve structure. Thirdly, any benefit arising from Corporation tax would not occur until 1966-67 and building societies did not know the precise amount of the benefit. It would be taken into account in considering interest rates at the time when the benefit was received.

The increases were accepted by the Press and by borrowers as necessary. The increase in the share rate brought an improvement in receipts but withdrawals increased at an even faster rate. Net receipts in the first half of 1965 fell by one-third compared with the first half of 1964. Soon there were murmurings that a further increase in the share rate must be made to counter the competition which building societies were experiencing. At the Annual Conference in May the Council rejected a proposal that the share rate should be raised to 4 per cent, leaving the mortgage rate unchanged. The Chairman (Andrew Breach) said, "When we last altered our interest rates we had to take a wider margin. If, as an expedient, we increase the share rate by $\frac{1}{4}$ per cent and cut the margin, it will surely destroy much of the argument we have used — and will inevitably lead to a rise in the mortgage rate in due course". This view was consistent with the arguments which Breach had used in discussions with the Chancellor and the statement which the Association had made in reply to the Chancellor's attack in January.

However, for some societies the need to remedy a rapidly worsening withdrawal situation over-rode the Chairman's logic. Within a matter of days several societies decided to increase the share rate to 4 per cent and some of them put the mortgage rate up to 7 per cent for new borrowers. Faced with this

situation the Council was compelled to change its stance and at the June meeting recommended members to increase the share rate to 4 per cent from 1st July, and added that in the light of prevailing conditions it was not intended to recommend an increase in the mortgage rate notwithstanding the reduced working margin which resulted.

The Second Confrontation

The increase to 4 per cent brought about a much improved flow of funds. Building Societies were once again competitive but there remained misgivings about margins. It was desirable that mortgage rates should soon be increased. But it was not going to be easy to bring that about. A rise to 7 per cent or more in a year when the rate had already been increased to $6\frac{1}{4}$ was not going to be welcomed by the Government. At the September Council meeting there was a "long intensive discussion" prior to which the Chairman (now Donald Gould) had had a discussion with the Chancellor who had outlined the state of the country's finances and asked that no change in mortgage rates should be made. The Council acquiesced and throughout the remaining months of 1965, although pressure was being exerted by some societies, continued to recommend that there should be no change in the mortgage rate. In March 1966 the Council stated that unless societies were afforded substantial relief from taxation in the forthcoming Budget it was inevitable that mortgage rates would rise.

The Budget provided no relief to building societies and opinion was hardening that a rise in the mortgage rate must be effected. The Chancellor wrote a letter to the Chairman of the Council arguing that societies had no cause for concern about their reserves. The Chancellor also met a deputation from the Council and there was a long discussion. Crossman was present and recorded in his Diaries ". . . today was the day when Callaghan and I were due to meet the building societies for our long-postponed meeting about the rate of interest. I have always held that the building societies have got to fix a rate of interest which enables them to compete with the local authorities, for example, who may be borrowing money at $7\frac{1}{2}$ per cent. If their offer is worse than the prevailing rate they go out of business and the whole private sector of house building collapses for lack of funds. This is a point at which the Treasury officials and mine, particularly my new Permanent Secretary, see eye to eye. And I agree with them against Callaghan, who hates high interest rates and likes to put the blame for them on somebody else. The rest of us all felt that this meeting with the building societies was going to be a waste of time. It was obvious that whatever

we said they are going to put the rate of interest up and all we can do is to refer the issue to the Prices and Incomes Board".*

Apparently Crossman's only reason for wanting the question of building society interest rates referred to the Prices and Incomes Board was to get it out of the way for some months without it appearing that the Government had endorsed or approved the rise. The building society representatives were firm and the mortgage rate for new borrowers was raised to $7\frac{1}{8}$ per cent with immediate effect. Existing borrowers were to be given notice of an increase to the same level.

The Government asked the Prices and Incomes Board to examine the justification for the increase in the light of the Association's contention that the increase was essential in order to maintain the growth of building society activity without an undue reduction in societies' reserve rates. Whilst this enquiry was being held the country's financial position rapidly deteriorated. A seven weeks seaman's strike which began in May demonstrated the vulnerability of the economy. Large amounts of money left the country in May and June. There were pressures from abroad for the Government to cut back expenditure and tighten the incomes policy. Accordingly, in July Bank Rate was raised to 7 per cent and deflationary measures announced. In addition, there was to be a complete standstill for six months on wages, salaries and dividends followed by a further six months of severe restraint. Prices were to be frozen for twelve months. Legislation to give effect to the standstill on wages, salaries and dividends and the freezing of prices was effected by the middle of August.

The question then arose whether mortgage rates charged to existing borrowers could be frozen. They were not covered by the new legislation. So once again pressure was brought to bear on the Council. Crossman saw the Chairman, told him of the importance the Government attached to the prices and incomes policy and emphasised the Government's wishes that the notices served on existing borrowers should not be implemented until the Prices and Incomes Board had completed its report.

In September the Council decided to recommend that the increase to existing borrowers should be deferred until 1st January 1967. The Council made it clear that this recommendation had been made as a result of representations from the Government that deferment would be in the best interests of the country. At the same time the Council warned that mortgage rates might have to rise yet again in 1967 if it became necessary to increase investors' rates. That warning was made because net receipts were steadily falling and continued to fall so that by December the Council felt obliged not only to recommend that the increase in

*Crossman op. cit. Vol. 1 p. 522.

existing borrowers' rates should take effect from 1st January 1967 but also that the share rate should be increased to 4¼ per cent to stimulate a better flow of funds.

In both these confrontations on interest rates the pressures brought to bear on the Chairman of the Council and on the other representations of the Association by the Chancellor, the Treasury and the Ministry of Housing were far greater than the apparent acquiescence of Crossman would indicate. The Chancellor was firmly of the opinion that building societies could manage for a time at least by leaving the mortgage rate unchanged and operating on a margin which left little or nothing to add to reserves or even meant operating at a loss. But for how long? That was the question which troubled building societies. They were unwilling to accept an uneconomic relationship between investment and mortgage rates for an indefinite period. To oblige the Government they did accept it temporarily. The course of events proved that they were right on both occasions to stand firm, for interest rates were to go on rising and the Government could do nothing about it.

The Prices and Incomes Board Report

Before the December decision on rates was made the Report of the Prices and Incomes Board had been published. On the immediate question of whether the mortgage rate for existing borrowers should be increased the Board gave a conditional answer. If no change in the investment rate was required on 1st January 1967 the Board was of the opinion that there need be no increase to existing borrowers. As related above an increase in the investment rate was needed and this disposed of the short-term issue.

The Board also examined the longer-term question of interest rates and the margin needed to cover taxation, management expenses and provision for reserves. The essential question was how much should be put to reserves. The Board saw no case for margins falling so low that there would be a temporary lapse from the appropriate reserve level. But was the reserve level to which societies worked a proper level or was it one which could with safety be lowered? Similar considerations applied to liquidity ratios. The Board was not prepared to impose its own solutions to these questions but recommended that the Association should commission a study of the real requirements of reserves and liquidity ratios in the light of past experience and likely trends. They suggested that the study should be carried out by independent persons chosen jointly by the Government and the Association.*

*This recommendation was adopted – see next chapter under heading "The Hardie Report".

A Change of Heart

The Government was still struggling to get the economy back on course. The deflationary package of July had helped to stabilise the pound and by May 1967 the Bank Rate had been reduced to 5½ per cent. There were those who wanted to know when the building societies were going to reduce their rates. It was now that it became plain that the Government was no longer pressing for lower rates. The Minister of Housing (now Anthony Greenwood) said that the "general view of the Building Societies Association is that to support a rising programme of house building the societies will have to retain their present investment and mortgage rates for the time being. My concern is that funds should be available for building private houses, particularly in anticipation of the operation of the Option Mortgage Scheme this year". And the Chancellor said in October "one difficulty that we have not been able to overcome is that your borrowing and lending rates are higher than you or I would like, but I fear that this is unavoidable at the present time. The world is going through a period of high interest rates and we are not exempt.".*

Devaluation

During the latter part of 1966 and early part of 1967 the freeze was holding and the deflationary measures were beginning to bite. There was an influx of funds and sterling strengthened. There was however no evidence of a sustained improvement in the trade balance and bad figures for April produced a massive run on the pound. This was followed by dock strikes and in June the Six-Day-War in the Middle East. During October and November the crisis built up resulting in the devaluation of the pound from $2.80 to $2.40 Bank Rate went up to 8 per cent and building societies found their buoyant flow of funds falling sharply. By March 1968 net receipts were down to a mere £22 million. A further increase in the investment rate was needed and this time there was no question but the mortgage rate must also be raised. Accordingly the Council recommended that 4½ per cent be paid to investors from 1st May and the mortgage rate be increased to 7⅜ per cent. No serious attempt was made to interfere with this decision. A few deprecatory noises were made, but the Government was having to face the fact that high interest rates were here to stay.

    Following devaluation the country started out on what the new Chancellor (Roy Jenkins) termed "two years' hard slog". Deflationary measures and higher

---

*J. Callaghan: at the opening of Alliance House, Hove, 23 October 1967.

taxation were announced with the aim of achieving a surplus on the balance of payments. It was achieved by 1970. But interest rates did not come down. There were two reductions of one-half per cent in Bank Rate during 1968, but by February 1969 it was back to 8 per cent and remained at that figure for a year. Competition from other savings bodies had cut into building societies' net receipts, and in March 1969 the Council recommended increases in the investment rate to 5 per cent and in the mortgage rate to 8½ per cent. On this occasion there was no hesitation on the part of the Council. Inflation was driving interest rates higher all the way round and the need for building societies to be competitive was becoming recognised by themselves, the Government and the public. The consolation for borrowers was that house prices were steadily rising.

Chapter 31

A DECADE OF EXPANSION 1961-70

In the 1950s building societies achieved a notable expansion which enabled them to double their assets and their mortgage lending. It was a favourable decade in which progress in real terms was made. Inflation had been running at no more than two or three per cent per annum, house prices had remained reasonably steady and mortgage interest rates had not risen above 6 per cent. In money terms the 1960s were years of even more spectacular progress. By the end of the period assets had more than trebled at £10,800 million and the amount advanced on mortgage had risen from £560 million to nearly £2,000 million a year. These increases were partly due to the accelerating tempo of inflation and the rise in house prices. Over the decade house prices doubled.* As house prices had risen, so had the amount of the average loan – from £1,670 (December 60) to £3,575 (December 70). Thus, the growth of building society business in real terms was not as great as would appear from the figures. Nevertheless the increase did represent a substantial measure of progress as is evidenced by the fact that the total number of borrowers rose in the decade from 2.3 million to 3.6 million.

Owner-occupation made a significant advance in the 1960s. Some 2 million houses were erected for sale and these houses, together with houses sold from privately owned and rented stock, resulted in an increase of some 2.5 million in the number of owner-occupied dwellings. For Great Britain as a whole the proportion of such dwellings rose from 42 per cent to 50 per cent. In England the proportion rose to 51.8 per cent and in Wales to 55.5 per cent. And Scotland, far behind in owner-occupation made a useful leap forward from 25.4 per cent to 30.9 per cent.

The expansion of business had brought an increase in staff numbers to approximately 25,000 and the number of branch offices had risen to about 2,000 by the end of 1970. The large societies had continued to increase their share of total

*According to the Nationwide House Price Index: December 1952–100; December 1960–123; December 1970–241.

assets. There were some changes in the leading ten societies due partly to differ-ing rates of progress but also because of mergers between sizeable societies.

Building Society Funds

During the 1960s the inflow of savings and investments from share-holders and depositors was such that by 1969 the funds held exceeded the sum total of all the various forms of National Savings (Savings Certificates, Premium Bonds, etc.). At December 1970 the balances of members and depositors in building societies amounted to £10,142 million compared with £8,589 million held in National Savings. Branch offices, advertising and a determination to maintain the inflow at an adequate level to finance the high demand for mortgage loans, all played their part. There were two other factors which were helpful.

The first was a revision of the limit of £5,000 imposed on investment at the composite rate of tax in any one society by husband and wife. With the fall in the value of money it was felt that this limit had become too restrictive. It did, after all, date from the 1920s. Accordingly agreement was reached in 1965 that the limit should be raised so that a man and wife could each invest £5,000 in one society. And in 1968 the limit was raised to £10,000 for each.* There has, of course, never been any objection to investment up to the limit in more than one society and it is by no means uncommon for investors to have accounts with more than one society. It was said that George Bernard Shaw had something approaching £100,000 invested in £5,000 lots with various building societies'! But there are many investors who prefer to deal with one society only and the raising of the limit has no doubt encouraged many of these to make additions to their accounts.

The other helpful factor was the introduction of S.A.Y.E. In 1969 the Government introduced the save-as-you-earn facility under which the saver would qualify at the end of five years for a bonus equivalent to one year's savings in the scheme; and that bonus was to be free of tax, surtax and capital gains tax. If the savings were left untouched for a further two years the bonus would be doubled. S.A.Y.E. was to be operated through the Department of National Savings, but the Government offered to extend the tax relief to a similar contractual scheme run by building societies. The Association accepted this offer on the basis that the interest or bonuses would not give rise to liability for composite rate and that they would be an allowable deduction for purposes of corporation tax. The scheme was readily taken up by societies and was

---

*A further revision was made in 1978 – this time to £15,000 for each and the figure was revised again (April 1980) to £20,000.

publicised not only by individual societies but also in the Association's collective advertising. It has proved popular with the public and in the first six months of operation some 150,000 accounts were opened*

Retirement of C. Garratt-Holden

In 1963 Mr Charles Garratt-Holden C.B.E. retired from the secretaryship of the Association after 26 years' service in that office broken only by his war-time absence. Warm tributes were paid to him at the Annual Conference. It had fallen to him to create a professional organisation capable of dealing with the many problems and negotiations entailed in a rapidly growing movement. He did so with skill, tact and great efficiency and created a smooth-working establishment. Not only did he serve the Council well but he maintained liaison with the District Associations and paid punctilious attention to the problems and queries of member societies. He also served as Secretary-General of the International Union for a number of years and on the Council of the Institute, of which he was President 1963-4. He was succeeded by the present Secretary-General, Mr. Norman Griggs.

Halifax Rejoins the Association

The defection of the Halifax in 1956 was a severe blow to the solidarity of the Association. After the tenuous link preserved by the two-years chairmanship of the Council of Bentley (1956-58) the Halifax remained detached from the Association's activities. After Denham's death in 1961 it was hoped that rapprochement might be possible. But no sign of a change of heart was immediately visible. In reply to a question at the Annual General Meeting of the society in May 1964, it was stated that there was for the time being no intention of rejoining. But the Council did not give up hope of persuading the Halifax Board to a change of mind. By the Autumn of 1964, the advent of the Labour Government, the financial crisis and the question of interest rates were showing the need for building societies to close their ranks. At the invitation of the Chairman of the Council (Andrew Breach), the President and the Vice-President of the Halifax met representatives of the Council to "discuss some of the current and future issues which are common to us all". As a result of that meeting the Chairman wrote to the Halifax President (Ian MacLean) saying that "it would give us all much satisfaction if the Halifax, by resuming membership of the Association, could join regularly with us in dealing with these issues to our mutual benefit". The Halifax accepted the invitation in December 1964.

*At the end of the 1979 there were some 533,500 S.A.Y.E. accounts.

Public Relations

The growth of the movement, its dominance in the field of owner-occupier loans and its need for ever larger funds meant that its operations needed to be explained to the public. With the Government's approaches on the implications of the Housing Plan, and, more importantly, the concern about higher interest rates displayed by not only the Government but by the Press and by borrowers, that need became more acute in the middle 1960s.

In 1955 the Association had begun the publication of a quarterly bulletin entitled Building Society Affairs of which about 50,000 copies were issued, and, as already noted, a collective publicity scheme had been commenced in 1957. From 1964 onwards a bigger effort was made. A second quarterly (Building Society Statistics) was issued, and regular Press conferences, which had already been instituted by one or two of the larger societies, were started by the Association.

Public relations need to be conducted in two ways. First, endeavour must be made to bring to the public generally better understanding of what building societies are, the scope and range of their services and the limitations imposed upon them by financial and economic conditions. This can be achieved by direct communication to the public by means of collective advertising, television and radio interviews, by reports of Chairmen's speeches at annual meetings and communications to members of societies. The second approach is directed to a smaller but influential group which is able to contribute to public discussion on matters affecting building societies and which in various ways can influence opinion and events. It is desirable that this group, among which may be numbered journalists and editors, members of both Houses of Parliament, academics and those responsible for news and features programmes on radio and television, should be properly briefed with facts and figures, and informed of the building society viewpoint. They may not necessarily agree with what building societies do or say, but it is desirable that they should know the facts and the thinking behind societies' decisions or pronouncements. That is the purpose of the Press conferences and of the publications issued by the Association. On a longer term view the Association also began in the 1960s to issue booklets and wall charts for use in schools and also pamphlets on careers in building societies.

International Union: London Congress

In October 1965 the triennial Congress of the International Union of Building Societies and Savings Associations, was held in London and every effort was made to ensure that it was one of the outstanding conferences of the series.

Princess Margaret opened the Congress, Richard Crossman made an important speech on housing, including his proposals for the Government's co-operation with building societies on the housing plan. And the Prime Minister (Harold Wilson) addressed the closing session. Although Crossman's address was designed for British consumption only and the Prime Minister had little to say but praise for both the movement at home and abroad, nevertheless the many delegates from overseas were gratified that a member of the royal family, the Prime Minister and a senior cabinet minister should be seen and heard. There was also a splendid banquet at the Guildhall in the City of London at which the Lord Mayor and Lady Mayoress were present. Hubert Newton (now Sir) presided over the Congress. Other Congresses during the 1960s were held in Washington (1962) and Sydney (1968).

The Hardie Report

When the Prices and Incomes Board reported on building society interest rates in November 1966 it recommended (as recorded in the last chapter) that a study on reserves and liquidity should be commissioned to be carried out by independent persons to be appointed jointly by the Association and the Government. A committee of five under the chairmanship of Mr (later Sir) Charles Hardie (a chartered accountant with wide experience of finance and industry) was set up to consider and to make recommendations on the determination of reserve and liquidity ratios of building societies, having regard to their commercial requirements (including the necessity of retaining the confidence of the investing public and the need to maintain and expand their mortgage lending) and to the acquisition and retention of trustee status.*

At the time of the enquiry the requirements for trustee status were: assets of not less than £500,000; reserves of 2½ per cent for the first £100 million of assets and 2 per cent in respect of assets over £100 million; and liquidity of not less than 7½ per cent. The Committee, in addressing itself to the question of reserves considered the two likely sources of losses for which reserves would be required — namely losses on mortgages and losses on investments. They dismissed both risks as minimal. In recent years mortgage losses had for all practical purposes ceased to exist, constituting (on average since 1952) .011 per cent of

*The other members of the committee were:— Sir Gordon Newton (Editor and Director *The Financial Times*): Mr E J N Warburton CBE (Vice-Chairman Lloyds Bank Ltd): Mr G D M Worswick (Director National Institute of Economical and Social Research) and Mr Kenneth Keith (now Lord Keith) Deputy Chairman Hill, Samuel & Co Ltd. The last named resigned during the course of the enquiry owing to pressing public and other duties).

total advances. The only probability of any increase in this rate of mortgage losses would be if there were a major and prolonged depression of the kind experienced in certain parts of the country in the 1920s and 1930s. While such an eventuality could never be dismissed with absolute certainty, it was no longer a risk which societies should endeavour to cover in their reserve policies. So far as losses on investments were concerned, the Committee were of the opinion that as the regulations imposed by the Registrar under the 1960 Act had ended the purchase of long-dated securities the risk of losses had been reduced to minimal proportions. But although they were minimal they were not zero and some cover was needed. In addition part of the reserves held by a society was represented by fixed assets (premises and equipment), and some allowance must be made for increases in these items as a society grew in size.

The Committee concluded that beyond a certain size a reserve ratio of 1 per cent for additional assets would be sufficient. Accordingly, a sliding scale was recommended beginning at $3\frac{1}{2}$ per cent on assets up to £500,000 and falling by stages to $1\frac{1}{2}$ per cent for assets between £100 million and £500 million, with a flat rate of 1 per cent on assets in excess of £1,000 million. In subsequent discussions between the Government and the Association, the principle of the sliding scale was adopted both for Trustee Status and membership of the Association, but the percentages finally agreed were as follows:

Up to £100 million ;	$2\frac{1}{4}$%
£100 to £500 million	2%
£500 to £1,000 million	$1\frac{3}{4}$%
Over £1,000 million	$1\frac{1}{4}$%

Although the building society movement acquiesced in the adoption of this sliding scale it was only because it was regarded as a minimum requirement and left each society to determine its own level of reserves at such higher ratio to assets as it deemed prudent. No one was impressed by the argument that no provision need be made against possible losses in mortgages. It was not so much a question of the possibility of a prolonged depression such as occurred in the inter-war years, it was the much more arguable possibility that once the housing shortage was overcome there could be a reaction in the housing market and prices might fall. Before the Hardie Report was published the Secretary General of the Association had pointed out that for the first time in many years Britain had more houses than householders, and that at some point in the 1970s, unless societies found some other outlet, the problem of attracting funds would turn into one of attracting mortgage business. And, at about the same time, Prof. J. Parry Lewis of Manchester University was forecasting that by about 1975 the demand for additional housing accommodation would drop by

about 30 per cent because of fewer marriages and more deaths. The Minister of Housing (Anthony Greenwood – later Lord Greenwood) said that we were rapidly approaching a watershed in housing; instead of a position of total shortage there would be a national surplus of housing. Such pronouncements were bound to make building societies ask what was likely to happen to house prices. They could not foresee what would happen to house prices in the early 1970s and they were unwilling to concede that reserves against mortgage losses were unnecessary.

Nor were they willing to concede that the risks of investing in gilt-edged were minimal. The violent fluctuations in interest rates which have taken place in the seventies have served to show how sharply short-dated gilt-edged securities can rise and fall in value.

The result is that societies have endeavoured to maintain their margins at a level sufficient to keep their reserves at about the same proportion to assets as they were before the new scale was adopted. In the long run the income from reserves enables societies to operate on a margin less than would be required if they had no reserves or considerably less than those they now maintain.

The other question the Committee was asked to consider was that of the liquidity requirements. On that they were of the opinion that the $7\frac{1}{2}$ per cent minimum should be retained. They also expressed the opinion that the larger societies maintaining liquidity ratios well above the minimum could well reduce them, although at times when there was little difference between mortgage rates and the return they were able to obtain on their investments there was little inducement for them to do so. This suggestion has not found favour with the larger societies, and indeed it is now thought desirable to regard liquidity as a means of stabilising mortgage lending. On this view liquidity will be increased when money flows in well and lowered when the flow slackens off.

Mergers

In the 1960s the number of societies fell from 726 to 481, a decline of over one-third far outstripping the 10 per cent fall which occurred in the 1950s. The fall was mainly due to mergers or transfers of engagements, mainly on the part of small societies deciding that it was no longer worth while to go it alone. There were a number of small societies getting together to form a more viable society. There were also a number of mergers among large or middle-sized societies. The Bradford Equitable and the Bingley merged in 1964 to form the Bradford and Bingley. In the same year the Northern Counties and the Rock (two societies in the North East) formed the Northern Rock. In 1965 the Leek & Moorlands and the Westbourne Park came together to form the Leek & Westbourne Park

(now Britannia). And in 1968 two Lancashire societies the Burnley and the Borough (operating in the same town) decided to throw in their lot together under the name of the Burnley. A number of the smaller London societies came to the conclusion that it would be to their advantage to form larger units; accordingly the Magnet, North West and Shern Hall merged, as did the Chelsea and South London and also the Church of England and Maidenhead.

The Chief Registrar has encouraged this trend. In his Report for 1969 he stated of small local societies "For many the future can only hold stagnation. Directors should reflect upon the future, and, where there is no longer a worthwhile part to play, should ask whether it would not be better to merge with another society".

A year earlier the Chief Registrar had expressed his views on the terms on which a society should transfer its engagements to another society, with particular reference to a distribution of part of the reserves to shareholding members. Where a transferring society has over the years accumulated a large reserve fund (the most obvious case being a society which has not been expanding but adding its surplus to reserves each year) the Chief Registrar conceded that there was a case for some distribution by way of bonus to the members, but thought it desirable that the reserves taken over by the transferee society should be at $2\frac{1}{2}$ per cent to 3 per cent calculated as for trustee status. He thought, however, that one of the dangers of regarding the payment of a bonus to shareholders as an automatic right was that the directors might be tempted to seek the "best terms" from two or more larger societies. And he went so far as to say that if he became aware of a case where dealings of this nature had taken place he would have to give serious consideration to withholding any dispensation (from getting consents of the holders of two-thirds of the shares), not only from the transferor but also the transferee society. He was of the opinion that a building society was a mutual organisation, not a property to be bought and sold or auctioned off to the highest bidder. But against this view it has to be said that the directors of a society which has accumulated substantial reserves and is about to be handed over "lock, stock and barrel" as it were to another society have a duty to get the best possible terms for the members. Faced with a take-over bid the directors of a company clearly have a duty to do their best for their shareholders, and if they can obtain a higher bid from another interested concern they will surely do so. Can the duty of building society directors be otherwise?

Computers

The 1960s saw the beginnings of computerisation by building societies. There was an obvious case for the use of computers to deal with the mass of transac-

tions arising on both investors' and borrowers' accounts, to say nothing of interest calculations and the printing of statements. For some time building societies waited to see how the banks fared with their first experiments with computers and what emerged was not always encouraging. But in the early 1960s there was a quickening of the pace at which computers were being installed by financial institutions and by industrial firms. So the larger societies began to study the possibilities and to investigate the various systems which were being offered.

The Leicester Permanent led the way and were the first society to instal a computer, which was housed in a specially built centre just outside Leicester. By 1963 they had taken delivery of their machine and begun the transfer of accounts. The Abbey National were second in the field, followed soon afterwards by the Co-operative Permanent and the Halifax. By 1968 the Woolwich, the Leeds Permanent, the Alliance and a score of other societies had either installed or ordered computers of one make or another. Centre-File Ltd (a subsidiary of the Westminster Bank) introduced a shared computer service for building societies not large enough to justify purchasing a computer of their own. At the outset some seven societies with combined assets of £200 million agreed to join this scheme and others followed.

This first generation of computers installed by building societies was designed to do no more than replace conventional accounting and registration systems. In those societies where the accounts had formerly been decentralised and as a result of computerisation were now centralised there were some disadvantages in dealing with members at branches. Up-to-date information relating to their accounts was not readily available as it had been. To solve this problem, societies began to consider the introduction of "on-line" equipment through which information could be obtained direct from the computer by the branch, and whereby the branch would transmit a record of its daily transactions direct to the computer. This was a development which has been realised in the seventies.

The Housing Corporation

The successful pilot scheme of 1961 under which £25 million was quickly absorbed in cost-rent schemes encouraged the Government to create the Housing Corporation for the purpose of financing cost-rent and co-ownership societies on a more extensive scale.

Since World War II a combination of political, social and economic forces had created a situation in which there had been a steady erosion of privately-owned middle-priced rented property. The main part of the country's housing

stock now lies in the sectors of owner-occupation and local authorities' housing. The Housing Corporation was designed to supplement the existing arms of housing with a third, which would broaden the choice for those who could pay their way and wanted to live in a decent modern home but for one reason or another did not wish to buy and were not eligible for a subsidised local authority house. Neither cost-rent nor co-ownership housing was to be subsidised.

The Government made £100 million available to the Housing Corporation for on-lending to housing societies. Discussions between the Government and the Association took place and arrangements were made under which a building society would lend two-thirds of the cost of a scheme on first mortgage and the Housing Corporation would advance one-third on second mortgage. In this way housing societies could look forward to a £300 million programme.

In the first three years the Housing Corporation approved projects for some 18,000 dwellings at a cost of over £75 million. But cost-rent schemes soon proved to be unviable owing to increases in interest rates and gave way to co-ownership schemes which were able to take advantage of the option-mortgage and therefore determine their repayment terms on a net basis. The co-owner was also entitled on leaving his house or flat, providing he had lived in the property for a minimum period of three years, to a "premium" payment representing his capital repayment plus a portion of any capital appreciation which had taken place in the meantime.

A number of building societies supported housing societies by making loans although some refused to participate. Those that did advanced considerable sums of money.

In 1973, by which time some 44,000 dwellings had been approved in either cost-rent or co-ownership schemes, the Housing Corporation's funds were greatly increased and its scope was widened. Subsidised housing to let at fair rents through housing societies became the Corporation's main activity and co-ownership housing was relegated to a minor role. The co-operation of building societies was no longer sought except for the comparatively few new co-ownership schemes.

Chapter 32

SOARING HOUSE PRICES 1971-73

What Happened

Throughout the 1960s house prices rose at a fairly steady pace. There was no acceleration of the rise during the closing years of the decade and there was nothing to suggest that an explosive situation was about to develop. However, towards the end of 1970, and more noticeably in the first half of 1971, house sales became more buoyant and prices began to advance at a much faster rate. The increases were most marked in the South of England where prices by the middle of the year were widely reported to have risen by 15 to 20 per cent. Demand for houses was such that there were often three or four eager would-be purchasers for every one available. And as early as this there was talk of "panic buying". Markets were active throughout the country with other regions following in the wake of the South. There were more buyers ready to purchase older houses and flats. Agents reported that their lists of properties for sale had been drastically reduced. As prices rose buyers became increasingly anxious to secure a house and a new word "gazumping" came into use to denote cases where a vendor, having agreed to sell to one purchaser, subsequently was tempted to accept a higher price offered him by someone else. Prices were moving so quickly and buyers were so keen that this became a frequent occurrence.

In 1971 the average rise in house prices for the country as a whole was 21 per cent. The following year produced a much greater increase. In the first half of 1972 the average rise was 18 per cent. The southern half of England still led the upward spiral but other areas were fast catching up. The climax came in the third quarter when prices rose by about 15 per cent. They continued to rise thereafter but the rate of increase began to slow down in the last quarter of 1972 and through the following year. By the end of 1973 the index for newly-built houses stood at 199, compared with 100 at the end of 1971. The corresponding figure for existing houses was 193. In three years therefore prices had all but doubled, an unprecedented and staggering rise in so short a time.

Why it Happened

To understand how this dramatic increase in house prices came about it is necessary to examine a number of factors:– the economic and financial backgrounds; the relationship between earnings and house prices; variations in supply and demand; and the substantial increase in building society lending.

First, the economic and financial background. The Conservative Government which came to power in June 1970 was committed to reducing the rise in retail prices and defeating inflation. It had also promised that there would be no statutory incomes policy. But the Government's stern resolution was soon weakened by the prospect of rising unemployment. In December 1970 the number of unemployed was below 600,000; by July 1971 it was nearing 800,000 and rising rapidly. A mildly reflationary budget in March 1971 was followed by a further reflationary package in July which was a direct stimulus to consumption: purchase tax was reduced by 20 per cent and all hire-purchase controls were lifted. It takes time for such measures to work through to the factories, and in the months following unemployment continued to rise.

By January 1972 the total was 900,000. The Government now became alarmed that it would rise to the dreaded figure of 1 million. In the Autumn of 1971 they embarked on still more reflationary measures. Bank Rate was cut to 5 per cent in September. Public expenditure was substantially increased. And the banks were encouraged to compete with each other and new rules of credit were introduced which enabled the clearing banks greatly to increase their lending. These steps were followed by an expansionary budget in March 1972 in which both income tax and purchase tax were reduced. All these reflationary steps were taken before the preceding ones had had a chance to work. They followed on each other too quickly and in any case were wrongly directed. They stimulated consumption, whereas the need was to encourage exports and productive investment.

The result of the measures taken was to increase demand, raise prices and induce more inflation. While it lasted the expansionist mood produced a feeling of confidence and well-being. These were the background conditions created by the Government which were likely to induce more families, especially those in secure employment, to think about buying a house or, if already owners, about buying a larger or more modern one.

The second factor was that of average earnings and the relationship the earnings index bears to the index of house prices. Over the long-term there is a fairly stable relationship between house prices and average earnings. Borrowers have to decide how much they can borrow by the amount of repayment that

they can afford to pay. And building societies, likewise, in deciding how much they can lend an applicant are concerned not only with the value of the property but with the size of his repayment in relation to his earnings. Accordingly if earnings are rising fairly rapidly there will be a corresponding rise in the amounts the recipients of those rising earnings can afford to borrow. They will therefore be prepared to pay higher prices for houses.

Earnings and house prices do not maintain a constant relationship. Sometimes the graph of earnings will fall behind that of house prices – then earnings will catch up and perhaps run ahead of the house price graph. In the immediate post-war years when the housing shortage was acute prices ran well ahead of average earnings. In the 1950s there was a gradual closing of the gap and for most of the 1960s the two graph lines ran more or less parallel. In 1966 the Labour Government introduced a statutory incomes policy which imposed a check on earnings until it was abandoned in 1969. Thereafter wages moved ahead sharply. As a result average earnings rose by about 12 per cent during 1970. They went on rising – in 1971 by 11 per cent and in 1972 by 13 per cent. These were substantial increases and the effect was initially to send earnings racing well ahead of house prices. It was not until the Heath Government (like its predecessor) was obliged to fall back on pay restraint at the end of 1972 that the increase in earnings was curbed for a brief period.

Thirdly there are some demand and supply considerations which should be mentioned. Demand for houses in these years was stimulated because there was a growing feeling that a house was the best hedge against inflation. And inflation was gathering momentum. As the Chairman of the Halifax (Ian Maclean) observed: "Home-ownership is a desirable social aim in itself and it is an indictment of our social and economic situation that it should at present be so heavily advocated as the best hedge against inflation".

There were some other factors of lesser weight perhaps but nevertheless helping to promote the wave of buying which took place. One was the growing tendency for buyers at the bottom end of the market to take option mortgages; 132,000 such advances were made in 1972 and 110,000 in 1973, the total sums involved being in both years 15 per cent of the total amount advanced by building societies.

Another contributory influence was the fear that the Housing Financial Bill brought in by the Government to introduce "fair rents" to the local authority sector would result in appreciable rent increases. This probably prompted a number of better-off council tenants to enter the house-market.

At the same time as demand was growing the rate of new building was falling. The total number of new houses (for sale and letting by local authorities)

built in 1971 was 364,000 and fell to 330,000 in 1972 and to 304,000 in 1973. The corresponding net increases in the total stock of dwellings (after allowing for houses pulled down, falling into disuse or used for other purposes) were no more than 280,000, 220,000 and 210,000. These net additions to the total stock of houses were less than could be absorbed when demand was more or less normal. When demand was increased by boom conditions, increased earnings and inflationary fears, there was no help coming from the supply side. Prices were bound to rise.

To what extent was mortgage lending responsible for fuelling the price rise? Building societies increased their lending from £1,950 million in 1970 to £2,705 million in 1971 and to £3,630 million in 1972. The figure for 1973 was slightly less than that for 1972 at £3,510 million. These substantial increases (the average for 1967-69 had been approximately £1,500 million) were made possible by a high rate of inflow of money from investors. Societies were offering 5 per cent from 1969 until January 1972 when the rate was reduced to $4\frac{3}{4}$ per cent. This rate proved attractive until the end of 1972 when it had to be raised again. As a result shareholders' balances increased by around £2,000 million in each of the three years 1971-3. Over the period total assets increased from £10,818 million to £17,545 million. Much of this was due to the substantial increase in the money supply, to increased earnings and to the resulting inflation.

The Criticisms

There were those who, disregarding the other causes of rising prices outlined above, were in no doubt that building society lending was primarily to blame. And blame it was labelled. The question whether there was a justification in economic terms for the rise was not seriously discussed.

But in 1972, while the rise was still in progress, the Government's representatives came to the defence of societies. Why? Because they were anxious that nothing should get in the way of increasing the house-building programme. In May 1972 a Labour Member of Parliament asked the Government to restrict building society lending to which the Chief Secretary to the Treasury (Patrick Jenkin) replied: "Building societies have a duty to hold a balance between encouraging the building of new houses by having adequate funds available and meeting reasonable demands on reasonable terms without adding to inflation. In the circumstances I think building societies are holding the balance very well".

Soon after (in July 1972) the Minister for Housing and Construction (Julian Amery) said "What would be the consequence if building societies tightened up

on house loans? The better-off would be all right. They can always find the increased deposit or afford the shorter repayment terms. But those on low incomes could not hope to meet the stricter loans and as the market dried up the builders would cease to build. I will have nothing to do with a restrictive policy of this kind".

It was in 1973 that the shadow minister of the environment (Anthony Crosland) began to hit out at the building societies. In February of that year he advocated the setting up of a stabilisation fund, and in the House of Commons said of societies "It is not my view that those who run them are evil men – of course not – or even profit-making men in the conventional sense, but they react like automata to changes in the inflow of funds and those changes are at times violent and totally unconnected with the housing situation". And in an article in the *Gazette* in April 1973 he wrote "They did not wonder whether they should put some of those funds into a reserve fund against a rainy day. They blindly, thoughtlessly and automatically pumped them all out". He was of the opinion that houses had been turned into a speculative investment and that there was a powerful case for a publicly-owned element in the industry which would operate in competition with the existing societies and provide a yardstick against which their performance could be judged. He concluded by asserting "the fact must be faced: the days of *laissez-faire* are over, and future Governments will insist on an ultimate control over the provision of housing finance".

There were many other voices raised to the same effect and even the Government, notwithstanding the defence they had put up, were inclined to be critical at a later stage. But Crosland's strictures were the ones that really mattered as he was to become the Environment Secretary in the next Government.

The Rise in Prices – Combination of Factors

The events of 1971-73 have been widely debated and the blame for the rise in prices was by many commentators placed not only on the readiness with which building societies made money available but the equal readiness with which they accepted escalating prices as the basis for loans. Certainly they were flush with funds and did appreciably increase their lending. There have been other periods, however, when they likewise were able to make more money available without any marked effect on prices. One could go back to the 1930s when building societies had more money than they could lend and interest rates were low; there was no price increase, rather the reverse. One could instance the considerable increase in lending which took place in the 1960s when prices were rising, but at a

steady 6 per cent. Prices do not rise simply because loans are more readily available. The other factors we have dealt with above must be present.

What the critics of building societies did not ask was whether the rise was justified in terms of demand and supply and with regard to the falling value of money. The answer to that was demonstrated in the ensuing years. For after 1973 prices did not fall back sharply as might be expected after a boom period. As a whole they went on rising at a moderate pace until 1978, when they leapt ahead by some 26 per cent as prices once again caught up with earnings and mortgage interest rates came down.

What can be said – and it is the most that can be expected – is that if building societies restrain their lending, price rises can be slowed down to a more orderly and less violent progression. But in the long run, house prices will find their own level.

From Feast to Famine

From the beginning of 1973 high interest rates and competition for funds produced a sea-change in building society fortunes. Already in September 1972 societies had put up the investment rate from $4\frac{1}{4}$ to $5\frac{1}{4}$ per cent and the mortgage rate had been increased to $8\frac{1}{2}$ per cent without in any way deterring new borrowers. The rise in investment rates did not produce more than a temporary improvement in the inflow. The share rate was raised to 5.6 per cent from 1st February and in April it was raised again, this time to 6.3 per cent. There was no increase in the mortgage rate on either occasion, but the Council said in April that an upward adjustment was inevitable. It had been deferred on account of the Government's counter-inflation policy. There had been a number of meetings with Ministers and Treasury officials who were concerned about the prospect of the mortgage rate going to a new all-time high. They were especially apprehensive about the possibility of a 10 per cent rate. For this was the figure the building societies had in mind,. They were having second thoughts about the share rate which they felt ought to have been raised to $6\frac{3}{4}$ per cent. They were also wanting to secure an adequate operating margin. Further talks were held with the Government at which the Council made clear its intentions.

The Government finally quailed at the prospect of 10 per cent and at the last minute offered to make up for three months the difference between $9\frac{1}{2}$ and 10 per cent by a grant estimated to cost £15 million. This, the Council were at pains to point out, was a subsidy to borrowers, not to societies. Societies had not asked for, nor did they want the grant. They had been prepared to put the mortgage rate up to 10 per cent believing that that was the appropriate level. But in view of the grant they raised the rate to $9\frac{1}{2}$ per cent and increased the

share rate to $6\frac{3}{4}$ per cent. The Government for its part was hoping that by the time the grant period of three months was over interest rates generally would be falling.

And by July short-term interest rates were falling and the inflow to societies had improved. The Council, therefore, decided in July to reduce the share rate to 6.40 per cent and to retain the mortgage rate at $9\frac{1}{2}$ per cent when the grant expired. But a shock was in store. The effects of the boom which the Government's financial policies had created were beginning to show in accelerating inflation, rising prices and a rapidly deteriorating balance of payments. So, on the Friday after the Council decision to reduce the share rate, Minimum Lending Rate was raised from $7\frac{1}{4}$ to 9 per cent, and on the following Friday it was raised to 11 per cent. The Government had panicked. The building societies were compelled to go into reverse; the decision to reduce the share rate was hurriedly retracted and the mortgage rate was raised to 10 per cent.

The increase in M L R to what was then a record 11 per cent meant that bank deposit rates, local authorities' borrowing rates and other short-term rates had all been sharply increased. In particular building societies were feeling keen competition from the joint-stock banks offering rates up to 13 per cent for deposits. Societies were simply unable to compete and receipts fell off in August and September. Discussions continued with the Treasury about the situation. The Green Paper on Competition and Credit Control had envisaged that some limits might need to be imposed on the terms offered by the banks if they were having too great an impact on the savings banks or on building societies. When the Chancellor heard from the building society representatives how severely they were suffering from the competition of the joint stock banks he decided to ask the banks not to pay more than $9\frac{1}{2}$ per cent on deposits up to £10,000. The Chancellor hoped that by this action building societies would be able to avoid a further increase in the mortgage rate.

Although the building societies were grateful for this decision they did not think it was going to make all that difference to their worsening situation. Shortly afterwards they decided to raise the share rate to $7\frac{1}{2}$ per cent (representing at that time a gross yield of 10.71 per cent to a basic rate taxpayer) and the mortgage rate to 11 per cent (which, like M L R was a record figure). The Prime Minister (Edward Heath) made clear his annoyance at the decision. He said that he had hoped societies would wait and see the result of the Chancellor's request to the banks. The Chairman of the Council (Leonard Boyle) commented, "Without the Chancellor's intervention the rates could have been higher . . . I had said earlier that the mortgage rate could go to $11\frac{1}{2}$ per cent".

Edward Heath also observed that the Government were not satisfied with the present system of finance for house purchase which they thought ought to be a good deal more flexible and imaginative. The Government could not really complain. It was not the building societies which had forced interest rates to new levels. M L R had been raised to 11 per cent by the weakness of the pound which in turn had been caused in large measure by the economic and financial policies adopted by the Government.

The Joint Advisory Committee

While these events were taking place discussions were being held between Government and Council representatives on what should be done to ensure a more even flow of money for house buyers. The criticisms voiced by the Opposition and the demands from various quarters for the establishment of a stabilisation fund could not be ignored. And, apart from meeting the criticisms, the Government themselves felt something ought to be done. But what? It was soon evident that there were difficulties about setting up a stabilisation fund.

The solution arrived at was the creation of a Joint Advisory Committee to consist of representatives of the Department of the Environment, the Treasury, the Bank of England, the Chief Registrar's office and the Council of the BSA. Its objectives were to be:–

(a)   to continue to support the growth of owner-occupation

(b)   to produce and maintain a flow of mortgage funds to enable the housebuilding industry to plan for a high and stable level of house-building for sale

(c)   to contribute towards the stabilisation of house prices

(d)   to maintain an orderly housing market in which, subject to (c) above, sufficient mortgage funds are available to allow purchasers a reasonable choice of owning the sort of house they want.

The Government recognised in the agreement to set up the JAC that building societies would continue to be the chief source of mortgage funds for house purchase. If the objectives were to be achieved then the borrowing, lending and interest rate policies of building societies must be designed to result in a stable supply of mortgage funds appropriate both in relation to the level of effective demand and the supply of new and existing housing. There was to be an order of preference for mortgages. First-time purchasers and purchasers of new dwellings were to be first and second priorities.

The establishment of the Committee was announced in October 1973 and it was agreed that it should meet monthly. It was to be supported by a Technical

Advisory Sub-Committee which would supply the main Committee with the necessary statistics, estimates and analyses relating to interest rates, inflow and outflow of building society funds, housing starts and completions and house prices. On the information before it the Committee would then provide the Association with a forecast of the level of investment receipts required to realise the objectives set out above.

The setting up of the JAC was probably the best solution that could have been devised. It avoided the problems of a stabilisation fund, but was a recognition of the fact that the Government wanted and believed that through this machinery they could have a say (though not an absolute control) over the volume of lending in relation to other factors in the housing and house-building equation.

Government Lends £500 Million

The setting up of the JAC had only just been announced in October, 1973 when the Arab-Israeli war broke out, which was to lead first to an oil embargo and then to a quadrupling of oil prices, a blow felt by rich and poor nations alike. The Government was in trouble with the trade unions over wages; the miners, the power workers and the railway engine drivers were all exercising industrial action. The three-day week in industry came into effect at the beginning of 1974. Minimum Lending Rate was raised to 13 per cent in November 1973 and the Chancellor introduced a mini-budget in December cutting public expenditure, tightening credit, reintroducing hire purchase controls and imposing a 10 per cent surcharge on 1972-73 surtax bills.

The outlook was gloomy and building societies were again finding the going hard. Net receipts fell sharply from £126 million in October to £39 million in December. In January they were down to less than £19 million and in February there was a net outflow of £15 million. Withdrawals of money to place in more remunerative investments were running at an extremely high level. Local authority yearling bonds were yielding $14\frac{1}{2}$ per cent and guaranteed income bonds were providing a return of $12\frac{1}{2}$ per cent.

The Prime Minister had by this time decided to appeal to the country for a new mandate and a General Election was held on 28th February, resulting in a Labour Government taking office but without an overall majority.

By this time the building society position was acute. Money was flowing out and the situation demanded a rise in investment rates. But what was going to be the reaction of the public and the Press to a further rise in mortgage rate, now standing at 11 per cent? And what of the new Government? The question was

discussed by the Council with a good deal of heart-searching. It was talked about in the JAC which now provided a line of communication with officials and the Labour Ministers. There was no proposal to put up rates. For the moment all that building society leaders were prepared to do was to explain the position to the Government and see how they re-acted. Like the Conservative Government when faced a year earlier with the unwelcome prospect of a 10 per cent mortgage rate, the Labour Government was unwilling to acquiesce in a 12 per cent rate so soon after taking office.

As the Conservative Government had done, the new Ministers decided to come to the help of building societies but in a different way. At the beginning of April they offered to lend societies £100 million during that month at a rate of 10½ per cent, to be followed by a further £400 million (if required) during the succeeding four months. As with the three months' bridging grant a year earlier, this five months' loan aid was a temporary means of helping out with funds for lending until, it was hoped, the level of interest rates subsided. The net inflow to societies would then improve and they would be able not only to maintain lending but also to repay the Government loans. The loans were of course made on the condition that societies did not increase their interest rates to investors or borrowers. Repayment of the first £100 million was to start in October provided the net inflow of funds into societies exceeded £50 million and was to amount to half the excess. Subsequent loans were to be repaid in November and succeeding months. As a result, a substantial part of the £500 million was repaid before the end of the year and the remainder was repaid in the early months of 1975.

Significant Years

House prices, mortgage interest rates and the availability of funds for lending are the three features of building society activity which arouse most public attention. Each in turn served to keep the spotlight on building societies in the four years 1971 to 1974. The dramatic rise in house prices came first. This was followed in 1973 by the raising of the mortgage interest rate from 8½ per cent to 10 per cent, and soon afterwards to 11 per cent. Then came the severe fall-off in the net inflow of funds at the beginning of 1974 leading to an actual net outflow in the months of February and March. There was an imminent threat of still higher rates or a sharp and unwelcome drop in mortgage lending. This was resolved by the Government loans of £500 million which staved off a further rise while maintaining lending at a respectable level.

That there was a great deal of comment and criticism on all three issues was

only to be expected. Some of the comments on the part building societies played (or were alleged to have played) in the house price explosion have been related above.

A fair amount of criticism was ill-informed, superficial or politically-motivated. The more responsible critics were concerned mainly with two issues:

(a) the capital structure of societies – that is the borrowing short, lending long syndrome

(b) the future relations between building societies and the Government.

The first of these questions was widely debated. The Chief Registrar summed up the general view in the following statement:* "I think it can now be seen that there is a need for greater flexibility with regard to methods of attracting and retaining funds. To obtain the funds which may be required for the future may well require a wider and more sophisticated approach than societies have hitherto been accustomed to employing – not only with regard to differentials the rates offered to attract various kinds of investment over different periods, but also with a view to tapping sources which at present lie outside those upon which societies have traditionally relied in the past, including possibly sources from outside this country".

It is not however an easy matter to alter radically a financial structure such as that of a building society. Discussions have been held between the Association and the Bank of England on the possibility of setting up a Housing Finance Agency which would provide funds from banking, insurance and other financial sources. Nothing has come of it. So long as this kind of potential lender can lend money at higher rates than building societies can afford to pay they will not be interested in what would (after all) be a philanthropic undertaking. Nor is it easy to borrow funds abroad which the Chief Registrar suggested as a possibility. The prime difficulty here is to guarantee repayment at a fixed exchange rate.

Another idea much canvassed when inflation was running at its highest levels was that of granting index-linked loans to borrowers which would enable some of the benefits borrowers were securing from inflation to be passed on to investors. The Association spent some time on drawing up a practicable scheme but when the rate of inflation began to slow down nothing more was heard of index-linking.

The real promise of a more stable structure lies in the development of term shares†.

The second subject of criticism was the relations between building societies and the Government. There were those who said that after the £500 million

*The Chief Registrar. Address to North-West Association, April 1974.

†See chapter 34.

loan in 1974 building societies would never be free of the Government again and that they had, by accepting the loan, taken the first step upon the road to nationalisation. The contrary view is that building societies are now so big in the savings and housing fields that they must expect Governments to take some interest in their operations and policies without necessarily wanting to impose detailed controls or nationalisation.

It was fortunate that the Labour Government in 1974 were content to continue the JAC along the lines which had been established by their predecessors. And it was also fortunate that Crosland in office displayed a desire to co-operate with the movement he had so fiercely criticised in Opposition. Speaking at the Annual Conference in May 1974 he said "Some societies may feel resentful at what they may consider to be the unjustified intervention of successive Governments in their affairs. The Government does not overlook the fact that building societies have statutory legal and moral responsibilities towards millions of small savers and mortgagors. But I am sure building societies would not want simply to sit in the stands and watch the struggle to work out new social problems on home-ownership. You surely want to be part of that struggle. You have been too successful to be ignored by any Government in any conceivable circumstances. You are responsible for assets in excess of £17,000 million. You are therefore one of the major financial institutions of the country".

The years of the house price explosion, of high inflation and volatile interest rates were of great significance to building societies. They gave rise to much self-examination and to the re-appraisal of building society methods And they produced in the JAC a means of a continuous dialogue with Government which has led to a better understanding between the parties to the arrangement of each other's problems and needs.

Chapter 33

BUILDING SOCIETIES IN TROUBLE

The Wakefield Society

Founded in 1846 the Wakefield was one of the earliest permanent societies and, although it was not one of the fastest growing Yorkshire societies (its assets in 1976 were some £24 million) it was nevertheless considered to be eminently sound and capably managed. Its two more recent managers had both served on the Council of the Association and had been closely connected with the Yorkshire District Association and the Building Societies Institute.

Great was the dismay of the building society movement when, in 1976, newly appointed auditors discovered that certain advances previously regarded by the Society as secured mortgages were not supported by appropriate deeds and advance records. The resulting losses and over-statements were initially estimated at £600,000. The reserve funds of the Society amounted to £1.4 million and the losses could have been absorbed by these reserves and still left enough to enable the Society to maintain trustee status. But the eventual size of the losses was uncertain. There was a risk that, once the facts were made known, there would be a loss of confidence in the Society and its directors. To avoid panic and the danger of a run on the Society the directors of the Wakefield, following discussions with the Chief Registrar and the Building Societies Association, agreed to recommend a merger with the Halifax Society. This was duly effected in October 1976 and thus the members of the Wakefield were quickly relieved of any anxieties regarding the safety of their funds.

The man responsible for the frauds on the Society was William Robinson, manager of the Society since 1949 and a director since 1954. He was a man apparently of great rectitude, well respected in building society circles, a worker for charity and a Methodist local preacher. In the Wakefield office he had a complete grip on his subordinates. His final safeguard was the auditor who always dealt with him rather than the directors of the Society. This auditor was an elderly man who wanted to resign in 1974 but was persuaded to go on in 1975 to complete 50 years as auditor. There was a second auditor who appears to have taken little or no part in the audit.

Robinson was approaching 70 years of age when in 1974, an appointment was made of a general-manager-designate who was a chartered secretary and had served with two other building societies. He was soon asking questions about certain transactions, to which Robinson gave somewhat unconvincing replies. Then, in 1976, in succession to the aged auditor whom it had not been difficult to hoodwink, new and competent auditors were appointed. With the assistance of the newly appointed officer they had soon discovered enough discrepancies to challenge Robinson. At first he refused to meet them, but in the end confessed to the fictitious accounts. He was subsequently jailed for six years and a criminal bankruptcy order was made against him.

Robinson appears to have spent the money he stole living above his legitimate means and laying out a good deal of money on football pools. Involved in his machinations' was the estate of Robinson's predecessor, G.E. Jackson, who died in 1970. Robinson was the executor of Jackson's will and his children were to be the eventual beneficiaries of Jackson's estate. Jackson's mortgages with the Society had been manipulated by Robinson. Precisely how has never been made clear, but there was sufficient evidence to enable an amount of £238,000 to be recovered. This sum was distributed to members of the Wakefield Society.

The Chief Registrar's Advice

The Chief Registrar was concerned about the Wakefield fraud, and especially how in this and some other minor cases sums had been misappropriated over periods of years without detection. In September 1976 he wrote to all chairmen of societies drawing attention to directors' duties under Section 76 of the Building Societies Act 1962. That section places on the directors the duty of taking all reasonable steps to ensure that the society has established and maintains a system of control and inspection of its books of account and also a system for supervising its cash holdings and all remittances and receipts. And the Registrar pointed out that while a society's auditors are required by the Act to consider whether a society has maintained a satisfactory system of control and to report if in their opinion it has not, nevertheless it was the directors' responsibility to ensure that compliance with Section 76 was effective. The fact that the auditors may not have reported to the contrary does not absolve the directors.

Each chairman was asked by the Chief Registrar to bring the letter to the attention of the board at its next meeting.

The Grays Society and the Registrar

The Grays was to prove one of the societies where the directors had taken no steps to fulfil their obligations under Section 76, nor, as it was shown

afterwards, were they permitted to see the Chief Registrar's letter in 1976. And as it was to prove, the Grays was one society where there was need for something to be done.

Although there was at the time no suspicion of defalcations, the Registry had begun to take an interest in the Grays towards the end of 1973. There were three matters about which there was concern: the average age of the board was 74; The Secretary (H.P. Jaggard) had been late with his monthly returns; and the Society's liquidity was only just in excess of the statutory minimum of $7\frac{1}{2}$ per cent. There followed visits to the Grays by officials of the Registry and meetings with Jaggard and members of the board. It was made clear that the Registry wanted to see some younger directors appointed, the liquidity ratio increased and some improvement in book-keeping methods, including mechanisation. It proved difficult to get the Grays to move along these lines. One younger director was appointed and the liquidity ratio was increased from 7.73 per cent to 10.15 per cent in September 1974. But on the accounting procedures and the introduction of mechanisation Mr. Jaggard proved obdurate.

The Registry continued to watch for improvements and to make enquiries. In 1976 representations were still being made about liquidity and the age of the board. Greater emphasis, however, was now being placed on the replacement of the antiquated system of book-keeping. In April 1977 a further investigation was carried out by the Registry's staff and was the subject of a confidential report to the Chief Registrar. Jaggard's replies had been unsatisfactory and it was found that nothing had really changed at the Society for the better since the previous visit two years before.

Harold Percy Jaggard

The root of the trouble at the Grays and the reason why the Registry made so little progress in persuading the board to make changes which were thought desirable was that for many years the Society was dominated by the man who ran and controlled the business, Harold Percy Jaggard. He had been in the employ of the Society for over fifty years – from 1927 as Secretary, from 1963 as Secretary and a director, and from 1974 as Chairman and Secretary.

Jaggard was reluctant to make any changes because it was only under the prevailing system that he could cover up the enormous thefts he had perpetuated over a long period of years, certainly back to 1938 and possibly before that.

To have had too many new, able and enquiring directors; to have appointed a qualified successor; to have introduced mechanisation of accounts: all these

would have endangered his position. Nor (although he was well on in his seventies) could he think of retiring.

The Defalcations

He had carried out an amazing fraud. This man — short, stout and rather colourless, irascible in early life but mellowing in later years — stole £2 million from the Society over a period of 40 years, and, with £5 million interest also lost, left it with £7.1 million missing at 31st December 1977. His gambling losses were thought to be £1.6 million.

The money was taken year by year in cash and the bulk of it went on gambling, on horses and dogs. Jaggard frequently attended race meetings in the company of his wife or mistress, carrying a brief case of bank notes from his private office safe. Indeed, in 1952, the directors of Grays were informed that he had been seen at a race meeting and instituted a special auditors' enquiry, but nothing came of it nor was anything recorded in the Society's minutes.

He was married three times and for a period supported two households, sending the children to private schools. Gifts of money were made to members of the family but none of them suspected that it came from the Grays. Jaggard lived very comfortably on a scale well beyond that which he could have sustained on the salary he drew.

How Jaggard Covered Up

Jaggard's thefts involved a three-stage operation. He would first misappropriate cash from the Society's takings. He would then cover up his misappropriations by accelerating the banking of cheques received in a subsequent accounting period — the practice known as 'teeming and lading'. And, thirdly, when his misappropriations had reached a level where they might become apparent he would abstract a cheque and use it to fill the gap. The cheques that Jaggard used to cover his thefts of cash were mostly those paid in redemption of mortgages, but there were times when he also took cheques paid in by the investors. It was necessary in both cases for him to make entries in the ledger accounts, either to clear off the mortgage balances or to enhance the amount standing to the credit of an investor. These were the day-to-day operations; but there was also the year-end balancing of the books to manipulate. At the end of each year there was an ever-widening gap between the total of the ledger balances and the total of such balances imputed by taking the opening balance from the control account and adjusting for the movements of cash and interest during the year. The gap

between the two totals represented the money Jaggard had taken and the interest which the missing money would have earned for the Society. The second factor began to assume far greater significance as interest rates rose in the 1960s and 1970.

By December 1976 the difference had become:

	Real value of ledger balances	Reported value in annual accounts	Difference
Liabilities			
Shares	£11,265,763	£9,158,764	£2,106,999
Deposits	1,588,514	1,259,514	329,000
Assets			
Mortgages	5,446,145	9,386,145	3,940,000
		Total deficiency	£6,375,999

Between 31st December 1976 and the time of his death Jaggard had helped himself to a further £85,000 and this, plus accrued interest, increased the deficiency to over £7 million.

There was a brown analysis book which served as the Society's nominal ledger. The totals had to agree with the summaries prepared each year by the staff working from the ledgers and passbooks. Jaggard therefore altered the totals on the year-end summaries, an increase in the case of mortgages and a decrease in the case of shares. The number of changes called for were enormous. Jaggard took the summaries home and worked on them night after night and as the years went on the task became even greater. By thus falsifying the summaries, the totals of the relevant columns agreed with the brown analysis book and hence satisfied the auditors. "His forgery was astounding in its scale, audacious in its execution and consistently successful, for by it he hoodwinked the auditors for over forty years."*

The Discovery

The discovery of the fraud occurred in March 1978 during the course of the audit of the 1977 accounts. An audit clerk found discrepancies in checking the share summaries back to the ledgers. Jaggard was in the room and realised that the game was up. He went straight to his house and committed suicide. A few days work convinced the auditors that there was a serious situation and that the deficiency could amount to at least £2 million. The Registry was called in and the Woolwich Equitable Building Society was approached with a view to taking over the Grays. The Woolwich were willing to help, but when told that the deficiency could be as much as £2 million, decided to send in their own officers

*Report of Inspectors: Grays Building Society (Cmnd. 7557, p. 46).

to make further investigations. They soon found that the situation was far worse than feared and that the deficiencies amounted to some £7 million. This was more than one society could be expected to bear alone.

The Rescue

There were two alternatives. Either the Society could be placed in liquidation and the losses borne by the investing members of the Grays, or the member societies of the Building Societies Association could be asked to contribute to a rescue fund. The Association in consultation with the Chief Registrar decided that in the interests of investors of a member society and in the wider interests of the movement as a whole a rescue operation should be put in hand. As a first step the five largest societies (Halifax, Abbey National, Nationwide, Leeds Permanent and the Woolwich Equitable) were asked and agreed jointly to give an assurance that between them they would see to it that the investors in the Grays did not lose their money. It was thought, however, that the burden of the losses should ultimately be borne proportionately in relation to size by all member societies. And when asked to do so, all members readily paid a proportionate part of the total loss into a compensation fund vested in Trustees. Before this could be done there was one obstacle to be surmounted. The rescue fund was to be set up under the provisions of Section 43 of the Building Societies Act 1962 which empowers societies, with the approval of the Chief Registrar, to enter into arrangements for the purpose of making funds available to meet losses incurred by persons investing in a society which is a party to the arrangements. An opinion was given that this provision of the Act was intended to apply only to losses incurred or coming to light after the arrangements were made; and that it was not legally possible to set up such arrangements, after the event, to meet losses already incurred. Others argued that it was permissable under the Act to make *ex post facto* arrangements. As it proved impossible to reconcile the opposing views it was decided to test the matter in Court. The case was heard by Templeman J. in May 1978 and judgment was given in favour of the scheme. The judge concluded his observations by saying "The directors of a building society are not going to enter into arrangements under Section 43 unless they are satisfied that the interests of their own building society so require and unless they are satisfied that the funds of their building society are ample for the purpose. Similarly, the Chief Registrar would not approve any arrangement which is not in the interests of building societies in general and of the building societies which participate in the arrangement in particular, and he would also require to be satisfied that the arrangement can be financed without prejudice to the financial

position of the participants and without danger to the investors in the participants.

In my judgment the present proposals constitute arrangements which do fall within the scope of Section 43 and there are no reasons why I should strive officiously to limit the scope of Section 43 in order perversely to forbid to be done that which plainly must and ought to be done, namely, the safeguarding of investors in a building society from loss".*

The way was thus cleared for the rescue operation to go ahead. Arrangements were made for the Woolwich Equitable to take a transfer of engagements and for the setting up of the compensation fund from which the deficiency was paid to the Woolwich Equitable. No money was lost by the members of the Grays (with the exception of the directors who were excluded from benefiting out of the rescue fund).

The Report of the two Inspectors appointed by the Chief Registrar to investigate the affairs of the Grays Building Society † was published in May 1979. It was a detailed Report on Jaggard's frauds and the manner in which they were perpetrated and concealed. The Report also examined the duties and responsibilities of the staff, directors and auditors, and the intervention of both the Registry and the Building Societies Association. The Inspectors concluded by making a number of recommendations for changes in law and practice in relation to building societies.

The Criticisms

(a)   The Staff

There were eleven full-time Grays staff. None had had professional training and none had worked at another building society or bank. The only long-serving staff member, and for 30 years the only other male employee, had joined the Grays as office boy in 1936 and was assistant secretary from 1947 onwards. The inspectors were satisfied that "none of the girls was knowingly involved in the fraud, and, given their background and experience, could not have been expected to detect what was afoot.†† Of the assistant secretary they were equally satisfied that he neither knew nor suspected what was going on, but should not, however, be absolved from all censure. He clearly had doubts and misgivings

---

*Halifax Building Society and Another v Registry of Friendly Societies [1978] 1 WLR 1544.

†Command 7557 – Report by J.H. Davison, FCA, and Murray Stuart Smith QC., HMSO.

††Ibid. p. 21.

about many of the things that were going on and should not have tolerated these abuses without demur.

(b)   The Directors

The inspectors had a good deal to say about the board of the society and their responsibilities. It was, they observed "one of the fundamental weaknesses at Grays, namely that the board failed to exercise adequate control over the affairs of the society. There was an almost total lack of forward planning; the board concerned themselves largely with the details of individual mortgage applications, but failed to devote themselves to important issues of policy that would enable the society to provide a satisfactory up-to-date service and to face the competition which sooner or later was bound to come. Although many of the directors disliked the fact that Mr. Jaggard was both secretary and chairman, they failed to exercise the additional measure of control which this situation called for; and failed to reach decisions in time or at all, or see that Mr. Jaggard as secretary carried them out".[*]

The inspectors felt that while all the directors must bear some responsibility, not all were equally to blame. But they were satisfied that none of the directors knew or even suspected that Jaggard was defrauding the society.

(c)   The Auditors

The fraud was uncovered in the course of the March 1978 audit and the inspectors say they would have liked to be able to report that the partner in the audit firm who was responsible for the Grays audit had devised an audit procedure which caught up with Mr. Jaggard, but this was not really the case. His approach to the audit of the 1977 accounts was basically the same as it had always been. But for reasons of health he had been relieved of some other work and for the first time he attended in person when he was not expected. Furthermore he supervised his staff who properly directed worked too fast for the ageing Mr. Jaggard.

But Jaggard's frauds had been carried out over a long period of years and the belated detection of the frauds in 1978 did not serve to excuse the defects of the audit in earlier years. The inspectors said "we would be very reluctant to criticise the auditors merely because they failed to take one or two steps, which, while we would regard them as standard procedures, and which might have led to the detection of the fraud, could be excused in the context of an otherwise well-planned and executed audit. But we have come to the clear conclusion that the combination of errors and failures add up in sum to a consistent failure of the auditors to discharge their professional duties properly". Having summarised

[*]Command 7557. p. 99.

their detailed criticisms of the auditors, the inspectors concluded "we are forced to the view that the auditors were negligent".*

(d)   The Registry

The inspectors, having examined at some length the steps taken by the Registry to suggest and obtain improvements in the Grays organisation, were not critical of the Registry, bearing in mind the provisions of the 1962 Act spelling out the duties of the auditors and the limited resources available to the Registry.

(e)   The Building Societies Association

The Association did come in for some criticism from the inspectors. Jaggard on two occasions (in 1974 and 1976) wrote seeking the help and comments of the Association in his dealings with the Registry. The Report observes: "Mr. Jaggard obtained support and comfort from the BSA which strengthened his resolve to resist the attempts of the Registry to institute reforms and which may also have afforded him some help in reassuring the board. But we do not think that this had much bearing on the course of events. We consider, however, as a general principle, that if the BSA is going to defend its members against the Registry, which in our view has a difficult job to do in attempting to monitor building societies, it is undesirable to do so in the absence of full information. The BSA's intervention in the Grays affair does nothing to justify the claim made in its evidence to the Wilson Committee that 'the Association closely monitors the accounts of each member society with a view to ensuring that difficulties do not arise which might jeopardise people's savings'.†

The inspectors were here making two criticisms. The first was that the Association in its replies to Jaggard was to some extent running counter to the efforts of the Registry and that it might have been wiser to have consulted with the Registry to clarify the position before replying to Jaggard. There is some force in this criticism although the Secretary-General did put the other side of the case by saying "I have a duty to my members as well as to the Registrar and the public and so on. I have to try to understand my members' point of view and not be too harsh . . . We told them to get their house completely in order, after which we thought the pressure from the Registry would die down. That was the advice we gave them at the time".

The second criticism, on the claim made to the Wilson Committee that the Association closely monitors the accounts of each member, is one which, it is submitted, was completely unjustified. For the Accountancy and Taxation Committee does closely monitor the accounts of each member and spends a good deal

*Ibid p. 152/3
†Ibid p. 165

of time on this task. But that Committee has to assume that the accounts it is examining have been properly audited and that it can rely on the auditors' certificate. The Association has never pretended that it carries out its own examination of the books of each member society.

The Inspectors' Recommendations

After their criticisms the inspectors had some recommendations to make for alterations in the law and for modifications to Registry practice. They said "Our proposals which follow are designed to meet the irregularities which occurred at the Grays. Our experience of building societies is largely confined to that institution and we are therefore unable to say whether measures which are clearly necessary to deal with the sort of situation that was present at the Grays should fairly be applied to all building societies, their auditors, directors and executives. However, the gravity of the crisis caused within the building society movement by the collapse of the Grays makes it clear that changes must be made in the Registry's monitoring procedures; and, while no changes can guarantee that a major fraud will never recur, those that we have in mind should at least ensure that the Chief Registrar is more likely to be forewarned of situations requiring his attention, and in particular those in respect of which there is *prima facie* evidence of defective auditing".*

One of the recommendations made was that the law should be amended so as to render an auditor an officer of a building society and thus require him to furnish information to the Registry if called upon to do so; in other words the Registrar should have direct access to the auditors and the auditors' working papers. Further recommendations were made that the scope of the auditors' report should be expanded; that the auditors should meet the board or a committee of the board at least once a year; that the Registrar should have power to monitor audits to ensure their adequacy, and that the Registrar should employ qualified staff for the purpose of carrying out Registry investigations of building societies.

The inspectors had some recommendations to make regarding directors. They thought the Registrar should provide guidance to newly elected directors as to the nature and extent of their duties, particularly under Sections 76 and 78; and that a new director should attend a short course on directors' duties within two years of his appointment, while existing directors should attend refresher courses.†But the most important recommendation was that, as under the Com-

*Cmnd. 7557 p. 168.

†Courses for new directors are already organised by the BSA with attendance on a voluntary basis.

panies Act 1948 directors should be required to resign and seek annual election upon reaching the age of 70. It may be wondered why this provision was not included in the 1960 Act; it will almost certainly be included in the next building society legislation, which may not be all that far ahead.

The inspectors believed that Jaggard's crime would have been much more difficult to commit had he not been at once chairman, chief executive, secretary and the sole executive present at board meetings. They proposed two measures to avoid such a situation. The first was that the chairman of a building society should never, at the same time, be the chief executive. The second was that there should be at least two executive directors on every board who should be familiar with the operations of the society. The inspectors recognised that this second requirement might present problems for smaller societies and therefore recommended that it should be required only of those societies qualifying for trustee status.

Lastly, the inspectors felt that their own powers were inadequate and that the law should be strengthened to give them greater powers to examine witnesses.

A Guarantee Fund

Following upon the Wakefield and Grays affairs the Labour Government then in office made it clear, through the Treasury, that they wanted building societies to set up a permanent investors' protection scheme. And it is anticipated that the Treasury will advise the present Conservative Government to make the same demand. If a voluntary scheme is not devised and adopted, legislation will probably be introduced to ensure that such protection is given. The Banking Act 1979 has already provided a scheme for protecting bank depositors for up to 75 per cent of losses. And an EEC Direction applying to all credit institutions will require in due course the setting up of a licensing authority which will not grant a licence to an individual credit institution, such as a building society, unless there is an investors' protective scheme covering the members of that institution.

One way or another, it seems that a protection scheme is inevitable. But there is a division of opinion as to what form a voluntary scheme should take. Should it be limited to covering 75 per cent of losses, or should it extend to 100 per cent of losses? A more vexed question is whether the scheme should embrace members of the Association only or include non-members. The Treasury and the Chief Registrar are of the opinion that it should be all-embracing. There are some building society men who would reject a voluntary scheme and let the Government impose one on the movement.

Chapter 34

BUILDING SOCIETIES IN THE SEVENTIES

Inflation

The 1970s have been years in which the high rate of inflation and the efforts made to control it have dominated financial and economic policy. We have seen in Chapter 32 how at the beginning of the decade the Barber boom increased the money supply, stimulated consumption and accelerated the inflationary spiral.

When the Labour Government took office in February 1974 it was committed to a large wage rise for the miners. That increase was followed by a general round of high wage settlements. The Government, like its predecessor, was eventually compelled to make an attempt at wage control – this time on a voluntary basis, the T.U.C. agreeing to a limit of £6.00 per week over the year to 1 August, 1976. A continuation of this voluntary pay restraint over the following two years did succeed in putting a brake on the rate of inflation and bringing it down to below 10 per cent.

But in the autumn of 1978 the Government was unable to persuade the unions to renew the compact. Despite Government exhortations and threats of sanctions against employers who settled wage claims above the norm, the unions began to obtain substantial increases accompanied by a good deal of industrial unrest. The troubles of the 1978/79 winter – strikes, secondary picketing and recriminations over alleged neglect of hospital patients – probably helped the Conservative Party to win a serviceable working majority over all other parties at the May 1979 General Election.

The new Government was committed to free wage bargaining, to firm monetary control, reduction of public expenditure and a shift from direct to indirect taxation. The hefty increase in VAT which the June 1979 budget imposed in order to reduce direct taxation, the abolition of price control and higher oil prices did nothing to reduce inflation. They were signals for enhanced wage claims and by the end of 1979 it was clear that the policies pursued by the Government would not bring down inflation in the short term.

The increases in the retail price index and in average earnings over the six years to the end of 1979 are shown in the following table:

	Retail Price Index (increase %)	*Average Earnings* (increase %)
1974	16.0	17.8
1975	24.1	26.5
1976	16.5	15.6
1977	15.8	10.2
1978	8.3	14.5
1979	13.4	15.6

Interest Rates

In Chapter 32 the course of interest rates was followed to the end of 1974, by which time things were improving and building societies were enjoying a satisfactory inflow of money. In fact, 1975 proved an excellent year. The inflow was good enough to enable societies to reduce the share rate from 7½ to 7 per cent from 1st June and still lent £4.9 billion to home-buyers compared with £2.9 billion in the previous year. In April 1976 the Council was able to recommend a further reduction to 6½ per cent and on this occasion a reduction in the mortgage rate from 11 to 10½ per cent.

But these reductions were short-lived. Once again, building societies' fortunes were determined by the measures taken by the Treasury and the Bank of England to deal with the worsening domestic situation. By September, M.L.R. had been raised to 13 per cent and it was clear that societies' rates must again be raised. In October, the Council was in the process of debating to what level rates should rise when the discussion was interrupted with the news that M.L.R. had just been increased by a further 2 per cent to a record 15 per cent.

There was on this occasion no hesitation on the part of the Council. If drastic measures were forced on the Government, it was necessary for building societies to take equally drastic steps. Accordingly, the share rate was raised from 6½ to 7.8 per cent and the mortgage rate from 10½ to 12¼ per cent; and as with M.L.R. these were record rates.

It was not until April 1977 that a reduction in rates could be made. In that year as a steadier economy enabled M.L.R. to come down to as low as 5 per cent in October (although it did not stay there long), building societies were able to make reductions in both share and mortgage rates, bringing them down to 6 and 9½ per cent respectively. In January 1978 further reductions to 5½ and 8½ per cent were made, but by the end of the year they were up again (in two moves) to 8 and 11¼ per cent. Thus in a little over two years rates had moved to record levels, been reduced by almost a third and then risen once again to more or less the same high levels.

From April 1976 to November 1978 rates were changed on eight occasions

and the inflow of money was thereby maintained at a rate which provided a high level of mortgage lending – £6 billion in 1976, £6.7 billion in 1977 and £8.8 billion in 1978.

The year 1979 was to see rates rising to new record levels. In the Conservative Government's first Budget (12 June) M.L.R. was raised from 12 to 14 per cent and the Association Council was faced with the problem of what should be done about building society rates. The increase in M.L.R. was imposed entirely for domestic reasons, the object being to restrain the growth of bank lending. It was expected to remain at 14 per cent for some time, although at the time there was a general expectation that M.L.R. and short-term interest rates would decline before the end of 1979.

On this view the Council decided that they would increase the share rate from 8 to $8\frac{3}{4}$ per cent from 1st August without calling for an immediate uplift in the mortgage rate. Societies were prepared to sacrifice their margins until January 1980. But the Government found that it was more difficult to control bank lending than they had hoped and in November 1979 M.L.R. was raised to 17 per cent. This called for a further increase in the share rate to 10.5 per cent and a rise in the mortgage rate from $11\frac{3}{4}$ to 15 per cent.

Not everyone thought that even these rates were high enough to produce an adequate flow of money but it was the majority opinion that an increase of $3\frac{1}{4}$ per cent in the mortgage rate was as heavy an imposition as could reasonably be made on existing borrowers.

Tax Relief on Mortgage Interest

Prior to 1969 all interest payable could be set against income tax in the year of assessment. The 1969 Finance Act limited tax relief to interest on loans for the purchase or improvement of land in the United Kingdom. The 1972 Finance Act restored tax relief to all interest payable except for the first £35 of interest but provided full relief for mortgage interest. The 1974 Act restricted mortgage interest tax relief to loans on the borrowers' main residence and restricted relief to £25,000. Since then the £25,000 limit has not been increased, although house prices and the size of the average mortgage advance have approximately doubled, and representations have been made by the BSA and others for an increase in the limit.

House Prices

After 1973, house prices settled down. There was a noticeable fall in prices at the top end of the market and housebuilders (faced with sharply increased costs) found that selling was not easy. For the United Kingdom as a whole, prices in 1974 rose by about 5 per cent whereas housebuilding costs rose by about 20 per cent and the Retail Price Index by about 18 per cent. The following year saw a fairly strong revival in the house market and prices rose by 12 per cent. Building societies increased their lending by some £2 billion. Prices continued to increase through 1976 and 1977, but were not rising at the same rate as building costs, average earnings, or the Retail Price Index as is illustrated by the following table:*

	House prices	House bldg costs (wages & materials)	RPI	Average earnings (all employees) seasonally adjusted	House price/ earnings ratios
1973	100	100	100	100	4.11
1974	105	121	118	125	3.47
1975	116	149	148	152	3.17
1976	125	177	170	171	3.08
1977	135	193	192	189	3.04
1978	172	209	208	218	3.39
1979	221	241	244	257	3.75

But in 1978 and 1979 there was a sharp advance in house prices, the average increase in both years being about 28 per cent. In 1978 the house price/earnings ratio rose to its norm of 3.4 but in 1979 the rise in house prices went well ahead of both the increase in retail prices and that for average earnings. At the end of the year the house price/earnings ratio was 3.7, higher than it had been since 1973, indicating the probability of a slow-down in house price rises. Over the decade, house prices had risen some three and a half times.

Competition for Funds

Since 1971 inflation has produced a vast increase in building society assets. The amount required to satisfy the demand for loans has resulted in societies seeking more and more savings and investments. The following table indicates the growth in money terms:

---

*(Housing Trends: First Quarter 1980. Issued by Nationwide Building Society).

Year	Advances £mill	Share rects £mill	Share wdls £mill	Total Assets £mill
1971	2,705	3,821	2,444	12,919
1972	3,630	4,965	3,467	15,246
1973	3,512	5,804	4,574	17,545
1974	2,945	6,126	5,375	20,093
1975	4,907	8,784	6,118	24,203
1976	6,183	10,146	8,200	28,202
1977	6,745	13,549	10,183	34,288
1978	8,807	15,684	12,769	39,538
1979	9,002	18,849	16,315	45,789

The competition for funds and the building society success in attracting an increasing share of what may be termed short-term financial assets from the personal sector (the building society share increased from 24 per cent in 1966 to 43 per cent in 1977) had aroused some criticism from the joint stock banks whose share had declined during the 1970s. The banks argued that the success of building societies was one reason for the low level of industrial investment and economic growth in Britain; funds had been finding their way into housing via the building societies rather than into industry via the banks. The composite rate had given societies an unfair advantage and there was some resentment over the restriction placed on the banks between September 1973 and February 1975, which limited to $9\frac{1}{2}$ per cent the interest they were permitted to pay on deposits of under £10,000.

In answer to these arguments building societies have a number of counter-arguments. A high proportion of building society lending is not financed by new savings received but represents existing loans being re-cycled. There is, first, the regular repayments of principal from borrowers. Secondly, there are families moving house who repay the loan on the house they sell and obtain a fresh loan on the house they buy. In 1979 these two kinds of repayment amounted to £3,500 million, representing 39 per cent of the total inflow.

There is also another kind of re-cycling to take into account. Not only do families change houses, eventually they die. At the end of their lives most home-buyers have paid off their mortgage or have very little owing in relation to the current value of their house. Of the 11.3 million estimated owner-occupied houses some 5 million are owned outright. Let us take a simple example. Mr and Mrs A bought their house in 1938 for £500. Both die in 1978 leaving their house and other possessions to their two children. The children are both married and buying their own homes. They therefore sell their parents' home for, say, £25,000 and the purchaser obtains a £20,000 loan from a building society.

Disregarding other savings and possessions left by their parents (and Capital Transfer Tax), the children each have now £12,500 to dispose of. They may decide to spend some of it on new furniture, a holiday or a new car. Let us assume that they each put £2,500 aside for these purposes. They thus each have £10,000 to invest. They may decide to reduce their own mortgages by that amount; or they may decide to invest the sum in a building society. Either way £20,000 will go into building societies' funds offsetting the £20,000 lent to the buyer of their parents' house.

Now this example is tailored to balance precisely the amount loaned and received from the purchase and sale of a house bought in 1938 and which has multiplied in value by fifty times. There are many variations; the appreciation may not always be as much; there may be other ways in which the children (or the beneficiaries) dispose of the estate; and some of the money may find its way into bank deposits, national savings, unit trusts or stocks and shares. But the fact of the matter is that each time a house without a mortgage or with a comparatively small mortgage is sold on the death of the occupant the mortgage required by the buyer is offset by the sale proceeds, much of which is likely to find its way back into one building society or another.

The amount of money realised from these final sales is not known with any certainty but has been estimated by the Association at £3.3 billion for 1979. To this figure must be added that released to landlords from the sales of rented houses, for that money is also available for re-investment in some form. There is also some movement of people from owner-occupation to other forms of tenure which likewise releases capital. The Association estimates that the total amount released from these three factors may have amounted to some £4.5 billion in 1979. How much of this money finds its way into building societies' investment receipts will vary according to the relative attraction of societies' rates compared with other investment rates. It may be about one-third of the total, but at times when building societies' inflow is buoyant, could be considerably higher.

On the question of the composite rate, societies have no difficulty in showing that this is in no way a subsidy but an average tax liability borne on behalf of their investors from which higher rates of income tax and investment income surcharge are excluded and which, where they arise, have to be discharged by the investor. The composite rate was not originally designed to give building societies a competitive advantage, but to be (as indeed it is) of great administrative convenience both to societies and the Inland Revenue. It has admittedly been an attractive selling point, but the only complaint which competitors for savings can legitimately make is that they have not the advantage of a similar arrangement.

If the banks can complain of the competition of building societies, societies can in their turn point out that they themselves have had to face in recent years extremely strong competition from the Government. What the Government has done is to attract savings by giving fiscal advantages to the number of people paying tax at above basic rate. National Savings Certificates offering attractive yields free of all taxes have been issued and drawn considerable amounts of money from building societies. Index-linked bonds and low yielding gilts (exempt from Capital Gains Tax after one year) have also been designed to attract higher taxpayers.

Term Shares

When interest rates were much lower than they are to-day funds held by building societies were much less volatile. Competition was not so keen, there were fewer large accounts and the investors were not so sensitive to interest rate changes as they are to-day. Following the fluctuations of the early 1970s in both interest rates and the inflow and outflow of money it was recognised by some societies (though not all) that it was desirable to encourage the intake of money which would be invested on the basis that it stayed longer. As we have seen, term shares yielding an extra quarter or half per cent over the ordinary share rate providing they were invested for a minimum period of one to four years were introduced by a few societies in the 1960s and at that time were frowned on by the majority of societies as likely to encourage transfers from existing accounts or from other building societies rather than attract entirely new money.

In 1974 when building societies were experiencing an acute shortage of funds a number of societies began to take the concept of the term share much more seriously and to promote them with a much higher differential. These societies offered one to one and a half per cent over the ordinary share rate for money invested for two or three years. If looked at in isolation this represents expensive money, but if the cost of all shares is averaged out a holding of say 10 per cent in term shares against 90 per cent at the ordinary rate appears much less onerous. And at the end of 1979 the amount held in term shares by the 17 largest societies was 13.43 per cent of total shares.

If term shares continue to increase as a proportion of total money the point may come when societies can take no more. On the other hand as term share money increases it may be possible to make a differentiation in a downward direction on ordinary shares especially for those accounts where balances are small and the number of transactions is large. This lies in the future, but it seems that opposition to term shares within the movement has now disappeared and that they will grow in volume. There is every likelihood that they will lead even-

tually to more diversified interest rates and to a more stable structure for building society capital.

Branch Offices

One of the criticisms levelled at building societies over the last decade has been that they have been opening too many branch offices. It is claimed that in many towns they unnecessarily duplicate each other and that as societies offer much the same terms they do not even offer competition. It is needless expenditure.

From the outside this is an understandable point of view. The building society sees it differently. The larger societies – those claiming to be national societies and those hoping before too long to be able to make the same claim – have found that by dividing up existing branch territories and creating new branches with smaller territories business is increased. They have found too that opening branches in small towns where twenty years ago they would never have contemplated doing so has proved rewarding. Smaller societies have found it profitable to open branches in towns adjacent to that in which their head office is situated.

In 1970 there were some 2,000 branches and this number had increased to some 5,000 by the end of 1979. If this seems an over large increase it must be borne in mind that the number of share accounts increased in the same period from 10 million to 27 million, and the number of accounts per branch was higher at 6,000 against 5,000 in 1970. One may argue that increasing the number of branches has led to an increase in the number of accounts, or, alternatively, that the increase in the number of accounts has led to the demand for more branches.

One thing more must be said. Building societies open branches because they believe that there is a need which they can meet. And results have proved that far from the country being over-branched by building societies there is still a need for more branches and will be for some time.

Mergers and Concentration

By the end of 1979 the number of building societies had been reduced to 287, which was a fairly steep decline from the 504 societies existing in 1969. The reduction was in the main due to mergers effected by way of transfer of engagements by one society to another. No more than 14 new societies were established. The requirements of the 1960 Act have discouraged the formation of new societies, as may be judged from the fact that in the eight years prior to

new statutory provisions (see part 3, ch. 6) 84 societies were registered.

Of the remaining societies the total assets are heavily concentrated on the forty-four largest societies. The degree of concentration is shown in the following table:

	Total Assets £ million	% of Total
5 largest societies	25,191	55.0
31 with assets exceeding £100 million	17,134	37.4
48 over £25 mill up to £100 million	2,357	5.1
123 over £2 mill up to £25 million	1,067	2.3
109 up to £2 million	40	0.1
All societies	45,789	100.0

(Chief Registrar's Report for 1979)

Thus, the 44 largest societies held over 90 per cent of total assets; and the 89 largest held over 97 per cent. So that less than 3 per cent was held by the remaining 198 societies – a long tail indeed. The number of societies in membership of the Building Societies Association is 210 and most of the 77 non-members are very small. Some 50 of them are moribund. The Association can claim to speak for 99 per cent of the total assets.

At the end of 1978 the following were the 10 largest societies:

	Assets (millions)
Halifax	8,943
Abbey National	7,251
Nationwide	3,935
Leeds Permanent	2,630
Woolwich Equitable	2,433
Anglia Hastings & Thanet	1,610
Alliance	1,543
Leicester	1,399
Provincial	1,398
Britannia	1,248

The Housing Survey

In 1975 Anthony Crosland, the Secretary of State for the Environment, set up a Review of Housing Finance by his Department and the Welsh Office aided by several expert committees whose members were drawn from outside Government. The study was subsequently extended from financial issues to social aspects of housing. The result was a comprehensive survey of housing, published in 1977 as a Green Paper under the title of The Housing Survey. The Survey with its three separate technical volumes made a detailed examination of

housing and housing finance and provided a wide range of economic and statistical information relating thereto.

From the point of view of building societies the Council of the Association welcomed the document as marking a great step forward in the field of housing policy. The Council was obviously gratified by the explicit statement in the Review that the Government welcomed the growth in home-ownership and recognised that the demand for it does not stem only from financial advantage but also from the sense of personal independence which it brings. The document also recognised that building societies were in the forefront of housing policy, their dominant role in financing home-ownership being probably unique among countries where home-ownership is the largest tenure.

There were some suggestions made as to how building societies' policies might be made more flexible. Some of these were particularly concerned with helping the first-time purchaser of limited means. The Survey stated that the problems of many potential first-time purchasers with modest incomes could be eased if building societies were more able and ready to provide low-start mortgages and offer higher-percentage advances for those who could not raise a sufficient deposit; and also extend their lending on older property, especially in inner urban areas.

The Association commented on these observations that it was not so much the terms on which money was lent as the volume of money available and the number of houses available for purchase which were the key factors. The arguments for low-start mortgages often tended to exaggerate their importance and to underestimate the adaptability of the normal annuity mortgage. If a building society regarded a low-start mortgage as appropriate it could grant it initially on an interest only basis and introduce repayment of capital at a later stage. The need for high-percentage loans was equally over-estimated. Most borrowers wanted to keep the debt down and were prepared to put in 5 or 10 per cent of the purchase price as their initial stake. But, in any case, arrangements were already in existence to provide insurance guarantees for covering loans up to 100 per cent on houses costing up to £14,000. Such guarantee arrangements were already extensively used by home-buyers; some 45 per cent of first-time buyers availed themselves of this facility to obtain loans of 90 per cent or more of purchase price.

So far as lending on older property was concerned this had become a matter of arrangements with local authorities and had given rise to some controversy before the Housing Survey was published. In April 1975 the Government as part of a general cut-back in public expenditure decided to restrict lending for house-purchase by local authorities. They asked building societies to fill the gap

by setting aside £100 million for making loans to home-buyers sent to them by local authorities. Arrangements were made on a regional basis for the administration of the scheme. It got off to a rather slow start. Some building societies were reluctant to divert lending from their normal channels in order to give preferential treatment to people sent to them by the local authority. The local authorities were perhaps resentful that they were unable to continue their own mortgage lending and were unable to appreciate the different lending criteria employed by the building societies.

For the Lending Support Scheme had high-lighted the whole question of lending on older houses. In making loans to house-buyers local authorities have tended to regard the operation as something of a social service and have had less regard to the prudential requirements of a mortgagee than a building society. This applied in particular to older houses. In agreeing to the Lending Support Scheme, societies reserved the right to assess each application by established lending rules. Soon charges were made by local authorities, housing organisations and politicians that societies were being altogether too cautious and restrictive in dealing with applicants sent to them by local authorities.

The further charge was made that societies were red-lining certain areas – that is drawing a ring round the worst inner housing areas and refusing even to consider a loan on any house within the proscribed area. This on the grounds that the houses within the area were aged and dilapidated and that the whole district was neglected and run-down. This charge was hotly denied, building societies asserting that they did not practise "red-lining" but considered each application on its merits. At the same time they pointed out that they were entitled to choose their own securities and make their own judgments. Moreover, they were at pains to point out that it was not in the interest of a purchaser to encourage him to buy a worn-out house in a decayed area which might possibly cost him a fortune in repairs, or, in a few years, be included in a clearance area. There were counter charges that building societies were more concerned about the safety of their own money rather than the interest of the applicant, that they were too rigid in their policies and too conservative in their valuations. Some thought that it would be simpler if building societies were to lend money in bulk to the local authorities and let them do the on-lending. But this would technically have increased the public borrowing requirement and was therefore ruled out.

Happily the Lending Support Scheme has overcome most of the difficulties encountered in the early months. At the request of the Government increased yearly allocations of money have been made available by societies and more societies are participating in the Scheme. Local authority and building society officers have been brought into close co-operation as a result of which they better

understand each other's attitudes and ways of working.

The Association

(a) *The Council*

Dissatisfaction with the constitution of the Council rumbled on after the failure of the proposals in 1962 to increase the number of district association representatives. Another attempt was made by the South-Eastern Association in 1972 and on this occasion the proposal was for all members of the Council to be elected by the regional associations. When the proposal was discussed at the A.G.M. of the Association it was not pressed to a vote but it was agreed that the Council should consider changes in the method of election and bring recommendations before the next A.G.M. Accordingly the Council came forward in 1973 with proposals to provide the ten largest societies with permanent seats by way of nominated members; fifteen nationally elected members and ten regional members. It was also proposed that the age for retirement from the Council should be brought down from 70 to 65 in one-yearly steps to 1979. These proposals were approved as from the Annual Meeting in 1973.

The provision of automatic representation from the ten largest societies was made because it was felt that when (as had been the case) one or two of the largest societies were not represented on the Council, decisions on such vital matters as interest rates could not be as decisive as when the voices of all ten of the largest societies were heard in discussion. Controlling as they do some 70 per cent of the assets of the movement it is desirable that they should all be participants. Nevertheless there were those in the movement who were still of the opinion that reform should have provided greater representation of the District Associations.

(b) *Public Relations*

Although much had been done in the 1960s to improve the Association's public relations and output of information, the events of 1971-74 gave rise to criticisms that not enough was being done. There were demands for the appointment of a Director of Public Relations and for a review of the administration. Faced with a certain restlessness on the part of a number of influential societies it was decided to call in management consultants to examine the organisation and make recommendations for improvement. In announcing this decision the Chairman of the Council (Leonard Boyle) recalled that it was Alexander the Great who said he was dying with the help of too many physicians – "We are not dying but I think we are suffering at the moment from the attentions of too many physicians. We have too many people telling us how we should run our business".

The management consultants reported in due time but apart from one or two minor suggestions the recommendations they made did not find favour, neither with the Council nor with member societies.

(c)   *The Joint Advisory Committee*
The Joint Advisory Committee, established in 1973, has now become a permanent feature of building society life. The Technical Sub-Committee is charged with the task of preparing reports and statistics and its work has led to the production of information on the housing and savings markets which were formerly inadequate, and, when available, insufficiently up to date. The Sub-Committee also prepares forecasts of the likely levels of supply and demand in the housing market over the year ahead against which actual experience can be compared and measured.

It was agreed in 1975 that as a further step towards achieving the stabilisation of the flow of mortgage funds and avoiding an excessive increase in house prices, the JAC should monitor the volume of lending by building societies. A close watch would be kept on movements in house prices, figures of housing starts and other factors affecting house building and purchase. The monitoring process would form the basis for regular discussion between the Government and the Association and guidance would be given to societies on any adjustments needed to their levels of lending. This has been done ever since and in 1978 lending was appreciably curbed in view of the rise in prices which was taking place. It is quite clear that this kind of action can have only a short-term delaying effect on prices, and the J.A.C. has now abandoned the idea of restricting lending in order to limit price rises.

(d)   *The Institute*
In 1971 the Association and the Institute jointly decided that there was a need for a permanent training centre for building society staffs. Accordingly it was agreed to purchase Fanhams Hall, near Ware, Herts, which had been used for staff training by the National Westminster Bank. Funds for the purchase were raised by loans from a number of societies. As part of the arrangement the Institute's administrative offices were moved from Central London to Fanhams Hall.

Until 1977 the Institute was financed by the subscriptions of members and by donations from societies. The Association, having become in some measure responsible for the Institute finances through its involvement with Fanhams Hall, decided that it would be preferable for the donations by societies to be replaced by an annual grant from the Association, paid out of the revenue raised

from members. The Association has, therefore, taken the Institute under its wing. The grant each year is determined on the basis of a budget submitted by the Institute. The Institute was granted a Royal Charter in 1979.

(e) *200th Anniversary*
The Queen and the Duke of Edinburgh attended a Building Societies Association reception at Guildhall, London, on 24th November 1975, to mark the 200th anniversary of the Building Societies Movement.

The Stow Report

Over the last twenty years building societies have been unable to meet the demand for mortgages simply because there have never been enough funds available. When, in 1979, the Conservative Government asked the Association how societies were going to meet additional demands which would arise from the projected sale of council houses it was impossible to give any firm commitment. The question posed by the Government did however prompt the appointment by the Association of the Stow Committee* charged with the task of estimating the medium-term demand for mortgage finance and considering the extent to which that demand could be financed from traditional and from alternative sources of funds.

The Committee examined the various factors affecting the demand for houses (and thus the demand for loans) such as population and household changes, the level of new housebuilding, second homes, the trend of earnings and, of course, inflation. Estimates of mortgage demand based on so many variables must necessarily be tentative. The Committee were in no doubt, however, that there would be a substantially increased demand not only in money terms but in the number of loans. The total amount advanced per annum could rise from £9 billion in 1979 to as much as £19 billion by 1985. And the number of loans could rise from 710,000 in 1979 to 940,000 in 1985. To meet demands rising to these levels would mean a massive increase in the funds deployed by societies. Moreover, a further sum of about £700 million per annum would be needed for advances to council house purchasers, assuming that building societies were called upon to provide about 85,000 such loans each year.

The Committee considered various ways of raising funds outside the traditional field of personal savings. They looked at the possibility of obtaining

---

*Mortgage Finance in the 1980s (Report of a Working Party under the Chairmanship of Ralph Stow (immediate past-chairman of the B.S.A.) Dec. 1979. Building Societies Association.

money from pension funds and life assurance companies and concluded that if building societies wished to raise substantial funds from these sources they would have to offer marketable securities at a premium over the rate offered by gilt-edged securities. Over the period 1973-79 this would have implied a rate between three and five percentage points above societies' grossed up share rate. This was so unattractive as to be no real alternative to raising an adequate volume of money direct from the personal investor.

Consideration was also given to the concept of a secondary mortgage market. Unknown in this country, a secondary mortgage market is one in which the lender (e.g. a building society) sells a batch of loans to a third party (e.g. an assurance company) to produce funds for further lending. Such markets are widely used in the U.S.A., France and other countries. The Committee concluded that a pre-requisite for such a secondary market was that the rate of interest on mortgages should be above other rates of interest. It would be impossible to sell mortgage loans at a rate well below the yield on more marketable assets, such as gilts.

Other possibilities were examined but the Stow Committee came to the conclusion that the essential way to raise adequate funds was to pay competitive rates in its traditional field, even if this meant higher mortgage rates. And higher mortgage rates were not without their compensations. An increased flow of money would encourage housebuilders to build more houses. There would be shorter chains of transactions and less need for expensive bridging finance. And higher rates might be offset by a curbing of the rise in house prices. "The major conclusion of the Committee's work is that building societies should experience no difficulty in meeting mortgage demand from their traditional sources of funds and that there are no alternative sources of funds that would provide more mortgage money at a lower rate of interest".*

And thus concludes this story of the building society movement. As societies move into the 1980s it is evident from the facts and figures assembled by the Stow Committee that they can anticipate further expansion and continuing useful service to the community. Over the past two hundred years they have had their trials and tribulations but on the whole they can look back with some satisfaction. They can also look forward with optimism.

*Stow Report, p. 44.

OFFICERS OF THE BUILDING
SOCIETIES ASSOCIATION

PRESIDENTS

W. T. McCullagh Torrens, MP 1869–1885
Sir John Lubbock, MP (afterwards The Lord Avebury, PC) .. 1886–1913
The Lord Emmott, PC, GCMG, GBE 1922–1926
The Viscount Cecil of Chelwood, PC, CH, QC 1928–1936
The Earl of Harewood, PC, KG, GCVO, DSO 1936–1939
The Viscount Sankey, PC, GBE 1940–1947
The Earl of Halifax, PC, KG, OM, GCSI, GCMG, GCIE, TD 1947–1954
The Duke of Devonshire, PC, MC 1954–1961
The Duke of Hamilton and Brandon, PC, KT, GCVO, AFC .. 1961–1965
The Earl of Selkirk, PC, KT, GCMG, GBE, AFC, QC 1965–

CHAIRMEN OF COUNCIL OR EXECUTIVE COMMITTEE

James Higham 1869–1883
Charles Binyon 1883–1903
Edward Wood, JP 1903–1913
Ezra Naylor 1913–1921
Sir Enoch Hill, JP, FCIS 1921–1933
Sir Harold Bellman, MBE, JP, DL, FBS 1933–1937
Walter Harvey, FBS 1937–1939
Thomas R. Chandler, FIA, FBS 1939–1940
Sir David W. Smith, JP, FCIS, FBS 1940–1942
William McKinnell, FFA, FBS 1942–1943
Sir Bruce Wycherley, MC, FCIS, FBS 1943–1946
Andrew Stewart, CBE, CA, FCIS 1946–1948
Sir Charles Davies, JP 1948–1950
William W. Wetherill 1950–1952
Sir Hubert Newton, MA, FCIS, FBS 1952–1954
Francis E. Lumb, DCM, FCIS, JP 1954–1956
F. Bentley, FCIS, FBS 1956–1958
Alexander Meikle, CBE, CA 1958–1960
J. R. Millican, FCA, FBS 1960–1961
John Dunham, FRICS 1961–1963
Andrew Breach, CBE, JP, FCIS 1963–1965
Donald A. Gould, FBS 1965–1967
Gilbert J. Anderson, BSC(ECON) 1967–1969
F. M. Osborn, CBE, DL, FCIS, FBS 1969–1971
Sir Stanley Morton, FCIS, FBS 1971–1973
Leonard Boyle, CBE, FBS 1973–1975

SIR RAYMOND POTTER. MA 1975–1977
RALPH C. STOW, FCIS, FBS 1977–1979
L. E. H. WILLIAMS, DFC, FCA 1979–

SECRETARIES

JAMES HIGHAM, Junr 1869–1874
F. M. WHITTINGHAM 1874–1880
G. W. PHILLIPSON 1880–1883
EDWARD F. BRABROOK, LLB 1883–1888
R. H. MARSH, FCA 1888–1936
CHARLES GARRATT-HOLDEN, CBE, TD, BA, MCOM 1936–1963
NORMAN E. GRIGGS, CBE, BSC(ECON), FCIS 1963–1967

SECRETARY-GENERAL

NORMAN E. GRIGGS, CBE, BSC(ECON), FCIS 1967–

A CENTURY OF GROWTH

Year	Number of Societies	Total Membership (000)	Total Assets (£000)	Amount Advanced on Mortgage during the Year (£000)
1870 *(circa)**	2,088	820	18,286	–
1900	2,286	584	59,767	–
1910	1,723	626	76,286	9,291
1920	1,271	747	87,060	25,094
1930	1,026	1,449†	371,165	88,767
1940	952	4,361,928	756,242	9,950
1950	819	4,417,941	1,255,872	269,717
1951	807	4,562,992	1,357,023	267,638
1952	796	4 728,096	1,478,068	266,090
1953	782	4,966,879	1,642,606	299,480
1954	777	5,271,562	1,867,353	373,201
1955	783	5,579,893	2,065,377	394,368
1956	773	5,845,728	2,230,134	334,947
1957	755	6,085,911	2,414,588	374,145
1958	744	6,336,252	2,621,337	374,757
1959	732	6,633,444	2,907,145	517,345
1960	726	6,838,294	3,165,938	559,398
1961	706	7,116,526	3,436,751	545,761
1962	681	7,578,798	3,815,332	612,983
1963	662	8,111,951	4,331,414	849,389
1964	635	8,632,983	4,862,633	1,042,543
1965	605	9,299,089	5,531,645	955,418
1966	576	10,144,189	6,305,840	1,244,750
1967	554	11,158,912	7,445,528	1,462,714
1968	525	12,131,040	8,298,273	1,589,884
1969	504	13,170,000	9,289,270	1,558,715
1970	481	14,538,000	10,818,772	1,953,708
1971	467	16,119,000	12,919,330	2,705,296
1972	456	17,675,000	15,246,462	3,630,431
1973	447	19,261,000	17,545,458	3,512,716
1974	416	20,747,000	20,093,500	2,945,102
1975	382	22,990,000	24,203,749	4,907,955
1976	364	25,312,000	28,202,445	6,183,300
1977	339	28,132,000	34,288,438	6,745,143
1978	316	30,888,000	39,538,356	8,807,765

*Estimated by the Royal Commission on Building Societies, 1871.
†Shareholders only: before 1928 borrowers who were not also shareholders were included. Subsequently, the figures include shareholders, depositors and borrowers.

MORTGAGE ADVANCES SINCE 1960

Year	Number	Amount (£000)
1960	387,406	559,768
1961	364,117	545,761
1962	378,145	612,983
1963	477,230	849,389
1964	535,289	1,042,543
1965	456,799	955,418
1966	535,512	1,244,750
1967	586,411	1,462,714
1968	594,660	1,589,884
1969	545,065	1,558,715
1970	624,289	1,953,708
1971	768,749	2,705,296
1972	892,522	3,630,431
1973	719,623	3,512,716
1974	545,906	2,945,102
1975	797,612	4,907,955
1976	912,767	6,183,300
1977	946,318	6,745,143
1978	1,183,961	8,807,765

INDEX